D1521850

Images of Older People
in
Western Art
and
Society

Images of Older People
in
Western Art
and
Society

HERBERT C. COVEY

New York
Westport, Connecticut
London

WINGATE COLLEGE LIBRARY

Copyright Acknowledgments

The author and publisher gratefully acknowledge permission from the Gerontological Society of America to use sections of the following journal articles:

"Historical Terminology Used to Represent Older People," by Herbert C. Covey, *The Gerontologist, 28* (1988): 291-297.

"Perceptions and Attitudes toward Sexuality of the Elderly during the Middle Ages," by Herbert C. Covey, *The Gerontologist, 29* (1989): 93-100.

"Old Age Portrayed by the Ages-of-Life Models from the Middle Ages to the 16th Century," by Herbert C. Covey, *The Gerontologist, 29* (1989): 692-698.

Library of Congress Cataloging-in-Publication Data

Covey, Herbert C.
    Images of older people in Western art and society / Herbert C.
Covey.
        p.   cm.
    Includes bibliographical references and index.
    ISBN 0–275–93435–7 (alk. paper)
    1. Art and the aged.   2. Aged—Public opinion.   I. Title.
N72.A33C68   1991
700'.1'03—dc20   90–38714

British Library Cataloguing in Publication Data is available.

Copyright © 1991 by Herbert C. Covey

All rights reserved. No portion of this book may be reproduced, by any process or technique, without the express written consent of the publisher.

Library of Congress Catalog Card Number: 90–38714
ISBN: 0–275–93435–7

First published in 1991

Praeger Publishers, One Madison Avenue, New York, NY 10010
An imprint of Greenwood Publishing Group, Inc.

Printed in the United States of America

The paper used in this book complies with the
Permanent Paper Standard issued by the National
Information Standards Organization (Z39.48–1984).

10 9 8 7 6 5 4 3 2 1

To
Marty,
Chris,
and
Kelly

CONTENTS

PLATES

PREFACE

This book was written to help us understand how older people were perceived in earlier periods of Western history. It draws on art, literature, and historical information from earlier times. The period that I selected for study ranges from the late Middle Ages through the nineteenth century. The late Middle Ages was chosen as the starting point because it represents a period of change in both artistic techniques and attitudes toward older people. It was at the close of the Middle Ages that artists began to portray the individual characteristics of their subjects, including age. In prior centuries, the individual was relatively insignificant, and artistic images of old age were rather sterile, shedding little light on perceptions of older people in the first millenium of the Christian era. The Middle Ages also gave rise to the use of perspective, and human subjects began to be shown in natural contexts. The thirteenth through the fifteenth centuries saw an increasing effort to depict subjects as individuals and as they actually appear (Hofstatter, 1968). This innovation allows us, despite some limitations, to obtain for the first time a good notion of how old age was perceived. It also means that, by the end of the Middle Ages, older people were being portrayed in sufficient detail to pick them out by their old age.

At the closing of the Middle Ages and especially at the opening of the Renaissance, a new orientation to life could be witnessed. Life in this world took on greater importance. The focus on the individual that emerged with the Renaissance brought attention to the older people. As Western society turned toward understanding humankind, a natural curiosity grew about aging. Older people increasingly became the subjects of art. Thus, beginning with this era, we can learn how older people were viewed by taking a look at Western art.

The Renaissance, and especially the Northern Renaissance, provides us with many important images of older people. The rise of portraiture and the emphasis on individuality contributed to the creation of many works of art involving older people. The fifteenth century marks a growth in a sense of individuality in literature as well (Tristram, 1976).

The centuries that followed the late Middle Ages and the Renaissance were characterized by accelerated social change and social upheaval, which in turn caused dramatic changes in many perceptions about older people. This was not a period that idly contemplated some static icon of old age, but rather a period of changing, refining, and recasting images of older people. To understand this evolution to the ideas of our own day, it is necessary to cover a fairly broad period of time.

The study ends with the nineteenth century for several reasons. First, the advent of pensions, industrialization, urbanization, social welfare, and the other major social trends of the nineteenth century caused fundamental changes to take place in the perception and image of older people in both art and society. Second, the nineteenth century can be seen as a clear line of demarcation separating the historical from the contemporary. I purposely avoided the twentieth century because I did not want inadvertently to allow its contemporary images of older people to overshadow my interpretation of earlier periods. Third, the 1980s produced such a vast amount of research on older people in the twentieth century that a separate volume would be needed to cover the subject.

The same cannot be said about periods prior to the twentieth century. Social historians writing on older people have focused on the nineteenth and twentieth centuries and, with few exceptions, have tended to avoid earlier periods. This is due in part to the relative lack of information about older people from these earlier times.

Some historians and scholars may take issue with the broad scope of this work, suggesting that both significant details and subtleties will be lost in a work covering the years from the late Middle Ages to the end of the nineteenth century. They may argue that each region, with its unique traditions and culture, or each of the periods or centuries encompassed in this book deserves intensive, thorough coverage in a separate volume.

Though both sides of this argument are valid, this work is not intended to be a detailed or period-specific historical piece, but an introduction to some of the basic images of older people over the centuries. Only by studying images and perceptions of older people over such a lengthy period is it possible to determine whether these views were fleeting or enduring. No other work presents such a social overview on which more detailed studies can be based. Therefore, this book is meant to be an introductory text and a catalyst for further research.

Its audience may be the interdisciplinary reader who wants to explore the roots of some of our current perceptions and images of older people. The book may also be of interest to students and academic researchers in the field of gerontology. It draws on various disciplines and has an extensive bibliography.

To the therapist and gerontological practitioner, *Images of Older People in Western Art and Society* will hopefully offer insights into the human side of aging and old age. Many of the socially influenced experiences in old age have roots in the Western tradition that are identified here. Older people may take comfort in the fact that some of their problems have been shared by others.

Actually, quite a number of the issues confronting older people in the past would be meaningful to today's elderly population. Insights into old age in earlier times will help older people put their experiences into a broader context. There is much that contemporary older people can learn from the old who have gone before—on such basic concerns as family, sex, death, and the aging process itself. It is the author's hope, therefore, that the art will capture the attention of older people and provide insights and answers to some of their questions.

My strategy has been to present snapshots of older people in art and literature and to fit these images into what social and art historians as well as the writers and historians of literature itself can tell us about the contexts in which these images were created. At times, I present only the historical and literary work, as I could not always find art that reflects known historical facts. An appreciation of cultural differences has been acknowledged whenever sufficient information was available.

Finally, I did not find it necessary to delve into art and literature created prior to the late Middle Ages. The biblical and ancient writings, although not included in the time frame of this book, were influential in shaping Western images of older people. Late medieval and Renaissance scholars often drew on the ancient works for insights into the process of aging and old age.

I am highly indebted to major literary scholars and social historians such as Andrew Achenbaum, Peter Stearns, Carole Haber, Philippe Aries, David Fischer, Simone de Beauvoir, David Van Tassel, John Demos, and others for their ground-breaking work on the subject of older people in earlier periods. Of these works, Philippe Aries' *Centuries of Childhood* (1962) was the most influential source of information and inspiration. Although it has been criticized, Aries' book remains a classic in the field.

I wrote each of the chapters that follows with a special area of interest in mind. Chapter 1 introduces the reader to the general topic of older people and their images in art. It provides some background information on aging in prior centuries.

Chapter 2 examines a number of models in the ages-of-life genre, which have often served Western culture as a means to divide the human life-span into distinct, comprehensible segments. Although older people in earlier times un-doubtedly experienced life and old age somewhat differently than we do, these ideal models provide important insights into how the aging process was viewed by intellectuals and, to some extent, the general public throughout the centuries and demonstrate how old age relates to the other ages of the life-span. What the ages of life represent is a set of stereotypes, abstractions, and perceptions of how and when aging occurred in the respective periods and how older people behaved. The extent to which these stereotypes corresponded with reality is arguable. A case could be made that they reflected only the musings of intellectuals. However, an equally credible argument could be made that they had an empirical basis.

Chapter 3, on symbolic representations of older people, is actually a collection of various images—some of them more symbolic than others. For example, portraits of older people are not always intended to be symbolic, but simply to capture reality. At other times, images of older people are highly symbolic in placement and characterization. Artists also included in their works symbols that had meanings of their own, some of which were strongly associated with older people. For example, the cane and the hourglass are still recognizable as relating to old age.

Several of the images that appear in this chapter were selected because of their special significance. They have become deeply ingrained icons, such as the old man as time. Others were very much like the images of contemporary pop culture, in that they were relatively transient in Western history. Nevertheless, despite the transformations in imagery, older people have symbolized very central values and enduring ideas.

Chapter 4, on older people and the family, was included because older people's central relationships were most often those involving the family, and artists and authors often chose the family as the context in which to portray them. In fact, the subject of older parents and their offspring have proven to be a lasting reflection in the cultural mirror of society. Although social historians and other scholars—who have written volumes on the subject—hold widely divergent opinions on the development of the family, the topic must be addressed here because of its importance in our understanding of older people.

The topic of sexual behavior was selected for Chapter 5 precisely because in contemporary society we do not associate older people with sex. We never see them as having sexual desires or feelings, but rather as being sexless. It is this very fact that makes the topic of sex in old age so important. Have older people always been viewed as sexless? No, at certain times in history, their sexuality was certainly acknowledged, if not so well accepted. Chapter 6 considers the topic of death for the opposite reason—because it is so strongly associated with older people in contemporary society. Is this association new, as some have suggested, or does it have roots deep in Western history? Death and sex provide two extremes, then. On the one hand, death is almost always associated with old age; and on the other hand, sexual activity is always associated with youth.

This book was written to increase our consciousness of images of older people in Western history and to fuel future inquiry on the topic. Many of our contemporary images and ideas cannot be applied to people who experienced old age in earlier periods, and hence the book debunks several contentions of modern-day popular wisdom. Also, it offers researchers on old age and aging background information on how Western society developed the perceptions evident today. Finally, it has been my hope to present the rich texture of imagery regarding old age and aging from earlier periods in such a way that these images are more meaningful than ever to older people, scholars, and other readers of this book.

ACKNOWLEDGMENTS

Many people contributed to this work by providing inspiration and assistance. I want to thank the numerous reviewers and journal editors who have provided guidance and input over the years, as well as Susan Holte, who assisted with an early version of the draft. My friends Drs. Scott Menard and Bob Franzese have always been supportive of my work. Another friend and fellow academic, Keith Meagher, was a sounding board for many of the ideas that have come to fruition here; and he too was very supportive. I also want to thank the editors of Praeger Publishers and in particular Alison Bricken, Pat Merrill, and Nina Neimark for their assistance and suggestions; their help proved invaluable to the production of this book.

I want to thank the Gerontological Society of America and the editors of *The Gerontologist* for permission to use sections from some of my earlier publications.

I want to thank the following museums, libraries, and publishers for their permission to reproduce the works included in this text: the Mauritshuis, The Hague; the British Library, London; the Library of Congress, Washington, D.C.; the National Gallery of Scotland, Edinburgh, courtesy of the Duke of Sutherland; the Prado, Madrid; the National Gallery, London; the Museo Civico, Vicenza; the Öffentliche Kunstsammlung, Kupferstichkabinett, Kunstmusueum, Basel; the Norton Simon Museum, Pasadena, California; the Rijksmuseum, Amsteradm; the Cummer Art Gallery, Jacksonville, Florida; the National Portrait Gallery, London; the Staatliche Museen Pressischer Kulturbesitz (Berlin-Dalheim Museum), Berlin; Pushkin Museum of Fine Arts, Moscow; Metropolitan Museum of Art, New York; National Museum, Stockholm; the Philadelphia Museum of Art, Philadelphia, Pennsylvania; the National Museum and the per I Beni Artistici e Storici, Soprintendenza Naples; Macmillan Publishing Company, New York; the Boston Museum of Fine Arts, Boston; the Louvre, Paris; the National Gallery of Art, Washington, D.C.; the Art Institute of Chicago; the Royal Museum of Art and History, Brussels; Conservée au Musée des Beaux-Arts, Strasbourg; the Bibliothêque Nationale, Paris; and the Kunsthistorische Museum, Vienna.

My grandparents served as its most basic source of inspiration. It is through them that I developed my love for older people. I am also deeply appreciative of my wife, Marty, my son, Christopher, and my daughter, Kelly. They provided great encouragement and understanding and never questioned the time I devoted to this project.

Images of Older People
in
Western Art
and
Society

1

ART AND OLDER PEOPLE: AN INTRODUCTION

Older people of earlier eras did not especially attract the interest of historians or gerontologists until the past decade and a half. Very little thought has been given to the study of older people in different historical periods (Dahlin, 1980). Consequently, we know very little about the experience of old age in earlier times—and in particular, preindustrial society (Stearns, 1982). We are left to speculate about aging in prior centuries. It is almost as if old age and older people were an invention of modern times. Nevertheless, to truly understand our place and time on earth, we must dig deeper into our images of older people than what contemporary modern society has to offer.

The neglect of contemporary scholars is partly due to the fact that older people were no more visible in the past than they are today. Old age and the aged have never been a dominant theme in Western thought or literature (Charles & Charles, 1979–80; Fowler et al., 1982), although older people have always been a recognizable portion of the population. As Simone de Beauvoir (1972) and others have observed, written and documentary evidence about the aged is relatively scarce. Rarely is there much mention of them in the literature. (As we shall see, though, there have been times, such as during the eighteenth-century Restoration, when old people were popular as subjects in the comedy of manners.) In contemporary Western society, we still pay little attention to our aged population, and consequently know almost nothing about its lives and experiences. We know considerably more about the first years of life than we do about the last.

Neglect in art and literature does not mean that cultures have not formed strong opinions, however. We should not confuse neglect with perception: Societies did develop strong images and perceptions of older people; and these perceptions are indeed reflected in art and literature, even when they play only a supporting role there to another theme. Some of these perceptions lasted only briefly, while others persisted for centuries and continue today. Some are positive, and other negative. They run the gamut of Western experience.

It is noteworthy that the definition of old age—and its starting point—has varied over the centuries, a point developed further in Chapter 2. In contemporary society, old age is defined as starting at age 65. This arbitrary age would not have been meaningful to people in prior centuries. Old age is an abstraction; its boundaries are indistinct, and its definitions differ. For our purposes here in reviewing art over the centuries, it will be unnecessary to use chronological age to separate older people from younger. Rather it is more important to focus on what the artist or writer conveys about old age.

Contemporary social scientists say that old age has become roleless. We are told there is now an apathy and indifference toward older people that at times borders on neglect. We shall discover here that prior societies prescribed roles for their older people, perceived them according to some fairly rigid guidelines, and certainly formed strong opinions of and expectations for their behavior and position in society. In fact, Western society has maintained a well-defined—and perhaps even now restrictive—image of its older people.

The suggestion has been made that our lack of knowledge regarding older people in earlier times is due to their scarcity in the general population then. In other words, so few of them existed that little can be known about them. The question then becomes, How common was old age in the past? Information on the prevalence of older people in earlier societies is limited. Simone de Beauvoir (1972) claims that they barely existed prior to the late eighteenth century. Those who did survive to old age were primarily from the upper classes. In his work on older people in rural nineteenth-century France, Peter Stearns (1976) observes that, although relatively rare, older people were in sufficient numbers not to have inspired awe from their younger counterparts. In any case, it is important from the start to realize that older people have always been a part of society. Old age is not a recent invention of science, medical advancement, and better living conditions. Rather, older people have always represented a proportion of the population in whatever societies they lived. Old age was not so rare in earlier periods as some might think.

Our misconception about the prevalence of old age in earlier times is due in part to a lack of understanding about life expectancy. Life expectancy at birth has increased with the improvement in the quality of our lives. Advances in medical technology and better diet, sanitation, working conditions, and the like have led to increases in life expectancy, but not in the length of life (the life-span). Indeed, many of the reported increases in life expectancy are due to advances at the other end of the life-span continuum. That is, infant mortality rates have dramatically declined, resulting in greater life expectancy at birth.

The average life expectancy at birth was 35 years in the thirteenth century, and 33 years in the fourteenth century. Life expectancy was about 40 during the Renaissance (Gilbert, 1967). After the Renaissance, mortality rates declined and the chances of reaching old age improved (Hendricks & Hendricks, 1977). In

England, life expectancy ranged from a low of 34 to a high of 45 for the periods 1538–1598 and 1750–1799 (Laslett, 1977). In eighteenth-century Massachusetts and New Hampshire, life expectancy was placed at 28.15 years (Vinovskis, 1971), and at 28.8 in France (Laslett, 1977). These sample studies indicate that life expectancy at birth was low; thus when compared to contemporary times, there were fewer people reaching old age.

Another way to view life-span is to see how many people actually reached old age. The data are incomplete and scattered, however. Historians have found that in 1371 older people represented about 3.8 percent of the population in Prato, Italy (La Ronciere, 1988). In 1480, they represented about 4.8 percent of Florence's population, and as much as 11 percent in Tuscany in the fifteenth century (La Ronciere, 1988). In sixteenth-century York, England, 10 percent of the population lived at least to the age of 40 (Smith, 1976). And Steven Smith (1982) found that in the seventeenth century a fair number of people made it to the age of 60 or over. Lawrence Stone (1977) reports that persons over 60 comprised about 8 percent of the population of England from 1500 to 1800. Similar figures are reported by John Demos (1986), who found that between 4 and 7 percent of the total population in late-seventeenth-century New England were over 60. Demos concludes that old age was a better than even prospect in colonial New England. David Barash (1983) reports that in 1789 America a 60-year-old male could expect to live another 15 years.

Peter Laslett (1977) pulled together numerous studies on the numbers of people surviving to old age. He found studies that report 10.1 percent in Italy for the year 1427, 11 percent in Iceland in 1787, 3.1 percent in Hungary in 1816, 6.1 percent in France in 1690, 7 percent in France in 1778, and 1.4 percent (for the year 1599) to a high of 11.2 percent (in 1698) in England. John Faragher (1976) reports that more than half of the women in seventeenth-century New England lived beyond 70 years and that 70 percent of the men lived to 50, and 30 percent to 70 years. Thus, while the percentage of people reaching old age does not match contemporary experience, older people were present in sufficient numbers to merit attention from their respective societies.

THE LIMITATIONS OF ART

The reliance on art as a source of information does have its limitations. We must always be judging whether the images we find in art are generalizable to the society as a whole or merely exhibit the biases of the artist; the age portrayals of old age in literature and art may not always be reflective of social reality (see Kebric, 1983). In addition, art is often biased toward the upper classes (see de Beauvoir, 1972). Art portraying the upper echelon of society was more likely to be commissioned than art of the general populace. Typical and ordinary members of society were rarely the focal point of the artist until the late Middle Ages, and even then on a very limited basis. By the late Middle Ages all social classes began to shape culture and art, more so than they had in the past (Hofstatter, 1968). However, this influence should not be overstated. High position and status in society still played the dominant role in dictating what was or was not captured by the artist. Yet works did surface—rarely—that give us a glimpse of how life might possibly have been.

Another major limitation of relying on art is that art commentary is a relatively recent phenomenon. Contemporaries of the artists of the late Middle Ages and other later periods provided no explanations or interpretations of their art (Martindale, 1979), and thus we know very little about earlier people's reactions to art, especially during the Middle Ages.

We do know that art has been biased not only toward the upper classes, but toward major events and secular topics rather than on the ordinary aspects of everyday life. Private life was not really examined by artists until the sixteenth and seventeenth centuries (Aries, 1962). Exceptions to this are rare in prior periods. Activities tied to the seasons, like harvesting and butchering animals, were quite common subjects in the arts of the Middle Ages. But these are exceptions to the rule, nonetheless, and this rarity of everyday life in the art of so many early periods limits our understanding of the older people in their respective societies.

Another limitation is that of survival. We have little choice but to rely on the art that has survived time. Much of what was painted, sculpted, drawn, and so on has been lost. This is particularly true of folk art and the art of the commoners. The art that does remain may actually slant our view of life in earlier periods. Furthermore, art of the masses is less likely to survive than art of the upper classes and of the Church. One could argue, however, that the art of the Church was in fact the art of the masses. Religious images were available to all in the form of architecture, stained glass, statuary, and murals.

Then too, the artist has not always been committed to showing life as it really is. For example, Gothic artists had little concern for showing things as they really were, but rather showed how they were to be viewed spiritually. The twelfth-century artist was more obsessed with the afterlife than with the reality of twelfth-century life.

WHY ART THEN?

This book draws primarily on a vast array of art and history and secondarily on the literature created over the centuries. The immediate question that comes to mind then is, Why use art to understand the past, and in particular older people? Of all the possibilities for information, why rely on art? Given its limitations, why bother with art at all?

Yet art does form the basis for much of what we know about prior societies. It served as the foundation of this work for several reasons. First, every major work of art is an expression of the people and society that produces it. Art does not develop outside of the social context, but as an integral part of it. The arts can help us understand what society was like during a historical period. Trewin

Copplestone writes, "The social conditions, intellectual climate, and the attitudes of mind that they sponsored make each work of art, as a product of its own history, and as a potent expression of its own cultural context" (1983:10).

Social attitudes and perceptions shape and guide art, and art shapes social perceptions and attitudes. Reviewing art, thus, provides insights into how people view their world. For example, the relative heights of the figures in a painting can be a clue to their status. A case in point is family portraiture. Throughout the centuries, family portraits have displayed a period-wise awareness of the position of the members in the family. The higher the status, the higher the individual's position in the work of art, the one exception being the era when the patriarch was always shown seated in the center of the work. The social activities being performed by the older people depicted in art also shed light on social perceptions and status. The activities and roles of older people are quite definite in art. Some roles are almost never performed by the old, while others are quite common. The artist selects what we want or need to see, but also what society encourages us to see (Copplestone, 1983). Therefore, art is a reflection of society, and society reflects art.

Second, as Patrick McKee and Heta Kauppinen (1987) observe, the selection by an artist (and for that matter, a writer) of old age as a topic attaches significance to it. In creating art and literature, the creator makes the subject matter significant to the host society. What Andy Warhol did for the soup can in contemporary society, the artists and writers of prior centuries did with their own cultural topics. The fact that older people were selected as topics and symbols by artists and writers added meaning and significance to their existence. Furthermore, because all of the aspects of old age are too complex to be captured in one story or one work of art, the creator had to focus on certain aspects of old age. In a sense, old age as shown by the writer or artist is an abstraction. Its perceived essential characteristics are brought to the fore. In a sense, the artist or author often works with and creates stereotypes of aging and old age. Stereotypes themselves as we all know, influence social attitudes and behavior and hence are important to understand.

Much of art throughout the Middle Ages and up to the nineteenth century followed certain well-defined rules. Artists did not have much freedom to vary from the social prescriptions and perceptions of their times. Naturally there were exceptions to this but on the whole art has towed the line and followed the rules. And many of these rules have been dictated by religion. During the Middle Ages, social and religious values guided what the artist was allowed to represent. In order for images to be presented, social expectations had to be met. In other words, the society had to be tolerant of an image before it could be created by the artists. Anything not prescribed by society was subject to criticism and the accusation of heresy. Again, art often mirrors its host society, its values and attitudes. Hence, the art of the past can be a reliable source of information on major social perceptions. In a sense, artists have been keeping a record of the social images of the old.

In fact, the use of art as historical evidence has been relatively common in many areas of study, although its use by gerontologists is still uncommon (Philibert, 1974). The French historian Philippe Aries (1962; 1985) relied on art in several of his works on death, childhood, and other topics. Other examples include David Fischer's (1978) study of family portraiture; Lynn White (1962); Donald Weinstein and Rudolph Bell (1982); Alison Stewart (1979); Philippa Tristram (1976); Samuel Chew (1962); John Antony Burrow (1986); Mary Dove (1986); and several others. A few researchers have even focused on understanding older people through art (Achenbaum & Kusnerz, 1978; Berg & Gadow, 1978; McKee & Kauppinen, 1987; O'Conner, 1979). Their efforts prove the value of the method. Since the artist's work is confined to the restrictions imposed by society, the dictates and perceptions of society are reflected in the art. The more exacting the dictates, the more restricted are the artist's images. When, say, society views older people in the context of a particular ages-of-life model—as described in Chapter 2—the artist who works with this subject is usually rendering a rather literal interpretation of the social prescriptions of the times.

It is important to note that the masters such as da Vinci, Tintoretto, and Rembrandt were passionately concerned with old age and the process of aging. Da Vinci's sketches and extended works contain several renditions of the older human body. Tintoretto, according to Murray (1967), is unsurpassed in his portraits of old age. But when it comes to the number of paintings involving older people and the process of aging, no artist exceeds Rembrandt (see Ranum, 1989). More than half of his known works are of older people. On this theme alone, his works could easily fill a volume of art.

Rembrandt's portraits of older men show them deep in thought or study; as scholars, dignitaries, grandparents, and religious figures; and from various walks of life. His older women, too, are shown in contemplation or reading, and with great dignity and self-reflection. He emphasized a realistic characterization of old age in his portraiture.

The artist's interest in old age—and specifically, in his own aging—is most obvious in his self-portraits. Rembrandt periodically took stock of his own life and painted self-portraits from 1629, when he was 23, to 1669, when he was 63. No other artist has recorded the subtle changes in the aging process with the dignity and perception of Rembrandt. In his self-portraits we witness the evolution from youth, with all its optimism, to the resolve and serenity of old age. His early canvases depict youth as a time of plumes and velvet jackets and steady gaze. His older self-portraits show a man whose watery eyes convey a life of personal misfortune. Rembrandt van Rijn was declared bankrupt in 1656, more than ten years before his death in 1669. Thus, one of the world's greatest painters spent the last decade of his life in financial distress, and died poor and unappreciated. Yet although there is a sadness to this life story, there is also a dignity. Rembrandt captured an important essence of aging: with the acknowledgment of decline, a growth in wisdom and dignity. As the artist ages, we watch this maturity develop.

The self-portrait in Plate 1, from the Mauritshuis in the Hague, was one of

Plate 1. *Late Self-portrait.* 1669. Rembrandt van Rijn. Courtesy of the Mauritshuis, The Hague.

the last two he painted. Here Rembrandt shows himself in serenity, solemnness, and self-reflection—as a man who has weathered the storm. This is a lifetime apart from the youthful optimism and flamboyance illustrated in his earlier self-portraits.

Despite the limitations of art, then, social historians can discover much about an earlier period by reviewing its art and other cultural artifacts. In fact, art can be particularly valuable when used in conjunction with other sources of information such as literature and historical evidence. The chapters that follow will present a sampling of images of older people. To some extent the previously mentioned limitations must be taken into consideration. All the same, however, many of these images were relatively common in their time and reflected, as the evidence will indicate, some fairly standard and accepted perceptions of older people and old age.

Undoubtedly, other images that were equally common have been excluded here. In addition, to every rule and example one can always find exceptions. We should therefore proceed with caution. Perhaps the most we can hope for is to reach some speculative conclusions about how older people might have been perceived within their respective societies. Even so, we will have come further than ever before in trying to understand historically our Western images of old age. We will know what images existed in earlier periods, but we will not know the extent to which they applied across the general population and various societies.

In any case, we are not working alone. In recent years social historians have started to investigate the evidence on older people in earlier periods; and humanists, historians, and gerontologists have begun to lay the foundation for the historical study of the aged. This relatively new work has already uncovered important insights into the nature of aging and old age, some of which may prove meaningful to our growing population of older people.

The status of our knowledge will eventually change as older people become more demographically prevalent in modern societies. Taking the United States as an example, current projections estimate that between 20 and 25 percent of the population will, in the immediate decades, be over 65 years of age. It will become increasingly difficult to ignore the role that the aged are playing in contemporary societies, and increasingly important to understand their role in the societies of the past.

2

THE AGES OF LIFE

Describing and explaining the human life-span has captured the attention of Western writers, artists, and scholars for centuries. This attention has spawned a multitude of ages-of-life schemes, which divide the human life-span into distinct phases of life. These distinct phases not only serve to describe the life-span, but also to explain the course of human existence (Burrow, 1986; Dove, 1986; Haber, 1983). In fact, the ages of life were so accepted and generalized that the historical evolution of civilization itself was viewed as analogous to the progression through the human life-span (Chew, 1962).

There is considerable evidence to suggest that the ages of life have had a long tradition in Western history. Over the centuries, a variety of schemes has been used to divide the human life-span into meaningful segments. For example, Roman calendars contained illustrations of human activity that might be considered forerunners of the ages-of-life genre (see White, 1962). And the French historian Philippe Aries (1962) has traced the ages of life back to Arabian frescos of the eighth century. Murals in the twelfth-century baptistry at Parma, Italy, also depict this theme (Aries, 1962; de Beauvoir, 1972). Andrew Achenbaum and Peggy Kusnerz (1978) provide recent historical examples of the ages-of-life theme in the United States during the eighteenth and nineteenth centuries, as has Michael Kammen (1980). The Puritan writer Anne Bradstreet's *The Four Ages of Man* and Cotton Mather's *To Old Men, and Young Men, and Little Children* are based on certain presumptions about life's phases (see Demos, 1986). Even the twentieth century has its portrayals of the ages of life, such as the one found in the lobby of the Waldorf Hotel in New York City (see Chew, 1962).

This chapter describes some ·of the main ages-of-life themes involving older people in Western history. As with all the other chapters, our information here was drawn from the work of historians, writers, and artists. Literature from the late Middle Ages through the nineteenth century abounds with the ages-of-life theme. Its study by the modern scholar can provide a sampling of perceptions about older people during earlier historical periods.

Many intellectuals of the Middle Ages and Renaissance wrote about the ages of life. Among them were Isidore of Seville (560–636), Avicenna (981–1037), Peter Abelard (1079–1142), Roger Bacon (1214–1298), Saint Thomas Aquinas (1225–1274), Dante (1265–1321), Petrarch (1304–1374), and Chaucer (1340–1400). Outstanding examples from the medieval literature include William Langland's *Piers Plowman*, John Gower's *Confessio Amantis*, Dante's *Convivio*, and Chaucer's *Canterbury Tales*. In the thirteenth century, particularly, there was a large body of literature on aging (see Freeman, 1965). During this period, old age was variously characterized as a state of reflection, an outward spectacle, a macabre state of being, a prototype of death, and the realization of God's plan (Tristram, 1976).

In later centuries the ages of life continued to be important to Western scholars and artists (Achenbaum & Kusnerz, 1978; Kammen, 1980). Kammen (1980) notes that American colonial views of the life cycle were based on earlier European models, there being a continuity of thought from the Old World to the New. Another sort of continuity was exhibited by the influential eighteenth-century author Daniel Defoe, who used the Biblical life-span of three-score-and-ten and the ages of life to organize his classic *Moll Flanders* published in 1721 (Sokoloff, 1986). Although the ages of life continued to be developed by scholars and artists over the centuries, such schemes had diminished in their relative importance by the twentieth century.

As noted earlier, the writings and artworks depicting the ages of life ranged all over Europe. The theme became a common topic of medieval thought among both intellectuals and the masses (Aries, 1962; Burrow, 1986; Herlihy, 1982). Although most people during this period were illiterate, it would be wrong to conclude that they did not know about so prevalent an idea in their culture. John Burrow (1986) indicates that the ages of life commonly shown in paintings were shared through spoken language and incorporated into folk wisdom. This is not to say, however, that the masses of people outside of intellectual circles would have understood the ages of life in great detail. Their understanding was probably very basic. Even among intellectuals there was confusion and disagreement on the subject. Mary Dove (1986) warns that the ages of life were sometimes used inconsistently by scholars. For example, Renaissance scholars used various names for the several ages of life; and even when the same names were used, they might have different meanings.[1]

It is important to note also that opinions have varied as to when old age beings. Chaucer put it at about 50 (Coffman, 1937). Dante thought old age starts at 45 (La Ronciere, 1988). Official England in the late medieval period considered old age to begin at 60, but the church placed it at 50 (Hanawalt, 1986). Erasmus in his *On the Discomforts of Old Age* (1506) complains of old age's beginning at 40. Cervantes' Don Quixote sees himself as being old at 50, whereas Shakespeare spoke of old age in a 40-year-old (Gilbert, 1967; Smith, 1976). In his second sonnet Shakespeare writes, "When forty winters shall besiege thy brow / and dig deep trenches in thy beauty's field." Cotton Mather believed that old age begins at 50 or 60, and Increase Mather considered himself old at 59 (Faragher, 1976). In nineteenth-century France, old age was felt to begin at 55–60 for men and 45–50 for women (Stearns, 1976).

The only safe conclusion, then, is that opinions about the beginning of old age have varied over the centuries. Regardless of where old age was thought to begin, moreover, there has always been a certain amount of built-in imprecision due to the fact that people did not always know their exact ages. Birth dates were not always considered important or recorded.

FOUNDATIONS FOR THE AGES OF LIFE

It is important, first of all, to review some of the factors that influenced the development of the ages-of-life concept in general. Some of its advocates based their models on natural events such as the changes in the seasons, astrological phenomena such as the number and movement of the planets, and religious writing. The ancient writings of the Greeks and Romans also provided inspiration on the ages of life.

Another influential factor must have been the high mortality rate in earlier times. The ages-of-life models that developed during the period from the late Middle Ages to the nineteenth century should be viewed within this context. Throughout most of Western history, life expectancy at birth was very low (see Dublin, 1965; Herlihy, 1982; Kastenbaum, 1979; Thomlinson, 1976). From the thirteenth to the seventeenth centuries, life expectancies are estimated to have been between 20 and 40 years (Goldscheider, 1971; Smith, 1978). Although the life-span itself was about as long as it is today, a person's chances of living a full life were unfavorable (Kastenbaum & Ross, 1975). Given such high death rates, there may have been little attention paid to old age simply because most people did not believe that they would live to see it.

Therefore, high mortality rates caused a mixed view of death, old age, and the ages of life. There are numerous depictions of death touching all people during all ages of life. This theme—discussed in more detail in Chapter 6—is most clearly presented in the dance-of-death illustrations that were popular in the fourteenth and fifteenth centuries. In these illustrations, death is seen touching people from all ages and walks of life. Most of the ages-of-life art, however, seems to contradict this view of death. Generally, it shows death as coming near or within the final ages of life. Death and preparation for death were usually the province of older people. This dual image of death and age may be due to a distinction made between the full life-span in which death naturally occurs in old age and catastrophic death, which can occur at any age of life.

BIBLICAL AND CLASSICAL INFLUENCES

Certainly, one major influence on the perception of the ages-of-life models in Western history must be the Old and New Testaments. The Old Testament placed emphasis on life in this world and how to prolong life. It held that a righteous life in this world would be rewarded by longevity. Life could be prolonged—through the grace of God—by the doing of good deeds and living righteously. Many Old Testament figures achieved great ages, at least figuratively. For example, Adam lived to be 930, Seth 912, and Noah 950. Great age was the reward for their good lives in this world. Therefore, old age was looked on as a positive state of being, and longevity was evidence of divine blessing. Importantly, however, the Old and New Testaments rejected the proposition—popular in later times—that chronological age was the reliable measure of a person's individual and social value (Kastenbaum & Ross, 1975). Instead, the Scriptures focused on one's functional rather than chronological age.

Classical Greek, Roman, and Alexandrian literature also provided guidance to those later Western thinkers who were seeking to understand the human life-span. Ancient scholars wrote extensively about the ages of life. For example, Pythagoras, Ovid, and Horace divided the life-span into four ages. Hippocrates and Ptolemy saw it as seven ages. Medieval scholars such as Saint Thomas Aquinas and John Duns Scotus drew on the ideas of Aristotle, Plato, and other earlier scholars to develop their concepts about the ages of life. The same was true for Renaissance intellectuals, who often turned to antiquity for ideas on the aging process and life's phases (Stern & Cassirer, 1946).

Of particular importance is Hippocrates, the fourth-century-B.C. Greek physician, who influenced many later ideas on the ages of life. Hippocrates described the life-span as a ladder divided into many stages. The final stage at the end of this ladder begins at the age of 90. Hippocrates believed that at this final stage death is welcomed by the older person. It was apparently also the Greeks who provided Western culture with the concept of *coup de vieux*. This idea, deeply ingrained in later thought, holds that healthy adults quickly change to unhealthy ones as a result of the rapid onslaught of old age (see de Beauvoir, 1972). There is evidence, however, that ancient scholars may actually have viewed age-related changes in the individual as being gradual and smooth, rather than rapid and dramatic (Dove, 1986).

One of the major concepts with an origin in Greek thought is that of moderation. Among the earliest proponents of moderation was Aristotle (384–322 B.C.) whose *Rhetoric* was influential during the late Middle Ages, the Renaissance, and later. Aristotle's central principle was that aging is a natural and inevitable process. The individual moves over the course of life from one extreme to the other, with middle age representing the perfect balance (Chandler, 1948). Aristotle referred to this perfect age as status. He also proposed that the body loses heat and moisture throughout the life-span (see Fowler et al., 1982): During the early part of the ages of life, the primary characteristics of the human body are heat and moisture. As the person ages, these characteristics are replaced by coldness and dryness, leading to the diseases of old age (Freeman, 1965). This idea, known as the humoral theory of aging, dominated as the model for future ages-of-life schemes.

And in the second century A.D., the Roman physician Galen concurred with Aristotle, perpetuating the humoral view of aging. Galen's works had a lasting influence on the Middle Ages and on up to the nineteenth century. To Galen, humors and heat were the foundation for understanding aging. He believed bodies ought to be warmed and moistened. Actually, the fact that so little changed from Galen through the nineteenth century is indicative mostly of the lack of medical progress over the centuries.

It is an essential feature of this view of aging held by Aristotle and Galen that one can reduce the negative effects of the aging process by living one's life in moderation. Too much of anything, they said, can upset the balance of the body humors and result in such undesirable effects as premature aging or death. The theme of moderation was given new life during the Middle Ages and Renaissance. Drawing from Aristotle and other sources, the Renaissance scholar Liugi Cornaro (1464–1566)—when himself an old man—adopted the theme of moderation and argued that energy should be retained at all costs (Haber, 1983; Miles, 1965). Cornaro believed that death results from the exhaustion of bodily energy. In general, then, although classical ideas offered a foundation to build on, its adherence to Greek theories effectively stagnated Western thought on the ages of life for many centuries.

MOTIFS AND THEMES WITHIN THE AGES OF LIFE

There were several major themes and motifs within the ages-of-life scheme that remained fairly constant not only throughout the period from the late Middle Ages to the nineteenth century, but also prior to the late Middle Ages. These included the cycle, the staircase, the bridge, physical decay of the individual, ambivalence to old age, age-appropriate behavior, the various linkages of the ages of life to natural and supernatural phenomena. Some themes actually declined over time, such as the emphasis on the zodiac as a means of understanding the human life-span, in favor of more natural world explanations of the ages of life.

Certain themes were very short lived. For example, the voyage of life as motif was quite popular in the nineteenth century. According to Kammen (1980), the voyage of life displaced the seasons of life as the dominant image of the life cycle. The nineteenth-century artist Thomas Cole's popular *Voyages of Life* series is a case in point. An earlier but somewhat similar motif was that of the traveled pilgrim, sometimes illustrated by an old man walking alone in a forest. As youth and vigor escape the old man and pain sets in, he faces the last confrontation: death. Thomas Cole (1984), after reviewing Protestant sermons from 1800 to 1900, concluded that nineteenth-century Protestantism viewed old age as a spiritual journey from this life to the next. Life was then seen as a great pilgrimage, and the pilgrimage was enjoined to flow with life. In the last important stages of the journey, the pilgrim would be preparing to meet with the creator God. By the twentieth century, the voyage of life motif had all but disappeared.

Analogies were often made between the ages of life and cycles, staircases, bridges, and the wheel of fortune (Chew, 1962). Many artists and writers have illustrated these four basic themes. In the cyclical motif, the cycle was considered to begin in childhood and come round again in extreme old age with its childlike behavior. This model was based on the perception that very old people become dependent on others, as if they were children. Shakespeare's Rosencrantz in *Hamlet* viewed old men as twice children, a theme that Smith (1976) believes can be traced as far back in Western literature as the ancient Greek Aristophanes. The model invariably assumes a helplessness and limited functioning in old age. Occasionally, the cycle-of-life view on aging also carried a very heavy religious connotation. The birth–life–death–resurrection–rebirth life model can be seen as a religious view of the cycle of life.

Plate 2, a page from the fourteenth-century English *De Lisle Psalter*, provides us with an illustration of the cycle of life. It shows ten ages, using a cycle as its basic design. The Deity is located in the center of the wheel, with the caption, "I see all at once; I govern the whole by my plan." The cycle starts with the mother holding her baby in the lower left-hand corner of the wheel. By the sixth age, we see the beginning of decline. In the seventh age, a child must lead the old man. In the eighth, a doctor examines the old man's urine. A funeral service is shown in the ninth age, and a tomb in the tenth. Four figures in the corners of the illuminated page represent the aspects of the man in the ages of his life: infancy, youth, old age, and decrepitude. The cycle depicts the rise and decline of the ages (Sandler, 1983).

The wheel of fortune was very similar to the cycle motif, with a key difference being that various figures turned the wheel. These figures represented Death or Fortune. And one could take little comfort in Fortune's turns, which were seen as arbitrary and often meaningless.

The staircase also conveyed a negative view of the life-span and its corresponding ages of life. The basic assumption of this model was that from birth on, the individual increases in ability, strength, knowledge, and other desirable features until a certain peak is reached. This pattern was sometimes characterized as being an arc or bridge (Burrow, 1986). Its peak was usually set at between the ages of 35 and 40. Once having reached the peak, the individual then declines physically and mentally, according to this model. Old age was generally positioned at the foot of the bridge on the right side of the drawing, visually the point of maximum decline. Individuals are shown stepping up the staircase through progressive ages of life.

As with the other motifs, these staircase patterns and images of the ages of life, though varying to some extent over the centuries, have been remarkably

Plate 2. *Wheel of Life*. 1339. Madonna Master. From the *De Lisle Psalter*. Courtesy of the British Library, London.

similar in their most basic assumptions: The decline of older people, older people's increased dependence, and age-appropriate behavior are present whether the version be medieval or of the nineteenth century.

Achenbaum and Kusnerz (1978) identified two nineteenth-century prints by James Baille, reproduced here as Plates 3 and 4, that depict the ages of life using a staircase. Actually, versions of the staircase model were popular and abundant during the nineteenth century. Michael Kammen (1980) shows four representative works from this period, all remarkably similar. Some staircases, such as Baille's *The Life and Age of Woman* (1848), show a separate staircase for women, as

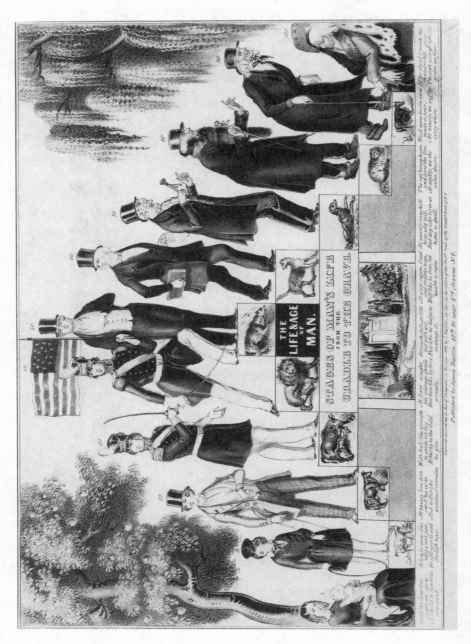

Plate 3. *The Life and Age of Man: Stages of Man's Life from the Cradle to the Grave.* 1848. James Baille. Courtesy of the Library of Congress, Washington, D.C.

Plate 4. *The Life and Age of Woman: Stages of Woman's Life from the Cradle to the Grave.* 1848. James Baille. Courtesy of the Library of Congress, Washington, D.C.

women were thought to age differently than men. Baille's prints continue to fit the pattern of ascent, peak, and descent typical in all the ages-of-life art. The artist shows 11 ages each for man and woman; both wind up, however, in same-looking grave sites. Every age in the man's life corresponds with an animal figure, such as a bull, a lion, and finally a goat for the old man. Each of the ages is captioned. For the oldest man, the caption reads: "If we should reach the hundredth year though sick of life the grave we fear." Interestingly enough, the woman's ages of life are not connected with animals, but rather plants and landscapes. Why this distinction is made between man and woman remains unclear. Where the old man is symbolized by the goat—a traditional symbol for old age—the old woman is symbolized by what look like knitting tools used to work yarn. For the oldest woman, the caption reads: "Chained to her chair by weight of years, She listless knits till death appears." The visible signs of aging are dramatically illustrated—the cane, bent posture, stooped shoulders, and gray hair. And in the end, both of the oldest figures are shown sitting down, after their climb through the ages of life.

There is remarkable consistency between these and other versions of the ages of life that use the staircase model. For example, in the late sixteenth century the Italian artist Christofero Bertello used a staircase for his *Nine Ages of Man* and *Nine Ages of Woman* (see Chew, 1962, figs. 101 & 102). Apart from the difference in the number of ages and the emphasis placed on death (which is more evident in the sixteenth-century work), the ages of life are very similar to the nineteenth-century prints. The animals used for the ages of man are virtually the same, with the goat representing old age; the peak of life occurs at about the same age; and the rise and decline of the individuals are parallel. Bertello used a hen with her chicks to represent the motherhood age of life, and a goose symbolizes the old woman. Cupid appears at age 20, fortitude at 40, and an hourglass at 50. Bertello's 80-year-old man has one foot in the grave. It is almost as if the nineteenth-century artist used the sixteenth-century work for a model and simply updated certain sections. More importantly, the similarities show a consistency of thought regarding the staircase-of-life motif over the centuries. Use of the staircase eventually died out in the nineteenth century, however (de Beauvoir, 1972).

Simone de Beauvoir (1972) makes an interesting point about staircase-of-life models. She observes that rarely did people in real life actually reach the old-age end of the staircase. There was, in fact, a lack of correspondence between the model and and actual experience. De Beauvoir concludes that these images were not based on life observation, but on archetypes. And it is true that all the age-of-life motifs were nothing more than ideal models of the life-span and had little correspondence with reality. However, a case could be made that the stereotypes symbolized by each of the different ages were abstracted from observation and experience. Artists based their images on general patterns that they witnessed in society or had gathered from scholarly writings on old age.

Ambivalence

One theme present in the ages-of-life genre was an occasional ambivalence toward older people (Hendricks & Hendricks, 1977–78; Kastenbaum & Ross, 1975). The ancient world caricatured old men as being pale and on the decline, but at the same time praised their old age (de Beauvoir, 1972). Traditional societies had a dual image of older people. They thought of old age as a downward movement toward debility, but also as an upward movement toward knowledge and wisdom (Moody, 1986; Tristram, 1976). Youth was seen as short and foolish, whereas old age could draw on the wisdom of experience. On the one hand, older people were respected for their perceived moral and spiritual superiority— as they were most dramatically in Anglo-Saxon England (Burrow, 1986)—yet on the other hand they were also sometimes characterized as losing their wits and becoming senile. On the most basic level, this ambivalence arose from a sense that older people experience bodily descent while they ascend spiritually.

The Bible and its teachings are very ambivalent toward the old with regard to the ages of life and age-appropriate behavior. The Bible makes reference to the liabilities of old age, but also to the dignity of the older person (Griffin, 1946). It expects older people to contribute to society, but in different ways than when they were younger. The old are expected to contribute their wisdom and experience to the good of society. Also, certain ages must be attained before certain behaviors are permitted by the Scriptures. For example, Christ had to be at least 30 before he was baptized—which was later taken to be the minimum age for becoming a priest, according to the medieval scholar the Venerable Bede (673–735; see Burrow, 1986). The Bible also indicates that the old are too old for certain activities, such as marriage (Kastenbaum & Ross, 1975). Thus, the Scriptures were prescriptive with respect to age-appropriate behavior.

Christianity itself exerted influences on thought about the ages of life. For example, the body was viewed as moving independently of the soul. Saint Augustine (354–430) held that decay brings men down but spiritual perfection lifts them upward (Dove, 1986; Folts, 1980). Viewed as wise and knowledgeable, older people were also seen as unable to escape the physical decline that accompanies old age (see Haber, 1983). Basically, they were perceived as being in a state between youth and death. Old age was certainly an alternative to death, but was undesirable nonetheless (Kastenbaum & Ross, 1975). To some, old age was almost a prototype of death. Philippa Tristram, for instance, argued that old age in Chaucer's *Pardoner's Tale* and Langland's *Piers Plowman* serves as the messenger or prototype of death (see Tristram, 1976). In addition, there was also the theme of tension between the ambition and desires of the individual and the reality of physical decline (Cole & Gadow, 1986). These aspects of ambivalence characterized much of the early literature and art on the ages of life.

Although physical decay is predominant in the ages-of-life literature and art, however, there is also a sense of mental and spiritual growth. This understanding has had a lasting impact on perceptions of aging. Many examples depicting the inner growth of older people can be found in the works of artists such as Rembrandt, Titian, and Van Dyck. Rembrandt's series of self-portraits (see Plate 1) imparts a good sense of physical decay over time, but also of inner growth.

Older people thus face the dilemma of physical decline being accompanied by intellectual and spiritual growth. Examples of this dilemma have been noted in seventeenth-century Puritan society by David Stannard (1977), John Faragher, (1976), and others (see Moody, 1986). The central point is that one could very well experience ambivalent feelings about aging, as it was considered a process of both decay and growth. In early America, old age was viewed favorably in terms of knowledge and experience, but also negatively because of infirmities and decline (Haber, 1983). Faragher (1976) found this ambivalence in the writings of Cotton Mather, for instance.

The theme of ambivalence continued into the nineteenth century. Even though old age was viewed with gloom, it was also seen as full of optimism for mortals, as the time when heaven would be near at hand (Kammen, 1980). In the nineteenth century, one could take pride in the accomplishments of a lifetime. Thus, old age was a blessing and a time of harvest, though also a time of physical decline and diminished activity. And so it was an ambivalence toward aging and older people that endured in Western thought. It may be, as Robert Kastenbaum and Barbara Ross (1975) suggest, that the diversity of attitudes and conditions among older people themselves, the competition for scarce resources, and the status of old age as an imperfect alternative to death—in the absence of external youth, that is—all contributed to ambivalent perceptions in regard to older people.

Lawrence Stone (1977) makes an important point about ambivalence. As long as older people maintain their mental capacities and contribute to the community, they are venerated. But when these faculties fail and diminish, older people become despised and ridiculed by their societies—sometimes, as will be noted in Chapter 4, to the point of being considered outcasts and left to die. The key point is that general attitudes toward older people depend on their perceived value to society. This is a very familiar concept to contemporary gerontologists.

Physical Decay

Physical decay became a major motif during the Middle Ages (Huizinga, 1952; Tristram, 1976), an era in which the passage of time was strongly associated with decay (de Beauvoir, 1972) and death (Aries, 1985; Stannard, 1977). Thus it is with the aging process, the medievals would say: As time passes, the individual decays. During the fifteenth and sixteenth centuries (and perhaps earlier), this decay was interpreted as a sign of human failure. According to Philippe Aries (1974a), the French had a view euphemistically termed *les oeuvres naturelles*, the operations of nature. This view held that all human bodies contain worms that eventually, in old age, consume the individual from within. Elizabethan playwrights also often wrote of the physical infirmities that were considered an inevitable accompaniment to old age, and by the end of the seventeenth century this theme seemed to be an obsession of Restoration writers of comedy (Mignon, 1947). In later centuries decay continued to be viewed as a product of aging, each progressive age of life bringing its share of dreaded decline to the individual.

The connection between physical decay and the ages of life was linked to the processes in nature. Plants and animals were observed to grow and then decay. The four seasons of the temperate-zone year also provided a basis for the concept of decay. Spring with all its new growth, summer with its maturation and continued growth, fall with its harvest and decay, and winter with its death—together they served as a model for understanding the ages of life.

The life-span regarded as a process of decay appears in several works that influenced Western thought over the centuries. For example, the book of Ecclesiastes characterizes old age in terms of physical decay (Kastenbaum & Ross, 1975), as do other sections of the Bible (Griffin, 1946). In his influential work *De Senectute*, the Roman orator and writer Cicero acknowledges the operations of decay. However, Cicero departed from most other writers in his emphasis on attitude. Cicero believed that one's attitude toward aging and lifestyle is more important in the aging process than the passage of time. The physical decline can therefore be mitigated through a positive attitude.

Another example of the decay theme is Langland's *Piers Plowman*, which identifies the miseries of old age. And during the thirteenth century, Roger Bacon thought—as did others of his time—that every day is a step toward old age and that disease accelerates this process (see Freeman, 1965). Chaucer wrote of decay in his *Knight's Tale*: "This world but a thoroughfare full of woe, And we been pilgrims to and fro." Indeed, most of Chaucer's fourteenth-century contemporaries viewed life as a continual process of decay (Tristram, 1976). Much later, in the seventeenth century, Shakespeare maintained the same focus. In *As You Like It*, his character Jaques states: "And so from hour to hour we ripe, and ripe, And then from hour to hour, we rot, and rot, And thereby hangs a tale" (act 2, sc. 7).

In fact, English literature has on many occasions contained the theme of decay and often in association with older people (Freedman, 1978), along with the theme of fear of aging. Elizabeth Mignon's 1947 book on Restoration comedies of manners cites several seventeenth-century treatments of the theme in the works of Etherege, Congreve, Wycherley, Dryden, and others. Richard Freedman (1978) indicates that William Congreve's eighteenth-century *The Way of the World* as well as Jonathan Swift's *Gulliver's Travels* and Jane Austen's *Sense and Sensibility*—both eighteenth-century works—all contain the theme of decay associated with old age.

Early New England writers also acknowledged the process of decay and viewed aging as a time of misery and pain (see Fischer, 1977). Demos (1986) provides examples of the "natural infirmities" of old age identified by Cotton Mather. Mather went into great detail: He spoke of weak teeth, weak backs, buckling legs, and other aspects of physical decline (Demos, 1986). People in seventeenth-century England viewed old age in a similar fashion (Smith, 1979). In fact, there were some in both England and America who thought of old age as a disease in its own right (Smith, 1978a; Thomas, 1976).

The most dramatic eighteenth-century presentation of the theme is in Jonathan Swift's *Gulliver's Travels*. Gulliver visits a country inhabited by people—the Struldbrugs—who experience aging but never die. These aged Struldbrugs display the effects of aging and decay in the most extremely negative light. Swift basically characterizes their lives as a disaster. Voltaire would write, "The heart does not grow old, but it is said to dwell among the ruins" (cited by Barash, 1983:12). In any case, by the nineteenth century, old age had in effect become diagnosed as a disease (see Haber, 1983; Miles, 1965). The medical profession increasingly cited it as a disease and cause of death during this period.

Predictable and Appropriate Behavior

Many Western writers and artists have believed in a natural order that governs the physical and behavioral development of the human being (Burrow, 1986). This natural order is reflected in the ages-of-life schemes. During the late Middle Ages, the Renaissance, and the periods that followed, people felt there was a natural order in the life of the individual from infancy to old age (Burrow, 1984). The ages of life were logical, sequential, and predictable. There was a mechanical certainty to the aging process similar to a clock. In fact, predictability was an important feature of all the ages-of-life motifs (Haber, 1983). Each of them provided a meaningful explanation of the life-span for people in its era or location of popularity. In chaotic times, the perceived predictability of life offered some sense of order.

The ages of life similarly reflected what artists and writers defined as age-appropriate behavior. The ages were described or portrayed with their corresponding activities, passions, preoccupations, virtues, and vices (Burrow, 1984). As a matter of fact, age has been used throughout history as a basic determinant of what people can or should do. For example, sexual activity has been considered inappropriate behavior for older people. Chapter 5 will detail some of the social restrictions that have applied to sex in old age.

On the other hand, avarice or greed was thought during the Middle Ages to be quite appropriate—though shameful—behavior among older people. The medieval scholar Petrarch viewed avarice as the chief sin of old age (Folts, 1980). Artists and writers often portrayed older people as clutching their worldly possessions, holding, grasping, hoarding; and old age was often symbolized by hands (May, 1986).

This emphasis on associating older people with an overriding concern about their worldly possessions is really not so surprising, if you think about it. In preparing for death and/or arranging for their care during old age, people do have to take stock and then part with their possessions. Then as now, they had to make difficult decisions about surrendering their monetary worth to the next generation. And in many cases, there was indeed cause for great concern, with so few guarantees for family care in periods like the Middle Ages (see Hanawalt, 1986). Undoubtedly, the arrangements were not always smooth, and offspring and others found older parents reluctant to surrender their property and security. After all, wealth was an assurance of care in old age. If such a scenario were common enough, it is easy to see how older people would become associated generally with a reluctance to give up their worldly possessions and then the reluctance would be interpreted as selfishness and avarice.

In a more agreeable vein, contemplation was also viewed as an age-appropriate behavior for old age. Ancient and medieval societies placed a high value on contemplation (Moody, 1986). In fact, there was a bias toward the contemplative over the active life during the Middle Ages (Regnier-Bohler, 1988). However, there is also evidence from medieval England that older people were as active as their health permitted (Hanawalt, 1986).

Contemplation was certainly expected during the last ages of life—although it was not always possible, due to socioeconomic reasons. Old age was seen as the appropriate time for life review and melancholic reflection (Dove, 1986). Saint Augustine's *Confessions* (397–401) is an example of the early Christian emphasis placed on contemplation. This work was influential for centuries afterward. Augustine saw the spiritual review of life as the path to salvation or deliverance (Moody, 1986). His vision of contemplation maintained its influence well into the nineteenth century (Kammen, 1980). Augustine defined old age as the time to sum up one's life. He also thought that a new man of spirit is born during old age. The person's life can come into full view for the first time (Moody, 1986), having enough experience to give it context. This contemplation was sometimes regarded as being not only a way to fulfillment, but also preparation for death.

One of the major behaviors that has been viewed as appropriate for older people is the preparation for death. In the art of the period under consideration, children are generally shown at play. Middle-aged persons are involved with business, work, romance, work, and war. Meanwhile, older people are shown hobbling along, stooped over, leaning on their canes, and contemplating their deaths.

Titian's 1515 painting of the three ages of life, reproduced in Plate 5, illustrates the older person in the contemplative mode. The old man, whom Titian consciously places in the background, holds a skull, a symbol of death that was common in the sixteenth century and was to become even more common in the eighteenth (Whittick, 1972/1935). The old man is deep in thought and seems to be resolved about the end of his life. In contrast, the middle-aged man is involved in courtly romance, and the child sleeps comfortably in the front of the painting.

The theme of contemplation persisted in the centuries that followed the Middle Ages. For example, in seventeenth-century America, Cotton Mather suggested that people withdraw from activity and take up contemplation during old age

Plate 5. *The Three Ages of Man.* 1515. Titian. Duke of Sutherland Collection, on loan to the National Gallery of Scotland, Edinburgh. Courtesy of the Duke of Sutherland.

(Faragher, 1976). Thus, while it is certainly not the sole province of older people, contemplation has nonetheless been much encouraged in the Western world as an appropriate pursuit for older people. Apart from its edifying features—religious or philosophical—however, contemplation may also involve coming to terms with regrets, for some of life's goals must no doubt always remain unmet.

There have been exceptions to the implied determinism in the ages-of-life concept with its emphasis on age-appropriate behavior. For example, in Puritan America the actual age of older men was less important than their physical condition. This attitude can be traced back to biblical teachings and in particular to the Old Testament, which viewed older people as playing a number of positive social roles. A certain looseness and flexibility characterized the application of age norms and attitudes toward growing old in colonial America.

As mentioned earlier, some activities such as sex, war, and work were almost universally considered inappropriate for older people. For example, in Chaucer's *Merchant's Tale* (which will be discussed more in Chapter 5), the marriage between the old knight January and his young bride May flies in the face of fifteenth-century attitudes (Covey, 1989b; Tristram, 1976). January's sexual interests are definitely not in sync with the medieval idea of age-appropriate behavior. As a result, the knight winds up being the butt of the narrative joke, in his sexual inability to satisfy his younger wife.

The timing of events and age-appropriate behaviors were clearly defined by the various ages-of-life schemes. An individual would progress from one age to the next at certain—although not always agreed-upon—age intervals. Women of the period were portrayed less often than men as the subject of the ages-of-life art and literature. In general, women were regarded as aging much quicker than men (Roebuck & Slaughter, 1979) and were therefore thought to move through the ages at an exaggerated pace (Dove, 1986). This may have been due to their perceived societal value as bearers of children and as sex objects. In addition, unlike men, women receive a message loud and clear from the aging process when they pass through menopause (May, 1986; Roebuck & Slaughter, 1979). In any case, there is some evidence that this perceived gender difference was present in nineteenth-century thought (Stearns, 1980), as well as earlier.

THE NUMBER OF AGES OF LIFE

In Western thought, there were four major traditions regarding the number of ages of life. These traditions contended that the life-span could be divided into three, four, six, or seven distinct periods (see Burrow, 1986; Chew, 1962; Dove, 1986). There were also other less popular schemes involving five and 12 ages. But while the number of ages has varied, the basic assumption that the life-span can be divided remained constant. In fact, Carole Haber (1983) has observed that there was a great deal of precision in ancient medical thought regarding the divisions of the life-span.

Furthermore, medical authorities and scholars regarded specific years as being

more important than others. They divided the life-span into numerical intervals—
such as seven, ten, and even 20 years—to denote these critical years. Thus, if
the ages of life were based on the number seven, then the ages of seven, 14,
21, and so on would mark major changes in the life of the individual. Finally,
it is important to note that the various number traditions used to understand the
ages of life coexisted during the same historical eras. Thus, one can find schemes
built on three, four, five, six, or seven in the same place at the same time. Artists
such as Titian and Hans Baldung show different numbers of ages across several
works, suggesting that artists of the genre did not strictly adhere to any one
numerical scheme.

The Three Ages of Life

A popular and widely accepted way to organize the ages of life was to divide
the life-span into the three categories of youth, middle age, and old age. Numerous works of art and literature follow this pattern. For example, various
renditions of the gift of the Magi, a popular subject for centuries, were designed
around it. Traditionally, the three wisemen represent the three ages of life (Sill,
1975). The wiseman Gaspar stands for youth or *juvenis*, Balthazar for middle
age or *media aetas*, and Melchior for old age or *senex*. This symbolic representation of the ages of life is very old, having existed since at least the sixth
century (Burrow, 1986; Schiller, 1971). And in contemporary society, the three
Magi continue to be shown as three different ages.

Old Melchior is portrayed with little variation throughout the genre. His old
age is shown by a long white beard and hair. Generally he kneels before the
Christ Child and is located at the front of the group. Examples of this arrangement
can be found in the twelfth-century Cathedral of Notre Dame in Paris. The
fifteenth-century Limbourg brothers' *Très riches heures du Jean duc de Berry*—
the Duke of Berry's *Book of Hours*—contains a nativity scene that also fits the
general format of the three ages with Melchior kneeling in front. Gentile da
Fabriano's *Adoration of the Magi* (1423) and Quinten Massys' renditions of the
theme are also representative of this pattern.

The Holy Family itself has often been used to illustrate the three ages of life
(see Chapter 4). Joseph is traditionally portrayed as considerably older than
Mary. He often wears all the trappings of old age as it was perceived during the
artist's period, including at times a stooped posture and a cane. The Virgin Mary
appears in her youth or occasionally middle age. And the Christ Child, of course,
is the picture of childhood or infancy. Examples of the three ages represented
by the Holy Family are numerous throughout the period studied here, as this
too was a popular subject. And in fact, these portrayals do all tend to follow a
rigid prescription based on age differences.

Hans Baldung of the sixteenth-century German school provides a very different
and remarkable view of the three ages of life. In Baldung's *Death and the Ages
of Women*—see Plate 6—a baby sleeps at the feet of three standing figures: a

Plate 6. *Death and The Ages of Women*. C. 1541–44.
Hans Baldung Grien. Courtesy of the Prado, Madrid.

young woman, an old woman, and Death. Death is holding an hourglass and a broken staff that is also grasped by the sleeping infant—which is perhaps meant to suggest the high infant-mortality rate of Baldung's time and the fragility of life in infancy. An owl, possibly representing wisdom, is in the foreground. Overall, the work displays a remarkably grotesque realism.

The differences in age portrayed in this work are described by dramatic changes in the figures' physiology including the old woman's sagging breasts, bent spine, and wrinkling skin. The young woman is the only figure with clothing; Death, the baby, and old age are nude. A sense of the entire life-span is given by an interlocking of the three standing figures. The old woman holds on to the young woman's clothes, perhaps in an attempt to retain her youth. Death's arm passes through the old woman's arm while she looks back at the young woman. The baby is not entwined in the standing threesome; this may be suggesting a lack of attachment to the life-span and could possibly allude again to the high mortality rate among infants.

The three-ages pattern was also an element of popular literature. In his *Knight's Tale*, Chaucer divides his characters into three ages (Burrow, 1984). Saturn is the father of Jupiter and the grandfather of Venus, Mars, Diana in this fourteenth-century work. Chaucer's view of old age comprehends wisdom but also malignancy. His Old Egeus preaches of the vanity of all things and the inevitability of death.

The artist Titian in the sixteenth century worked with the three ages of life in at least two paintings. In his *Three Ages of Man* (see Plate 5 earlier in this chapter), Titian shows three man at different ages of the life-span. As was common for the period, the old man sits in the background holding a skull and presumably contemplating his coming death. He shows the deleterious effects of age in his bent posture—contrasting sharply with the other humans in the painting. Titian's *Three Ages* served as a model for later renditions by other artists. For example, in 1682 the French artist Lefebre copied the painting and—interestingly—removed the old man from the scene, but kept the same title.

In another painting, *An Allegory of Prudence*—shown in Plate 7—Titian again reflected the three ages of life, this time styled as an allegory. The painting contains three human heads and corresponding heads of three animals. It bears the inscription: "From the past, the present acts prudently, lest it spoil future action." This reflected the sixteenth-century view that older people are wise due to the experience of their advanced years.

In sharp contrast to the young man's illuminated face, which conveys bright prospects for the future, Titian portrayed the old man's face in the shadows. The old man is above the head of a wolf, the middle-aged man above a lion, and the young man above a dog. Animal heads such as these carried special meaning to the sixteenth-century mind. According to David Rosand (1978), images of the dog, lion, and wolf date back to at least the fifth-century writer Macrobius. The dog, which represents youth and the future, is always eager to

Plate 7. *An Allegory of Prudence*. C. 1570. Titian. Courtesy of the Trustees of the National Gallery, London.

please. It signifies the uncertainties in the future about which hope, nevertheless, always presents a pleasing picture. The lion stands for middle age and the present, the condition between past and future. It symbolizes strength and present action. The wolf represents old age and symbolizes things of the past that have been devoured and carried away.

The Four Ages of Life

From the twelfth century onward, four became very popular as the number of ages of life (Burrow, 1984), particularly in Elizabethan and Jacobean England (Kammen, 1980). Elizabethan scholars of the sixteenth century relied on the Greek heritage of the four bodily humors and then elaborated on it themselves (Hendricks & Hendricks, 1977). Thus, the theory of bodily humors lasted on through the seventeenth century (Dove, 1986). And the notion of dividing the life-span into four ages was still very common in the sixteenth (Aries, 1962) and even the nineteenth centuries (Kammen, 1980). It seemed only natural to classify the ages of life into four categories, with old age being one of them. In Romanesque times, toward the beginning of the late Middle Ages, much emphasis was placed on organizing concepts into groups of four: the seasons, the elements, and the bodily humors as well (Burrow, 1984; Kaufmann, 1975). Indeed, the correspondence between the ages of life and the elements, seasons, and humors was the subject of considerable investigation by scholars of the period (Dove, 1986).

One of the strongest connections was between the four ages and the four seasons (Smith, 1976; Tristram, 1976). As far as old age is concerned, several works linked it to the winter season. For example, Shakespeare wrote in *As You Like It*, "Therefore my age is as a lusty winter, frostly but kindly" (act 2). Like many another poet, the Bard connected winter metaphorically with old age because of the season's association with the end of the year, death, and coldness.

In contrast, spring has often been symbolic of renewal and baptism. Summer is associated with heat and light. Autumn is the season of grain and grape, the season of harvest and reckoning—when we reap what we sow. Winter is the shadow of death that awaits every creature, every human being, in the world. And there are often reasons, too, that old age would become associated with winter. During old age, the body is more easily chilled, partly because of slowed metabolism and a corresponding decline in body heat. Thus, older people have a harder time keeping warm compared to their younger counterparts. This may also explain the association made by Aristotle and others after him between old age and the loss of hot body humors.

This theme of old age and coldness can be found in many places. In the cathedral at Amiens, for instance, an old man who represents the month of February is shown sitting before a fire (Tristram, 1976). Several medieval images show old men warming themselves in front of fires. Another example of this enduring theme is a woodcut by Robert Vaughan and Robert Farley dated 1638. Under the image of old age is the caption "Winter and chilly old age." Again we find an old man warming himself at a fire.

The idea of four ages was propounded by several important writers on the ages of life. For one thing, Aristotle had adopted this view. Later, in the eighth century, the Venerable Bede also held that the life-span consists of four distinct ages and that the process of aging involves a loss of heat and moisture. Avicenna

in the eleventh century and Philippe de Novare in the thirteenth century both
wrote of the life-span as comprising four distinct ages. Elaborating further,
Philippe de Novare divided life into four periods of 20 years each. The four
ages were also mentioned in the influential writings of Dante, for instance in his
Convivio.

Among artists, the seventeenth-century Le Valentin chose to work with four
as a pattern in *The Four Ages of Man*. And also in the seventeenth-century Van
Dyck too linked the life-span to four distinct and even disjointed periods. In his
painting titled *The Four Ages of Man*—see Plate 8—he shows an old man in
deep contemplation, a child asleep, and a middle-aged man in a soldier's breast-
plate making a selection from a younger man's hand. The old man and child
are all but oblivious to this central activity. The old man apparently ponders
some question, as he points his finger toward the unknown.

Often cited as an example of the four ages of life is another seventeenth-
century work: the Otho Van Veen print *Time Leading the Seasons* (Dove, 1986;
Chew, 1962; Kammen, 1980). This work from the *Emblemata Horatiana* shows
Time at the head of a procession of the four ages of life. Old Age ends the
procession, and he carries a pot of fire, which may possibly represent wisdom
here. A cane supports his bent, robed frame. A serpent lies coiled in the right
foreground, symbolizing the cycle of life. The four-ages pattern remained a
popular subject of art as recently as the nineteenth century, typified in Thomas
Cole's *Voyages of Life*. Also very influential was the Currier and Ives print series
titled *The Four-Seasons of Life*; see Plate 9 for *Old Age—The Season of Rest*.
Although by this time the bodily humor theory was not generally accepted as
the basis for aging, a reliance on the four ages of life continued.

The older couple in Plate 9 are behaving in a manner that was considered
appropriate to their advanced years. They are shown at leisure, relaxing by the
fireplace. Thus, the age-old connection between fire and old age is present. The
season is winter, as we see through the window where a leafless tree and a horse-
drawn sleigh are shown. The couple is resting; they have done their life's work.
Serenely, now they await their Maker. A granddaughter gazes up at the old man.
Thus, the generations mix in kindness and affection, and a deference to old age
is conveyed by the girl's sitting at the grandfather's feet. This is a comfortable
picture of aging and old age. Its caption reads:

> Last comes the winter of life's circling year.
> And strength departs, but love and joy abide,
> That "perfect love" which "casteth out all fear"
> That joy, that lives beyond life's restless tide.
> Grateful for mercies past, and trusting still
> In him whose goodness all our lives hath blest,
> We rest secure, and calmly wait his will,
> To call us hence, to his eternal rest.

Plate 8. *The Four Ages of Life*. 17th century. Anthony Van Dyck. Pinacoteca di Vicenza. Courtesy of the Municipal Museums of Vicenza.

Plate 9. *Old Age—The Season of Rest* from the series *The Four Seasons of Life*. 19th century. Currier and Ives. Courtesy of the Library of Congress, Washington, D.C.

The Seven Ages of Life

Burrow (1984) found that from the twelfth century onward the seven-ages pattern was very popular. In fact, according to Mary Dove (1986), versions based on the number seven were the most common of all of the ages-of-life models. Seven carried special significance in that so many phenomena were believed to be based on the number. It was easy to make analogies between the seven ages of life and such popular themes as the seven virtues, the seven vices, and the seven then known planets (see Tristram, 1976). Also, the standard biblical life-span amounted to three score and ten, or 70 years of age.

Proponents of the seven ages of life included the theologian Alcuin in the eighth century, who divided the old-age time into three categories of elder, old age, and decrepitude; the artist Giorgio Vasari in the sixteenth century, who divided old age into old age and decrepitude. In 1554 Vasari painted a house in Florence with murals illustrating the seven ages of life. In this complex work, described by Samuel Chew (1962), Vasari associated each age with one of the seven planets, virtues, liberal arts, and deadly sins.

Over the years, other artists and writers as well took up the subject of the seven ages. For example, a seven-age pattern appears in the work of Hans Baldung, who also portrayed the three ages of life, as noted earlier (see Plate 6). Shakespeare wrote of seven ages of life in *As You Like It*. And by his reckoning, it is the sixth age that brings on old age. Shakespeare's famous lines stand as one of the most widely known statements on the ages of life; they incorporate the themes of a cycle of life, physical and mental decay, and a return to childlike behavior:

> . . . The sixth age shifts
> Into the lean and slippered pantaloon,
> With spectacles on nose and pouch on side,
> His youthful hose, well saved, a world too wide
> For his shrunk shank, and his big manly voice,
> Turning again toward childish treble, pipes
> And whistles in his sound. . . . Last scene of all,
> That ends this strange eventful history,
> Is the second childishness, and mere oblivion,
> Sans teeth, sans eyes, sans taste, sans every thing.
>
> (*As You Like It*, act 2, sc. 7)

The old pantaloon in the above passage is a significant character: He represents the comic old man of Roman comedies, the *senex iratus*, which is an enduring image in Western literature (Smith, 1976).

Other Ages of Life

During the Middle Ages and Renaissance, additional schemes of the ages of life were developed, based on the numbers five, six, eight, ten, 12, or 14. Schemes based on all but the number 12 were relatively rare in comparison with three, four, and seven (see Burrow, 1986; Chew, 1962; Covey, 1989b; Dove, 1986; Kammen, 1980).

Petrarch recognized six ages of life (Folts, 1980). And there is an example of the six-ages scheme in the stained glass windows at Canterbury Cathedral, which show *senectus*, old age, as a bald, bearded old man with a crutch in his right hand (Burrows, 1986). Saint Augustine's division of temporal history into six ages corresponded to his model of the six ages of life. Augustine viewed the last stage—senectus, again—as one of outward decay but inward renewal. This dual image of aging left a strong impression on thought in the following centuries. Aging could never be described solely in negative terms for it was also felt to involve spiritual development and growth.

To some, 12 ages of life made sense in the context of the 12 months of the year and the 12 hours of the day (Tristram, 1976). The number 12 was also significant because of the 12 apostles and the 12 tribes of Israel. During the fourteenth century, some people divided the ages of life into 14 ages (Aries, 1962). One example described by Philippe Aries shows 14 figures representing the ages ascending and descending a staircase. Physical decline of the individual is an element in this example. The top of the staircase represents the peak of life, and at the bottom of the stairs is death.

CLOSING THOUGHTS ON THE AGES OF LIFE

The ages-of-life literature and art provide insight into the process of aging and old age. These models were used by intellectuals and lay persons alike as tools to make sense of the human life-span. The Middle Ages and the Renaissance generated numerous such schemes, many of which traced their foundations to earlier biblical and Greek explanations of the life-span.

Thus, the approach here has been to view the ages-of-life models simply as heuristic devices. Over time, their various elements exhibited both a remarkable continuity and abrupt change. Sometimes they were ambiguous and inconsistent. There is a clear consistency, however—regardless of the model—to what was defined as age-appropriate behavior. All the ages-of-life models characterized old age as, on the one hand, a time for contemplation, spiritual restoration, repentance, and wisdom. On the other hand, miserly behavior, lust, foolishness, childishness, decay, dementia, and poor health were also considered characteristic of older people.

Age-appropriate behavior for older people has always been restrictive. The best example in our own time is the advent of mandatory retirement laws. Perhaps it is this restrictiveness coupled with the association with decay and impending death that makes old age the least favorite age of life, generally speaking. Yet were we to ask older people if they would like to return to childhood, many of them would probably answer no.

Although Western culture has been restrictive and prescriptive regarding older people, it is replete with famous examples of older people who have broken society's dictates. Michelangelo painted the Sistine Chapel during old age and continued to work on other projects afterward; Verdi composed *Falstaff* at 80; Titian painted *Christ Crowned with Thorns* at 95; Victor Hugo was writing and actively engaged in politics well into his old age; Voltaire wrote up to his death at 84; and Claude Monet painted his *Water Lilies* series at 83. In fact, there is evidence to suggest that creativity may actually increase with age (Edel, 1977–1978; Woodward, 1978). Furthermore, throughout the centuries, older people in all walks of life have continued to function as productive members of society—often out of economic necessity. Thus, while the ages-of-life models did serve to guide and enrich our understanding of the human life-span, they were never fully adhered to by older people themselves.

Regardless of the number of ages recognized, certain themes endured and were universally applied. For one thing, the number of ages was often arrived at by analogy to medieval perceptions of the spiritual and natural worlds as they were then known. Thus, the life-span might be divided perceptually like some natural phenomenon such as the change in the four seasons of the year, or to show a connection with elements of the belief system, such as the 12 apostles of Christ.

Another enduring theme was that of physical decay. Aging during the latter half of the life-span and in particular old age has long been caricatured as a downhill slide. Decay is portrayed a variety of ways in Western art and literature from the late medieval period to the nineteenth century. The trappings of old age usually included a crutch or cane and spectacles. After all, medical science did not offer the bone repair and other healing techniques known to modern medicine. Until the modern era, in fact, once a bone was broken it was not likely ever to heal correctly; thus, over a long life a crutch or cane could very well become a necessity for older people.

Counterbalancing the theme of physical decay was an acknowledgment of the intellectual and spiritual growth that comes with old age. Sometimes it was even said that the true meaning of life can only be understood by one who has the experience and wisdom of a long life. Old age, then, was interpreted ambivalently, with the individual ascending and descending simultaneously. What remains unclear and is certainly worthy of future inquiry is the seemingly contradictory relationship between the state of senile dementia that some writers make a point of mentioning, and the perceived increase in wisdom and spiritual understanding believed to be characteristic of older people.

Michel Philibert (1974) contends that there are two basic, logically separable types of images involved here: (1) images that emphasize the predominantly physical and largely negative, terminal, universal, necessary, and gruesome characteristics identified with aging; and (2) images that stress the differentiated and controllable dimensions of aging, and perceive it as an opportunity for growth. This summation finds support in many of the ages-of-life models created over the centuries.

The predictability of life is another theme in the ages-of-life genre. The ages of life gave an aura of natural order to human existence at a period in history when life was generally chaotic and mean. The predictability of the model had its limitations, though. At any time, sudden death or illness could undercut the logical progression through the life-span. Furthermore, the predeterminism implied by the ages-of-life models sometimes obscured the individual experiences and life processes that make each older person's life unique (Hendricks & Hendricks, 1977). However, the various models did go a long way toward fulfilling people's need—right or wrong—to attach meaning and understanding to their lives.

Contemplation was one of the most commonly admitted age-appropriate behaviors for older people throughout the period under consideration. For one thing, contemplation itself appears to have been a valued pursuit, especially in the Middle Ages. Perhaps, as Harry Moody (1986) suggests, contemplation was thus a more acceptable form of activity in old age than it is in contemporary times. In our day the emphasis is on staying physically active as long as possible; our image of successful aging calls for continued engagement in physical and social interests. Thus, old age may no longer give us time for contemplation. But from the late Middle Ages to the seventeenth century, a very different view of aging and its appropriate behavior prevailed (Moody, 1986). Contemplation and idleness were much more common among the old then, as witnessed by the ages-of-life art and literature. Repentance was another expected behavior, as was preparation for death.

When reviewing the art and literature of the ages-of-life genre, one is tempted time and again to compare these representations with how older people are viewed today. Certain themes of the genre seem to parallel contemporary views on old age. Today as yesterday, older people are at times seen as decaying and as limited in their age-appropriate behaviors, and are approached with ambivalence. And in fact, the past does have much in common with the present. Our perceptions about aging and older people run deep into Western history.

NOTE

1. Disagreements have arisen among modern scholars on how to interpret the ages of life. Two recent publications by John Burrow (1986) and Mary Dove (1986), for instance, propose different interpretations of the ages of life during the Middle Ages. From Burrow's (1986) perspective, individuals might age at their own paces, but the ages-of-life schemes established norms to which everyone generally conformed when their time had come. Thus, the ages of life were prescriptive in their message to people of the Middle Ages. Individuals were criticized for straying from or praised for conforming to the ages-of-

life norms or what might be called age-appropriate behavior. In addition, the ages of life conveyed a single, inevitable, predictable, natural order to life. According to Burrow, human beings were perceived as going through the life-span in predetermined steps. These steps or ages represented major shifts in the individual's orientation to life. Burrow implies that the shift from age to age was often abrupt. And the most important age—in Burrow's view—was middle age, as opposed to old age or youth. He also makes a distinction between spiritual age and physical age. One could be spiritually old and yet young in years.

Dove (1986) departs from Burrow's perspective on several key points. For one thing, Dove interprets that the ages of life were less deterministic in real life than Burrow indicates. She questions the inevitability of the ages themselves as well as the adherence of people to the prescriptions for age-appropriate behavior. Dove argues that, in the ages-of-life literature and art, life is seen as an integrated experience, continuity is more prevalent than disruption, and there is no inevitable order to the progression of the ages (see Tristram, 1976). To her, the ages are consistently connected in the genre, and life gradually flows from one to the next. Like Burrow, however, Dove believes that a person could be young in years and spiritually old, or vice versa. And besides acknowledging the physical and spiritual aspects in general, Dove also sees wisdom as an element mapped by the ages of life during the Middle Ages.

As mentioned in the text, Dove (1986) further argues that there may have been confusion and disagreement over the names and boundaries attached to the ages of life. The ages were sometimes described inconsistently. For example, Renaissance scholars used different names for the same ages; and even when the names were the same, they might have different meanings. Another example is Henry Cuffe's (1607) inconsistent references to the age he calls "youth." At one point Cuffe proposes that youth ranges from 18 to 25, and in another section he holds that it extends from 25 to 40 years of age. Finally, Dove argues that the ages-of-life schemes were different for women than for men. Women were thought to experience each of the ages earlier in life.

The ages of life may be best interpreted as incorporating the conclusions of both Dove and Burrow. For one thing, the evidence does indicate that, as Dove argues, the ages of life were viewed as a continuum. However, it is also known that certain years were thought of as climacterics—that is, as times when critical changes would be experienced by the individual. Sometimes these climacteric years were said to occur in set intervals, such as every seven years. The point is that the evidence is mixed: One could see life as a continuous process, but also expect specific years to mark big changes. The extent to which the latter expectation actually became a self-fulling prophecy is unknown. Suffice it to say that, among those who looked for these critical years, there could very well have been changes in the individual's behavior at the right moment. Finally, it should be noted that, in art at least, continuity and gradual change are more difficult to portray than distinct stages. In this sense, the ages of life were intended to represent the aging process, not realistically describe it. They were simply heuristic devices used by intellectuals and others to make sense of the human life-span. In and of themselves, they were merely abstractions.

On the whole, there is an inevitability to the ages of life, whether one views them as continuous or dramatic. Some people, however, thought that this inevitability could be delayed. That is, a person could slow down the aging process either through proper living—moderation, in other words—or through restricted diet or alchemy. It is also true, as Dove (1986) suggests, that women were perceived as aging sooner than men. This attitude has had a long tradition in Western thought.

Both Burrow and Dove may be correct in concluding that the ages of life were not always considered dependent solely on chronological age. That is, a person could be young in years, but spiritually old. The ages-of-life models did allow people to become old before their "time." In contrast, older people who became young in their advanced years were considered exceptions, and were viewed askance. Childish characteristics in older people were especially frowned on because wisdom was expected to accompany old age.

In the final analysis, while Dove and Burrow differ on some points, they agree on others. And in fact, their perspectives are more similar than different. Besides the similarities mentioned above, they also basically agree on the sequence of ages, both allow for individuals to deviate from the norm, and they agree on many of the meanings and the relative importance they attach to the ages of life. Also, as the evidence indicates, the names used by scholars to represent the various ages of life were indeed ambiguous, as both Burrow and Dove suggest.

One thing is certain: The ages of life did illustrate age-appropriate behaviors for older people, and indeed for people of all ages. This is unmistakable whether one views the passage through the ages as gradual (Dove, 1986) or abrupt (Burrow, 1986). The overall conclusion reached by modern interpreters is that there was neither a blind adherence to the ages-of-life schemes, nor a total freedom to do as one pleased. The ages of life provided a summary of how life was to be perceived and how it should progress.

3

SYMBOLIC IMAGES OF OLDER PEOPLE

Throughout history, images of older people have served symbolic purposes. Old age has been used to symbolize a number of social concepts and themes, depending on the meaning attached by the society to the latter part of life. For example, when we in the West visualize the personification of time, we see an old man. When we think of the witch, we envision an old woman. God is always pictured as an old man. In addition, older people are often shown surrounded by symbols of their advanced age. The cane, the hourglass, winter, and the burnt candle are all associated with old age. Finally, older people have also been simply portrayed by artists as subjects in their own right—as human beings without symbolic representation.

Some of the general images involving symbolism and older people are reviewed in this chapter. Art historians and iconographers have provided us with a rich lode of information on symbolism in art, and this body of work serves as a useful starting point for understanding art from earlier periods. Before examining a few of the symbolic representations, however, let us begin with the art of direct portraiture.

PORTRAITS OF OLDER PEOPLE

Over the centuries beginning in the late Middle Ages and the early Renaissance, individual portraiture would become increasingly common, at least among the well-to-do. Art historians often link the development of portraiture to the rise of individualism in Western society. As portraiture evolved, artists paid increasing attention to the specific details and characteristics of the person. Thus, there was a steady advance in the realism of portraiture.

Realism in portraiture arose in the vicinity of the fifteenth century (Praz, 1971). Prior to that time, portrait painting was not meant to be realistic, but rather symbolic of the person's social rank. Emphasis was then placed on insignia and dress, instead of characterization. Thus, realistic portraits of older people—works that could tell us how they were perceived, and how they lived—were rare prior to the fifteenth century.

Following the rise in popularity of realistic portraiture, however, artists created numerous renditions of older people. In fact, individual portraiture became a major means of support for artists beginning in about the sixteenth century and continuing through the nineteenth. Many of those who commissioned the portraits were older aristocrats; thus, artists found themselves painting older subjects. This was certainly a common occurrence during the Italian Renaissance. It is important to note, however, that other portraits were noncommissioned. They tended to be not of specific individuals, but of older people in general. The Dutch artists of the seventeenth century, for instance, provide many characterizations of older people and everyday life in their period.

Examples of portraits of older people over the centuries include Hans Baldung's engraving titled *Bearded Old Man* (1508), El Greco's *Portrait of an Old Man with a Fur* (1590/1606), Rembrandt's painting titled *Portrait of an Old Man* (1633), Georges de La Tour's *Peasant Man* (1620), and *Peasant Woman* (1620), Frans Hals's *Malle Babbe* (1650), Edouard Manet's *Ragpicker* (1869), and Gaspar Felix Tournachon Nadar's early photograph of an old woman (1860). There are countless other examples from Rubens, Goya, and others. Of particular note is Leonardo da Vinci's collection of drawings of grotesque heads characterizing older people in a macabre and occasionally humorous fashion. Although anatomically correct and exacting, these drawings take on a cartoon character as da Vinci seems to be making fun of the effects of aging. In any case, all these works provide insight into how the process of aging was abstracted by the artists of the respective periods. Generally (and quite understandably), changes in physical appearance seem to be the focus of these particular artists, sometimes to the point of exaggeration.

Even within this realm of direct portraiture, symbolism has had its place. One of the most important symbolic elements has been the clothing worn by the older people in this as well as other forms of art. Clothing has long been used by social cultures and thus their artists to indicate position and status. Up until the fourteenth century, the predominant form of clothing had been the robe. During the fourteenth century the robe was abandoned in favor of the short coat for men, much to the dismay of the Church, which thought its tight-fitting shape evidence of immorality. Philippe Aries (1962) points out that "respectable people"—such as older people—continued to wear robes until the beginning of the seventeenth century because of their stations in life as magistrates, statesmen, and church officials. This adherence to tradition and a respectable image may explain why so many images of older people over the centuries show them as robed, regardless of the current period fashion worn by younger people in the mainstream of society. The robe itself can be thought of as being strongly associated with old age, and therefore its symbol. The hood was also popular for older women, as were the shawl and the long dress in later centuries.

In addition to clothing, other symbolic forms have also accompanied older people in portraiture and other forms of art. These symbols conveyed certain meanings to the audience of these works. For example, Frans Hals's *Malle Babbe* (1650) shows an old drunk woman with an owl on her shoulder. Traditionally, artists have used the owl to represent heresy and evil, an association that people of the time would have recognized.

Other symbols commonly shown in conjunction with older people include the goat, which stands for old age itself and for lust; the hourglass, time; the orb, worldly significance; the scythe, time; the can, old age; the skull, death and mortality; and the wolf, old age (Foote, 1968; Regnier-Bohle, 1988). The circle occasionally appears with older people, also. It is an ancient as well as early Christian symbol for eternity. Sometimes the circle was pictured as a serpent with its tail in its mouth, which represents Moses' serpent of brass (Whittick, 1972/1935). Those bitten by Moses' serpent were granted life.

As noted earlier, older people themselves have also served as symbols throughout the centuries. For example, in 1779 a London architect named George Richardson (1736–1817) published a book on iconography in which he discusses the use of older men and women in symbolizing certain concepts. Richardson's book (1979/1779), based on Cesare Ripa's 1593 *Iconologia*, provides insight into how basic themes in Western art were represented by older people and older people by symbols. Richardson states that old men should be used to personify winter, the cold north wind, misfortune, several major rivers, fate, a council, custom, treachery, and timidity. In contrast, old women are to represent longevity, drunkenness, avarice, malevolence, melancholy, and envy. According to Richardson, old age is an appropriate symbol for drunkenness because too much wine brings on the infirmities of old age and drunkenness hastens its onset. Richardson chooses an old woman to represent old age itself:

This subject is characterized by the figure of an old woman, dressed in a black mantle, or the color of withered leaves, to indicate the trouble and decay attending mortals at this age. In the right hand she holds a cup, and with the left she leans upon a staff, being in allusion to the support and nourishment necessary to the feebleness and infirmities of old age. An hour glass may be placed by the figure, with the sand almost exhausted, to denote the brevity of the remaining time. (Richardson, 1979/1779: vol. 1, 52)

In the following section, some of the more enduring symbolic representations of older people are presented. However, there are no doubt other symbols associated with old age and older people that have been omitted here. Furthermore, it is not always clear when these representations were first used. Some probably date to antiquity, but one can never be absolutely sure. Certain icons remain with us today, and they are as symbolic now as they were in earlier periods. The meanings may have changed, but the use of older people as their basis is just as familiar.

OLDER PEOPLE AS RELIGIOUS FIGURES

Older people have played many an active role in the evolution of Western spirituality. The Judeo-Christian tradition often acknowledges the special attributes of old age, and many Jewish and Christian teachings touch on this theme. For example, the Bible depicts the loss of power by the old kings Saul and David (Fowler et al., 1982). And many precepts and narratives of the Bible are devoted to showing honor and respect toward older generations. Elders were expected to be obeyed and venerated for their wisdom and closeness to God. Relatively few negative references intrude; older people are usually portrayed in a positive or at least ambivalent light. This is not to say that exceptions did not exist. In fact, Simone de Beauvoir (1972) discovered many negative biblical characterizations of older persons: Noah is overtaken with wine. Lot must be dragged away from the place of licentiousness. Joseph, the earthly guardian of Jesus Christ, sometimes comes across as a feeble old man. Clearly the Bible is ambivalent in this regard; but when the scales are finally balanced, the weight rests with a favorable view of older people.

In a different vein, older people have generally been perceived as intermediaries between humanity and God, and occasionally serve as His messengers. Their being closer to death and being the carriers of tradition enhances this association between them and God (Barash, 1983). In a sense, religion has been a main vehicle for integrating the old into society, a point sometimes neglected by historians (Smith, 1982). Not only has religion in the West been an influence on the old with its guiding principles and explanations and traditional structures, but it has also provided an enduring social role for older people—and especially men—among other younger age groups. Religious leaders and spiritual guides have most often been older persons. They were the ones considered wise enough to guide the unwashed and uninformed masses. It is no accident that Christian churches refer to their religious authorities as church elders. The term attests to the perceived connection between age (and to a lesser extent, being male) and religious authority (Covey, 1988).

God as an Old Man

Let us begin our exploration of religious images of older people by tracing the evolution of portraits of God. In medieval Christian art, God is usually found in the upper center of the painting or mosaic. Early in the Christian and Hebrew eras, the creation of human images of God was prohibited, being considered sacrilege (McKee & Kauppinen, 1987). Thus, in art before the twelfth century, the only symbol of God ever seen is a hand reaching down into the center of the religious scene, with open palm and the fingers at the bottom. This large hand is often shown emerging from stylized clouds.

After the twelfth century, it became more common to see heads and half-figures used to symbolize God. Thus, the open hand evolved into the head of

God. Again, the head of God was always located in the upper center of the art, frequently framed off from the rest of the scene. Two important assumptions about the nature of the Divine are present in these portrayals. God is always male, and always old; never is God portrayed as female or young. Over the centuries, these two assumptions have never wavered. God is, by Christian definition, the Father and is hence an old man.

In some of the early images, God is in the company of other older-male religious figures. Bearded ancients, old prophets and saints, elders of the Church, and elders of the apocalypse were commonly shown with God. In some portrayals of the apocalypse, God appears with 24 elders wearing crowns. The number 24 paralleled the signs of the zodiac (doubled, a common numerological device) and the 24 hours of the day. All such arrangements implied that these groups of old men were wise religious advisors. Thus, the association between old age and wisdom through nearness to God found early visual support in medieval art and manuscript illumination.

When the portrait of God evolved into a half-figure, it was still located in the upper section of the art. For example, the *Livre des Heures de Rohan* (1418–1420) shows a dead man's soul being given up to God. God is portrayed as an old crowned man, located in the upper right-hand corner of the scene. He holds an orb and a sword, symbolic of the dominance of Christianity over the world. From His position above, God can oversee the world He has created. In another interesting plate from this work, titled *Christ in Judgment*, Christ too is shown as an old man, although Jesus only lived to his mid-thirties on Earth. Harthan (1977) notes that the last judgment would unite God the Father and Christ into one, and thus Christ would naturally become older in appearance. Other books of hours, which were used by aristocrats to guide their daily prayers—such as the Duke de Berry—also contained similar images of God as an old man.

Artists would often picture God looking down on Old and New Testament scenes. For example, Albrecht Dürer's *Seventeen Illustrations of the Life of the Virgin* (1504) shows God as a bearded old man holding an orb with a cross on the top. God sits above the action, overseeing the events of the Virgin's life. Michelangelo's *Creation of Adam* (1508–1512) at the Sistine Chapel of the Vatican again uses the archetypical image of God as an old man, probably the most familiar image in Christianity. Michelangelo's God floats with the clouds accompanied by angels, as He reaches to give Adam life.

Plate 10 contains a very typical example of God as an old man, a 1513 rendition by Hans Baldung Grien called *God the Father*. God is an old man with a long beard, a crown, and an orb on a staff—symbolic of power over the world. Baldung's God is robed and majestic; He oversees the world from His throne.

Eventually, these images of God the Father became less prevalent in Western culture than those of Christ the Son. This transition occurred during the fourteenth and fifteenth centuries. It was increasingly the practice to focus on the annunciation, birth, miracles, passion, crucifixion, resurrection, and other events in Christ's life. Images of God as an old man would virtually disappear to the point

Plate 10. *God the Father*. 1513. Hans Baldung Grien. Kunstmuseum, Basel. Courtesy of Öffentliche
Kunstsammlung, Kupfersichkabinett, Basel.

of extinction. Although people continued to think of God as an old man and the father of all things, His image as such in art became rare as time went on.

Older Saints

Portrayals of the Christian saints have always adhered to a fairly rigid set of rules when it comes to age. Some saints are always shown in their youth, while others are always old. As we shall see, some of these rules remain with us today, but others have changed with the times. Prior to and during the Romanesque period, saints were predominantly shown as young or middle-aged men. This is because artistic images during the Middle Ages focused on social insignia, rank, and clothing. Individual characteristics such as the person's advanced years would have been relatively unimportant to the Romanesque artist, and thus absent. In any case, the model for most religious figures seems to have been middle age or sometimes youth, and rarely old age. There were exceptions; but in general, middle age predominates among religious figures and icons of the period. Byzantine iconography, during the eras when human images were allowed, also basically portrayed religious figures as either young or middle-aged. Older people might be present in the scenes, but were generally in the background and seldom the focus of attention.

Although, as mentioned above, manuscript illumination from the Middle Ages was virtually dominated by middle-aged saints, a review of early illumination turns up numerous examples of relatively young saints. For example, the *York Gospels* of Mont Michel (966–1100) show young-saint figures such as Ambrose, Augustine, Gregory the Great, Peter, and Stephen. The Morgan Library in New York contains one of these portrayals: the martyrdom of Saint Peter, definitely showing Peter as a young man. Later in the Middle Ages, the Duke de Berry's *Book of Hours*—for instance—shows many middle-aged saints such as Mathieu, Luc, and Marc.

The emphasis on young saints is interesting in light of the fact that many of them, according to Church history, lived to be quite old. The following is a list of some of the major saints and their ages: Augustine (354–430), 76; Ambrose, (334–397), 63; Gregory the Great (540–604), 64; Jerome (342–420), 78; Anthony Abbot (251–356), 95; Benedict (480–547), 67; Louis of France (1214–1270), 56; Martin of Tours (315–394), 79; Patrick (385–461), 76; and Thomas à Becket (1118–1170), 52. Unfortunately, the ages of many other early saints are unknown; that is, the year of death may be known, but not the year of birth. In those days, less emphasis was given to when one was born than to when one died.

We do know that many of the saints lived well into old age yet were seldom shown as being old when portrayed during the Middle Ages, whether the art was Byzantine, Anglo-Saxon, Celtic, Romanesque, or—for that matter—any other of the artistic styles prior to what we call Gothic. Even in much of the Gothic art, saints continued to be portrayed as young. And we can only speculate as to why, prior to the late Middle Ages, there was this bias toward youth in religious portrayals of saints and other religious figures. I will venture two explanations. First, old age may have been simply ignored by artists. Or maybe artists chose not to tackle its ambivalent characteristics (see Chapter 2). It is tempting to argue that they lacked the technical skill to illustrate old age, but the detailed work from this period would belie the argument. It is more likely that the features of old age were simply not recognized as important by those commissioned to represent religious images. This explanation would fit with the lack of attention paid to individuality by artists until the late Middle Ages. Individuality and personal detail were not a common element in any art until the late Middle Ages and the beginning of the Renaissance.

Second, youth has generally been considered the prime of life. It may be that portraying the saints as young implied power and energy, in which case it was preferable to worship and admire young saints and religious figures in the prime of their lives than to venerate older saints. Even when saints were known to have lived to old age, it was their youthful image that would be chosen for imagery.

This latter observation cannot be made, however, without acknowledging that older people traditionally serve as religious leaders in their respective societies. Generally speaking, religion has been a power base for older people. Then why were they neglected as religious figures in early Christian imagery? It may be that, when every image of the Godhead showed an older patriarch, it was necessary to picture saints and religious figures as younger. This would imply deference to God as older than everyone else and hence more wise and powerful. Old Testament teachings support this explanation. They often repeat the importance of reverence for old age and its assumed wisdom and power, a theme that was resurrected by the colonial American Puritans many centuries later.

Why had the portrayal of older saints become more prevalent by the close of the Middle Ages? For one thing, the Catholic Church was very much concerned with the rise of Protestantism and what it viewed as heresy. Martin Luther and others were challenging the very foundations of the traditional Church. What better way to associate itself with tradition and wisdom than to show major Church figures as old? Thus, it may be that old age became a political element manipulated by the Church in its war against Protestantism. Old age as a symbol for the traditions of the Church was to be respected and certainly not challenged. In short, the artistic representation of old age may have become a tool to sway public opinion.

Whatever the reason, the Gothic art of the late Middle Ages did begin to show religious figures such as saints as older people. For example, the London Library houses a portrait of Saint John from the *Sherborne Chartulary*, dated about 1146, that is a rare image of the apostle as an old man. In *Saint Anselm's Prayers and Meditations*, (1120–1130), we find an illustration of Christ handing the keys of the kingdom over to an old Saint Peter (Bibliothèque Municipale, Verdun, France). In the Duke de Berry's *Book of Hours* there are the old saints Pierre and Paul. These and other examples are the exception rather than the rule at this time, however. An openness to the subject of age would eventually come to full fruition during the Renaissance.

It is also interesting to note that the popes were once relatively young. Today we envision the Roman Catholic popes as old men, and generally they are. But this was not always the case. Following the Council of Trent in the sixteenth century and the Counter-Reformation, older popes became the rule. For one thing, it was expected that they would be less likely to break with tradition than their earlier, much younger counterparts. And the older popes were also seen as less likely to defame the Church through their sexual escapades (Barash, 1983). In other words, they would probably be more conservative. The Counter-Reformation endowed popes with high standing to combat the threats of heresy and the growth of Protestantism. Thereafter, they were required to be austere, and their old age was viewed as helping to assure that this would be the case.

During the Renaissance, the average age of the popes at death was 64, which was far above average for the general population (Gilbert, 1967). In seventeenth-century England, the comparable archbishops of Canterbury were also generally older men. The average life-span of nine archbishops in the seventeenth century was 73, and the average age of appointment 60 (Smith, 1979). Since 1800, the average age at death of the popes has been 79, again higher than the average for the general population (Gilbert, 1967). Thus, for the Catholic Church and its constituents worldwide, God's main representative on Earth is an older man. And this is true of other religious leaders, as well.

In the Renaissance, a major shift occurred in art—with regard to attitude toward age as much as in other ways. It became much more common for saints to be portrayed as older. Actually, certain saints were never depicted in any stage of life other than old-age. Saint Jerome is one good example of this. Jerome the old man is one of the most popular saintly images in Western culture. In fact, by the seventeenth century, Jerome—the fourth-century scholar who translated the Bible into Latin—was the saint most frequently portrayed (Chartier, 1989). He always appears as a bearded old man and is usually shown engaged in solitary study or looking toward the heavens. In other words, he is associated with spiritual retreat.

Many renditions of the saint have been created by major and lesser artists over the centuries. Jerome has been a popular image for several reasons, one of which is that he admirably overcame worldly temptation (Jacobowitz & Stepanek, 1983). Versions of Saint Jerome were executed by Domenico Ghirlandaio (1480), Albrecht Dürer (1514), Titian (1555), Paolo Veronese (c. 1580), Jusepe de Ribera (1640), El Greco (1610–1614), Hans Baldung Grien (1511), Antony Van Dyck (1641), Quentin Massys (1519), and Joos Van Cleve the Elder (1521).

Often, Jerome is shown with a lion—his symbol—a skull, a crucifix, and a Bible, either in the wilderness or in the study where he translated the Scriptures into Latin (Braunstein, 1988). Occasionally there is also a snuffed candle, which symbolizes life's impermanence. Over the centuries, but particularly in the sixteenth and seventeenth centuries, several variations on this popular religious story appeared. Saint Jerome was often depicted in the company of a lion because he is said to have once removed a thorn from the lion's paw and was thereafter faithfully followed by the grateful beast. A version by Peter Paul Rubens (1620) incorporates not only the lion, but also a skull symbolizing mortality. In sensuous Rubens fashion, the saint is portrayed as old, muscular, and half nude, dressed in a robe.

Plate 11 is a representative image of Saint Jerome, by the artist Francisco de Goya (1746–1828). Goya chose to show the old man with a crucifix, an open Bible, a skull, and a quill pen; he is dressed as a classic half-nude. The saint's bent posture, grey hair, and exposed ribs denote his old age. Along with the other renditions, this Saint Jerome helped create an archetypical image of the saint—and to some extent, old age—that was popular for centuries. It promotes a positive impression of old age as being a state of wisdom, repentance, the surrendering of worldly goods and temptation, physical decline and yet spiritual awareness.

Moses is always an old man, as well. Again, there are numerous examples in art of the Hebrew liberator and lawgiver as an old and bearded figure. Claus Sluter sculpted *The Well of Moses* (1395–1406) in Dijon, France, along these lines. Michelangelo's *Moses* (1513–1515) also follows the rule.

Older women, too, appeared in religious art. Certainly, Saint Anne—the mother of the Virgin Mary—is a prime example (see Chapter 4), but there were other images, as well. In the seventeenth century, for example, portraits sometimes showed older women saying their rosaries. This, as Roger Chartier (1989) suggests, exhibited a more personal form of worship than in prior centuries. The portrait in prayer was popular in the eighteenth century, as well. In fact, there are also examples in nineteenth-century art, such as Paul Cézanne's *Old Woman with a Rosary* (1896).

Older women were also shown reading religious books as was the case in several of Rembrandt's works. From the sixteenth through the eighteenth centuries, solitary reading was an activity commonly painted by artists. Rembrandt made several paintings of his mother reading religious materials. He also made numerous paintings of old men reading religious works. This solemn reading and reflection over religious writing, usually the Bible, was a popular image among artists. According to Aries (1985), during the late Middle Ages and the Renaissance, the act of reading and the book itself became a sign of piety for women. For men, it became a sign of intellectual and spiritual activity. In the seventeenth century—as indicated above—emphasis was placed on personal piety (Lebrun, 1989). Some artists chose to convey this in their portraiture. The artist Nicolas Maes follows the theme in his *Old Woman Dozing over a Book* (1655). Gerard Dou (1613–1675) provides another example of an old woman reading a Bible. In this and many other versions, the reading is being done aloud, as reading skills were generally not yet so refined (Chartier, 1989).

In 1631 Rembrandt painted a portrait of his mother as a prophetess dressed

Plate 11. *Saint Jerome*. 1798. Francisco de Goya y Lucientes. Courtesy of the Norton Simon Museum, Pasadena, California.

in an expensive robe and reading a religious text. The work is reproduced here as Plate 12. Rembrandt's unique manipulation of light draws the viewer into the solitude and personal piety of the subject. She reads the passages with her lips, in the common style of the period.

AVARICE

Older people have long been associated with miserly behavior or avarice. In fact, avarice has been called the sin of old age, just as—for instance—vanity is regarded to be a sin of youth (Chew, 1962; see also "Predictable and Appropriate Behavior" in Chapter 2 of this book). Avarice was often represented by human hands, the hands being the means to grasp one's worldly possessions. There are countless characterizations in Western literature and art of older people and the vice of avarice. In the twelfth-century Latin comedy *Alda*, a slave advises his master to prevent his father's miserly behavior from prematurely turning the master into an old man (Burrow, 1986). In the thirteenth century, Pope Innocent III said that old men are stingy, avaricious, sullen, and quarrelsome (Coffman, 1934). And the *ars moriendi* manuals on the art of dying in the late Middle Ages outright identify avarice as the chief sin of old age. The closer one comes to death, it is explained, the more fiercely does one desire to hold on to possessions (May, 1986).

This theme of avarice in old age has been reflected in several literary works over the centuries. In Shakespeare's *Merchant of Venice* (1600), Shylock is portrayed as a greedy, grasping old miser. He is a typical example of how avarice was associated with old age, although it should be noted that some people feel Shylock is more a product of Shakespeare's anti-Semitism than his attitude toward old age (Charles, 1977). At the close of the eighteenth century, George Richardson's guide to symbolism in art characterizes avarice as "an inordinate desire of riches; it is allegorically characterized by the figure of an ugly woman, meanly dressed, and of a melancholy aspect" (1979/1779:29). The theme persisted over the centuries and had many representations. One of the most familiar from the nineteenth century is Charles Dickens's (1843) *Christmas Carol*. Dickens consciously selected an old man to represent the miser Scrooge, just as so many of his counterparts from earlier centuries had done.

There may be some very good reasons why these earlier societies associated older people with the sin of avarice and miserly behavior. One reason may be that they often controlled property and wealth, the lack of which sometimes restricted younger people in their desire and ability to control their own lives. On occasion, older parents might be reluctant to surrender control over property to the family out of a concern for their own well-being, as was mentioned in Chapter 2. There is some evidence that this concern was justified, as parenthood was no guarantee of being taken care of during old age. In fact, children could be harsh and bitter toward their parents to the point of physically harming them. Thus, older people had to hold on tight to their possessions, this being their

Plate 12. *Rembrandt's Mother*. 1631. Rembrandt van Rijn. Courtesy of the Rijkmuseum, Amsterdam.

only protection against destitution and untimely death. The issue of inheritance, then—almost always a sensitive topic between generations—helped to fuel the association between old age and avarice. Older relatives often gave the impression of being stingy and miserly.

Another reason for the association has Christian roots. Death and dying, in the Christian context, is seen as the passage from temporal existence to eternal life. One acquires possessions in this world that must be surrendered at death. Thus, it is important not to become too attached to these worldly possessions, as they represent human weakness and allegiance to things other than God. One should be ready and willing to surrender them. Because older people were expected to be in preparation for the next life, they were logical candidates for criticism when they did not gracefully relinquish all properties at the first intimation of death's call. Such a willing abandonment of wealth is not always easy, however, when—as explained above—one's existence so depends on one's possessions. After all, people had survived what they mistakenly took to be their deathbeds.

The seventeenth-century painting by Paulus Bor reproduced in Plate 13 captures many of the stereotypical images and associations between old age and avarice. Bor's *Avarice* shows an old hooded woman who frowns out at us, conveying a strong sense of miserly behavior. She crouches beside her small accumulation of material possessions, symbolically represented in the pot of coins at her feet. Her small dog growls at the viewer, ready to snap if anyone takes a step closer. We are certainly not welcome into her world. Maybe she is a widow; clearly, she is poor.

Albrect Dürer, in his 1507 version of the subject, again uses an older woman to represent the sin of avarice. This very unflattering view shows the old woman with one breast hanging out of her blouse; her bare breast and missing teeth no doubt symbolize the transitory nature of feminine beauty. Neither smile nor posture is complimentary in the slightest sense. With both hands the woman clasps a bag of coins.

Again, the theme of old age and avarice surfaces in Hieronymus Bosch's *Death of the Miser* (1485–1490; see Plate 41 in Chapter 6). This work and others like it represent the multiple themes of death, old age, and avarice. It is important to note that older people did not monopolize all the images of avarice, but they certainly were its predominant symbol. Young misers are rare compared to older ones. In fact, the old miser is a tradition in Western art.

THE PURSUIT OF YOUTH

One preoccupation of certain scholars of old age and aging has been the prolonging of life. The seeking of ways to extend the life-span or recapture youth is a long tradition in Western history. Various potions and mixtures have been tried. Ironically, in spite of centuries of these concoctions, there is little evidence—as Jon Hendricks and C. Davis Hendricks (1977–78) contend—that

Plate 13. *Avarice*. 17th century. Paulus Bor. Courtesy of Cummer Art Gallery, Jacksonville, Florida.

the life-span has shown any dramatic changes. What has improved is the percentage of people surviving to old age. Likewise, the aging process has never been reversed and youth recaptured. What has happened is an increase in our knowledge of some of the health and diet measures that can lead to a healthier old age.

Early on, the Bible suggested that submission to God's authority might lead to a long life (Kastenbaum & Ross, 1975), thus lending religious support to the notion that life can be prolonged. The ancient Greeks had their own ideas. Aristotle believed that moderation in all things would prolong life. This early assumption periodically surfaced in the works of later scholars and continued through the nineteenth century.

One of the earliest works fully dedicated to the subject was Roger Bacon's 1267 publication *On the Retardation of Old Age: The Cure of Old Age, and Preservation of Youth* (Lawton, 1965). Bacon reiterated Greek thinking when he asserted that aging is pathological but can be delayed through moderation (Freeman, 1965). Arnoldus de Villanova (1235–1311), a contemporary of Bacon, also wrote on the prolongation of life in *The Conservation of Youth and Defense of Old Age*. Like Bacon, Villanova thought that life could be prolonged through correct living. The Italian Gabriele Zerbi wrote an early (1489) monograph on old age that addressed the problem of prolonging life (Freeman, 1965). Marsilio Ficino in his *Detriplici Vita* (1498) proposed that moderation and proper living would extend life. Another Italian, the Venetian Luigi Cornaro (1464–1566), built on the theories of the ancient Greeks and argued for a temperate life and the development of moderation. His own life serves as a model, as Cornaro lived to age 98.

Another outstanding example of the Western interest in prolonging life was written slightly later on by the Italian Andre de Laurens, sometimes known as Laurentis (1558–1609). He too said that aging would be delayed through moderation in exercise, air, food, and drink (Dannenfeldt, 1987). From the same period, the Englishman Henry Cuffe's work *The Differences of the Ages of Man's Life; Together with the Originall Causes, Progresse, and End Therof* (1607) advised those desiring a long life to be of sanguine humor because it was both moist and hot (Smith, 1976).

In the seventeenth century, the sensationally long life of one Mr. Thomas Parr—whose portrait by an unknown artist is shown in Plate 14—created quite a stir. His story was told in popular literature and journals of the period, and retold in those that followed (Hendricks & Hendricks, 1977–78). Parr reportedly married a widow when he was 120, and he died at the age of 152 in 1635. His long life supported the seventeenth-century conviction that longevity should be very possible (Smith, 1979). When Parr eventually did die, the noted British physician William Harvey performed an autopsy. Harvey claimed that the condition of the deceased was that of a much younger man (Lawton, 1965), and he attributed Parr's death to the deplorable urban conditions that were fouling the air, food, and drink.

It was in this same era that Francis Bacon's *History of Life and Death* (1638) was published. Bacon believed that aging is a process of the body's drying out. He thought that, if people could retard the drying-out process, they would prolong their lives. To this end, he recommended a moderate, moist, cool climate and the habit of moderation.

Eighteenth-century scholars such as the French Marquis de Condorcet also

Plate 14. *Thomas Parr*. C. 1635. Artist unknown. Courtesy of the National Portrait Gallery, London

sought solutions to the problems of aging. Condorcet thought that life expectancy would increase with the march of progress. He perpetuated the enduring assumption that moderation is the key to a long life. The eighteenth century also witnessed the vogue of an interesting practice in the use of wet nurses to prolong the lives of old men, who were convinced that breast milk was the very elixir of life. Charles Waldemar (1960) claims that the practice was common in France at the time.

Andrew Achenbaum and Peggy Kusnerz (1978) note that, during the early years of the American Republic, information was gathered on how long people lived. This would indicate that the forefathers wanted to demonstrate to their critics how life in the new America could promote longevity. Reports of extremely old people, such as the Puritan Ann Pollard, were welcomed and widely circulated.

By the nineteenth century, the bodily humor theory of aging had decreased in importance. The idea that life could be prolonged through moderation persisted, however. For example—as we shall see in Chapter 5—some medical experts thought that excessive sexual activity would speed up the aging process. Here again, although the recommendations may vary, there is the basic assumption that life can indeed be prolonged. And for centuries, moderation was considered the key.

The Fountain of Youth

For many long ages, folklore spoke of the fountain of youth that would restore vitality to its users. And this was a popular theme in the artwork of the fifteenth and sixteenth centuries, when the fountain appeared in many prints and paintings (de Beauvoir, 1972). Plate 15 shows a version painted by Lucas Cranach the Elder. In his *Fountain of Youth* (1546), older women arrive at the fountain by stretcher, on foot, and by carriage. Entering its waters with all the physical signs of old age, they emerge on the other side full of youth and beauty. There they are invited to dress and come to be waited on at a lavish feast. In the bushes, a couple glance amorously at each other, for love and sex are associated with the newfound youth.

The pursuit of beauty and the beautifying of oneself were viewed as entirely appropriate in the fourteenth and fifteenth centuries. Youth would be forgiven for wanting to flaunt its beauty, within the limits of reasonable conduct (Braunstein, 1988). Older people, however, were ridiculed for covering up their age to become beautiful (Braunstein, 1988). A later example of this motif is Bernardo Strozzi's (1581–1644) *Aging Beauty*, displayed in Plate 16. This fine work shows an older woman trying to enhance her appearance by covering up her age, all to no avail. Two assistants help her with ribbons and a feather for her hair. Their attempts only underscore her old age and fruitless vanity.

Other evidence for the bias toward youth presents itself over the centuries. For example, in the nineteenth century, this bias would surface in the newly

Plate 15. *The Fountain of Youth*. 1546. Lucas Cranach the Elder. Courtesy of the Staatliche Museen Preussischer Kulturbesitz (Berlin-Dalheim Museum), Berlin.

Plate 16. *Aging Beauty*. Date unknown. Bernardo Strozzi. Courtesy of the Pushkin State Museum of Fine Arts, Moscow.

flourishing graphic arts of advertising. Children appear very often as models on the product advertisements of the period, and older models were decidedly less common. This orientation toward youth has continued in the twentieth century.

Contrasts to Youth

Few would deny that there is today a social orientation toward youth in Western societies. Young people and, moreover, those simply younger than older people both enjoy favored status. That is, most people would say they prefer middle age over being older, since middle age is generally considered the peak of life— not so, old age. There are researchers who assert that our fascination and desire for youth is relatively new (Barash, 1983; Fischer, 1978). Some have even noted that youth tends to be exalted during particular periods, such as after the American Civil War (Achenbaum, 1978).

Others believe that this orientation toward youth and middle age is a very old notion in Western thought. With few exceptions, when a snapshot is taken in history, we find a bias toward youth. For example, the French *chansons de geste* tales from the Middle Ages glorify youth. And when Western artists have portrayed the human body, youthful appearance has often been their goal. This historical bias does not apply to children, however—as Aries (1962) demonstrated—since childhood is a relatively new concept in Western society. Rather, it is more the age from 20 to 40 years old that generally falls within the scope of youth.

Part of the orientation toward youth comes from the classical notion of what represents beauty. In this regard, Western thought has been greatly influenced by the ancient Greeks. The Greek notion of beauty did not incorporate old age into its formula. Rather, it looked for graceful lines and youth to match.

Western art abounds with examples of the youth orientation. To begin at the beginning, Adam and Eve are always shown as young or middle aged, though the Bible says they lived for 900 years. And although in the rendering of its features beauty is very much an age-specific phenomenon, by the time of the Renaissance the Western artists had clearly defined it as being youthful. Sculpted models of beauty such as the *Belvedere Apollo* and the other Apollos and Venuses of the Renaissance reflect the bias. Giorgione's (1478–1510) *Sleeping Venus* is the painting of a beautiful and youthful nude female figure, while his *Col Tempo* shows a time-ravaged woman. Leonardo da Vinci drew several comparisons between older and younger subjects. One of these drawings at the Uffizi in Florence—from about 1500—shows half-figures comparing old and young in exacting detail. Some of da Vinci's works take on a cartoonlike character, as the contrasts are exaggerated by the artist. In any case, this Renaissance exaltation of youthful beauty in the human body did little to improve the image of older people. Summarizing the literature, de Beauvoir (1972) proposes simply that older people were judged ugly in contrast to the beauty of youth.

The artist Francisco de Goya picked up this theme of contrast in numerous works. In the drawing titled *Caprichos* (1799), reproduced in Plate 17, the Spanish artist shows an old woman enviously looking at the beauty of a young maiden. The young woman elaborates on her charms while the old woman broods.

Beauty, moreover, is not the only dimension on which old age has been contrasted with youth. Other comparisons are also made. The Restoration comedies of the late seventeenth century (from 1660 to 1700) used age as a determinant in assigning roles and were unequaled in their brutality toward older people. These plays often contrast older people with youth. Their comedic characters are either young or old, with few falling in between. The young play off the foolishness of the old, and the old are the object of ridicule (Coffman, 1934; Hendricks & Hendricks, 1977–78; Mignon, 1947). The two ages are never presented as compatible, but always in contrast and conflict.

Not all juxtapositions of old age with youth have been negative, however; companionship between old and young has also been expressed in art and literature. Teaching youth about the world is another related theme commonly illustrated in art, especially in the art of the eighteenth and nineteenth centuries. At the Corcoran Gallery in Washington, D.C., there is a painting by Emile Renouf (1845–1894) of a young girl and presumably her grandfather rowing a boat; it very effectively conveys this element of friendship between the generations. Among the works of Currier and Ives there are several in this vein, including the lesson being learned in their *Trial of Patience* (1857). The positive relationship between young and old is also found in literature, as in Dickens's (1841) work *Old Curiosity Shop*, which is the story of Little Nell and her grandfather. Simone de Beauvoir (1972) notes, however, that for the most part Dickens deplored social relations between the young and old.

WISDOM AND SENILITY

For better or worse, older people have generally been judged on a continuum ranging from deep wisdom to profound senility and foolishness. On the one end, they have been perceived as having great wisdom due to their maturity and lifetime experiences. On the other end, they have been viewed as foolish, senile, lacking wit and awareness.

The Sage

The association of old age with wisdom surfaces in many forms. For example, the ages-of-life formulas linked wisdom and scholarship with old age. This fundamental understanding served as a source of respect for older people. And such respect was not limited to older men. Barbara Walker (1985) and Simone de Beauvoir (1972) both point to the roles older women have played in their societies as crones and sages.

The theme of wisdom and old age can be traced back to ancient times. The

Plate 17. *Caprichos*. 1799. Francisco de Goya y Lucientes. Courtesy of the Metropolitan Museum of Art, New York, Gift of Walter E. Sachs, 1916.

Bible—so especially influential through religiocultural groups such as the Puritans—equates old age with wisdom and spirituality. Wisdom often takes the form of an old man in biblical writings and interpretations. In early Hebrew society, the elders of the community were vested with wisdom and political power. Moses, David, and Solomon were and still are venerated for their wisdom in old age. The Bible repeatedly emphasizes respect for one's elders. One of the Psalms proclaims: "They shall increase in fruitful old age and shall be well treated that they may show that the Lord God is righteous."

The influential Roman statesman and author Cicero characterized old age as a period of wisdom and maturity in his work *De Senectute* (Stern & Cassirer, 1946). Cicero was of the opinion that the intellectual powers can certainly be retained by older people (Miles, 1965). Maturity, he believed, leads to greater creativity than is possible during other ages of life. Petrarch in the fourteenth century agreed with Cicero that old age is preferable to the pleasures of youth, partly because of the wisdom that comes with experience (Folts, 1980). Throughout Tuscany in the fourteenth and fifteenth centuries, older patriarchs were respected for their wisdom; they held an honored place in society (La Ronciere, 1988). Cicero's emphasis on the unique creativity of old age was picked up again by the sixteenth-century Italian scholar Gabriele Paleotti in his *De Bono Senectutis* (Stern & Cassirer, 1946).

Rembrandt and other artists of the seventeenth century made renditions of older scholars and wise older people. Rembrandt's *Two Scholars Disputing* (1628) is a typical instance: The scholars are old men—not young. Plate 18 is a reproduction of the painting titled *A Scholar in a Lofty Room* (1631). Here Rembrandt shows one old man in a dark room with a high ceiling. The solitude of the scholar and the typical Rembrandt style of lighting highlight the seriousness and concentration in the subject.

Aries (1962) suggests that the ages-of-life iconography of the fourteenth to the eighteenth centuries is remarkably consistent in showing childhood as the period of play and then schooling, followed by the age of love and then adventure and war, and ending with the stereotypic old and bearded scholar in the sedentary pursuit of law and science.

The wisdom of older people is also illustrated in several literary works during these centuries. Burrow (1986) notes that the Anglo-Saxons had often linked old age to wisdom because they assumed that the world was in its last stage and that only older men could understand it. This assumption may have stuck. Shakespeare's old magician in *The Tempest* is characterized as wise, kindly, and generally appealing (Charles, 1977). Two centuries later and across the Channel, the satirical writer Voltaire introduced several older characters through his eighteenth-century plays, novels, and philosophical tales. After reviewing Voltaire's portrayals of these characters during the 66 years of his writing life, Lorna Berman and Judy Nelson (1987) conclude that the most common trait attributed to older people by the wit is wisdom.

In late-sixteenth-century Oxford, older men were selected to hold leadership

Plate 18. *A Scholar in a Lofty Room* (St. Anastasius). 1631. Rembrandt van Rijn. Courtesy of the National Art Museum, Stockholm (Photo: Statens Konstmuseer, Stockholm).

positions because of their presumed wisdom (Smith, 1982). This same pattern held true in other times and places, as well. In early New England, older people were often considered the wiser for their years, and thus were often sought out for counsel (Demos, 1986), as well as judgment. In fact, older peoples' advice continued to be sought on a variety of subjects beyond morality, up until the time of the Civil War (Achenbaum & Kusnerz, 1978). And in antebellum America, the long lives of older people were thought to have given them the experience to live and die properly (Achenbaum, 1978). It was after the Civil War, however, that respect for the wisdom of older people began to decline—at least in the United States—as the focus moved to youth and away from old age (Achenbaum, 1978). Prior to this change, older people had frequently played an important sociocultural role; more than a few people regarded them as the only ones capable of understanding the ultimate meaning of life.

For centuries, because of their experiences and memory, older people had been perceived as the keepers of tradition. Today we have many ways to share and store wisdom, whereas in the past older people were the primary sources of wisdom and knowledge. Leo Simmons (1945) was one of the first social historians to suggest that, as the folk wisdom of older people declined in importance, so did their perceived social value as a generation and as individuals. Simmons also found that the control of information had been a major source of status and power for older people, and had ensured them care and respect during the last years of their lives.

In the past, then, this transfer of knowledge from one generation to the next was an important topic for writers and artists alike. Some of the most homespun as well as the most regal images of older people show the passing of wisdom, cultural knowledge, or status from one generation to the next (McKee & Kauppinen, 1987). In the seventeenth century, for instance, Rembrandt and Diego Velazquez were among the artists who worked with the subject. Some of the popular nineteenth-century prints of Currier and Ives also carry this theme.

A number of the great sages of Western culture have been honored by artists over the centuries. Aristotle is one good example. A subject of enduring interest, the Greek philosopher is always shown as an older man by artists, including Rembrandt. Another example—from the nineteenth century—is Benjamin West's *Benjamin Franklin Drawing Electricity from the Sky* (1805), shown in Plate 19. Franklin was perceived as a very wise as well as clever man in his day (which was also West's day) and was regularly consulted for his experience and brilliant mind. In fact, it is claimed that, at the Constitutional Convention, Franklin was given much say in the process of compromise largely on the basis of his 80 plus years (Barash, 1983).

West chose to depict Franklin as an old man in the painting, even though his work with electrostatics and his discovery that lightning is a form of electricity occurred when he was a relatively young man of 46. Here Franklin is portrayed as an elder statesman wise to the world and possessing the insight of his advanced years.

Plate 19. *Benjamin Franklin Drawing Electricity from the Sky*. 1805. Benjamin West. Philadelphia Museum of Art, Mr. and Mrs. Wharton Sinkler Collection. Courtesy of the Philadelphia Museum of Art, Philadephia.

And the Old Fool

In sharp contrast to the image of older people as sages and full of wisdom is the negative view of them as fools and senile. Older people have often been portrayed thus. To some people, being old means automatically being senile. And there is a long tradition of portraying old men as fools; one need not go far to find examples. The Bible refers more than once to the foolishness of older people (Griffin, 1946). For example, Paul instructs Timothy to "avoid foolish and old wives' tales" (1 Tim. 4:7). Examples from secular works also abound. Alexander Barclay's woodcut titled *Ship of Fools* (1509) shows an old man wearing a fool's cap and bells, with the caption: "Of Olde Folyes that is to say the longer they lyve the more they are gyven to foly" (cited by Smith, 1976). This view is typical of the attitude, and it has endured.

There have been periods when people of all ages were generally considered to be fools. In the Middle Ages, human beings were seen as struggling and blundering through life, forever committing foolish acts that the proverbs warned against. Older people simply had been foolish for a longer period of time, and the frailties of old age contributed even more to their foolishness. The sixteenth-century artist Peter Brueghel captured this theme and tied it to old age with his work *The Misanthrope* (1568). The work, reproduced as Plate 20, is captioned "Because the world is so faithless, I am going into mourning." It is clear, however, that the misanthrope's own faithlessness is what causes his misery. Even while the old man walks, he is being robbed by the wicked world. The glass ball is the symbol for vanity. In the background, a shepherd faithfully tends his flock, in sharp contrast to the faithlessness in the foreground. The old man's concern over worldly matters has cost him his faith in God, which makes him a fool.

The Elizabethans delighted in the foolish bewilderment of tyrannical old fathers and jealous old husbands. The comic plight of old men and old women was a popular motif in the drama of the period. However, the Elizabethans did also characterize older people as wise, while their later Restoration counterparts did not (Mignon, 1947). In Restoration comedies, older people were automatically fools, and the reason was their age. Often, older individuals were even viewed as culprits responsible for many of society's ills.

In the ages-of-life models, senility and foolishness are frequently identified as characteristics of old age. In seventeenth-century England, old age—as the final stage of life—was considered a time in which the individual was not expected to contribute much of anything (Smith, 1979). The assumed foolishness of old age contributed to this perception. For example, in William Wycherley's play *Love in a Wood* (1671), a character by the name of Lady Cockwood desperately searches for a husband. Wycherley portrays her as too old for anything but a wild-goose chase. Other seventeenth-century writers—Sir George Etherege, William Wycherley, William Congreve, and others—often based fool-

Plate 20. *The Misanthrope*. 1568. Peter Brueghel. Gallerie Nazionali di Capodimote, Naples. Courtesy of the Soprintendenza per i Beni Artistici e Storici di Napoli.

ish characters in their comedies on older men and women. And even Jonathan Swift in his *Gulliver's Travels* promoted this theme (Freedman, 1978).

VENERATION

Throughout Western history, older people have often been venerated because of their age. However, there is also evidence that this respect may have been present only so long as the older people maintained control over wealth and property, and hence controlled their offspring (Stone, 1977; Thomas, 1976). In early America, according to David Fischer (1977), veneration of older people could have existed independently of control over property, there being an abundant supply of the latter. In any case, veneration has been a fairly strong attitude toward older people in Western history, albeit selectively applied (Kastenbaum, 1979). Wealth, family, and education may actually count more than age and experience in this regard. Carole Haber (1983) notes that in colonial America age was not the ultimate source of respect, as status was largely a product of one's material worth.

The Bible, as mentioned before, has been a major influence on attitudes and behaviors toward older people. The fifth of the Ten Commandments dictates that parents should be honored and respected (Exod. 20:2–17), and the Law prescribes the most severe of punishments for rebellious sons (Deut. 21:18–21). Artists often picked up the theme of veneration. *The Story of Saint Nicholas* (c. 1425) by Gentile da Fabriano shows a daughter demonstrating deference to her aged father by removing his shoes while she sits at his feet (see La Ronciere, 1988).

In the sixteenth and seventeenth centuries, Puritan sermons and literature stressed the honor of old age (Demos, 1986). Increase and Cotton Mather both preached that old age is a sign of God's will and that older people should be respected. Being a manifestation of God's grace, a ripe old age was considered something to be much admired (Achenbaum, 1978). In 1690, Cotton Mather wrote that old men should be accorded much respect and honor (Faragher, 1976). However, public veneration did not always lead to a sense of security in private life (Demos, 1978). To enforce the issue, the Puritans felt it necessary to punish children for disrespecting their elders.

Often in Puritan America, the word "old" would precede a person's name to garner honor and respect. The word itself denoted social rank. But being honored did not guarantee leadership or power in the community, as wealth and property were major sources of prestige and status (Smith, 1978). Age would only take a person so far, and no farther. In the colonial period the veneration of older people tended to decline (Fischer, 1978). According to Andrew Achenbaum (1978), the early Americans exalted old age up until the end of the Revolutionary War.

WORK IMAGES

For most of us, work is a major preoccupation of life. The capacity of older people to put in a good day's work is well documented in the historical literature. Sometimes a shortage of labor, such as in early New England (Demos, 1986), would keep people working well into their old age. But most older people have had to work in order to survive. In fact, for the greater part of Western civilization, older people seldom retired; they worked until they wore out (Fischer, 1978).

In America, the concept of voluntary retirement has existed since early New England, but until recently people still tended to retire due to debility rather than choice (Demos, 1986). Generally, times have always been hard for most people.

And the aged have generally had to rely on themselves for survival. Although charitable economic-support programs were available even prior to the nineteenth century, they were relatively rare and insufficient. Not until the invention of serious social programs in the nineteenth century were some people released from the necessity of working in old age. Under the industrial working conditions of that era, people were fortunate to reach old age; those who did so were exhausted and often crippled.

As to the cultural representation of work, prior to the fourteenth century almost all art was sacred. After profane art started to become more common, it would sometimes involve work roles, primarily the crafts (Aries, 1962). In this context, the crafts were viewed with a certain degree of sentimentality, as a person's life in this world was essentially the trade he or she practiced. The value of life was linked to work.

Older people depicted in their work roles range from Quinten Massys' fifteenth-century *Banker and His Client* to Van Ostade's seventeenth-century *Herring Woman*, and countless others. Many different work roles have been available for older people, with some being more common than others. Certain roles have changed dramatically with modernization and industrialization. One common role of long standing has been that of assistant or caretaker. In the social record of art, older persons are often providing assistance to younger adults. This motif surfaces in both sacred and profane art. On the sacred side, Rubens' seventeenth-century *Entombment of Saint Stephen* at the Musée des Beaux-Arts in Valenciennes, France, is a fine example: An older man assists in lowering the saint into the tomb. In another of Rubens's works, *Samson and Delilah* (1610/1612), the artist captures an older woman in the act of aiding and abetting the crime of cutting of Samson's hair; she holds a candle. The caretaker role is also found in secular works, including Gabriel Metsu's *Young Lady at Her Toilette* (late 1650s). Here an older woman, possibly a servant, is shown taking care of a younger woman.

Another role long played by older people has been in the preparation of food, which historically is most associated with older women. Old men—or for that matter, all men—are not generally found in this role until the twentieth century. Older women in food-preparation roles are most evident in seventeenth-century art. Diego Velazquez's *Old Woman Cooking Eggs* (1618) is a fine rendering of this association; it shows an older woman cooking eggs for a young boy. David Teniers the Younger worked with the theme in his painting *Interior with an Old Woman Peeling Apples* (c. 1630/1640). A group of men playing a game in the background implies that the food-preparation role and the old woman are both subordinate. Other examples of older women cooking can be found throughout the centuries.

In early nineteenth-century American culture, older people were seen as productive members of society, and they continued to fulfill many work roles well into old age. Often these had to do with working the family farm. Their involvement in every rural family enterprise, be it farm or cottage industry, was important. Things may have been different in the urban setting, however. Even in preindustrial New York, the old represented a significant portion of the poor and dependent population of the city (Zimmerman, 1980).

The positive image of older people and work changed as the Industrial Revolution progressed. From the middle of the nineteenth century onward, experience became less important than physical ability. The work roles available to older people changed dramatically, even in agricultural endeavors and cottage industries. With industrialization came a change in attitude toward older people. People in general were a resource to be exploited and then cast aside. The idea that they could no longer contribute to the workplace in their old age became more common. Mandatory retirement was a natural outgrowth of this view. In 1900, more than two-thirds of American men over the age of 65 were in the work force; but by 1970, the number was down to only one-fourth (Back, 1977). This is a remarkable shift in the work role and the work image of older men. Gradually, older people were removed from the mainstream economic structure of Western society.

Their removal from the mainstream meant that they now had to take whatever limited work they could find. Some of the roles available to older people with the advent of industrialization were very undesirable. This observation is well established by some of the earliest photographic artworks ever made: images and engravings of industrial nineteenth-century European society made by the journalist Henry Mayhew (1950/1851). In his classic *Street Life in London* series, there are vivid photographic images of the types of work—or lack thereof—available to older people. The photo-essay shows old men serving as sandwich boardmen, crossing sweepers, and in other low-status jobs. Mayhew refers to an old woman beggar as a "crawler" because she and those like her were so destitute they barely had the energy to beg. Some of the crawlers described by Mayhew had not been poor originally, but old age left them in poverty. Manet's painting *The Ragpicker* (1864) is another example of a less than desirable occupation among older people of the nineteenth century.

OLD WOMEN AS WITCHES

The figure of a witch is easy for us to visualize: Most frequently perceived as an old woman, she is dressed in black with a pointed hat, has a black cat, and rides a broomstick. Although there have always been older women who were labeled as witches, their predominant association with the image is a recent development. Earlier in history, witches were shown as being all ages, such as in Dürer's engraving *Four Witches* (1497). They might be either sex, but were predominantly female as women were seen as the weaker vessel and thus more easily persuaded by the Devil.

There are accounts of older women in the eleventh, twelfth, and thirteenth centuries being accused of magic and sorcery in parts of Europe such as Tuscany (La Ronciere, 1988). Still, during these centuries older women were not particularly associated with witchcraft any more than the other ages were (Taylor, 1970). Certainly, the Catholic Church and later the Protestants regarded witchcraft as applicable to all people, regardless of age or gender (Bever, 1982). This broad application best served the interests of the Church, which wanted to punish deviants and heretics. Joan of Arc was burned at the stake in 1431 for heresy, sorcery, blasphemy, and witchcraft at the young age of 20.

In 1484, Pope Innocent VIII issued a papal bull that declared witchcraft to be a prime heresy of Christendom. Two years later the Dominican monks Heinrich Kramer and Jacob Sprenger published *Malleus Maleficarum* or *The Witches' Hammer*. This popular manual was an important guide used for hunting witches and religious heretics. *The Witches' Hammer* taught that all witchcraft comes from carnal lust (Stone, 1979), which is insatiable (Taylor, 1970). Witchcraft was thus associated with sexual deviance and problems such as impotence and miscarriage (Bullough, 1976b). Witches were viewed as erotic and were often assumed to have had sex with the Devil (Waldemar, 1960).

It was during the fifteenth century that witchcraft became associated with various kinds of stigmatizing behavior (Bullough, 1976b) and with women (Holmes, 1974). *The Witches' Hammer* did not isolate older women as witches, however, because of the Church's interest in having a broad-based definition of the witch (Bever, 1982). Rather, as noted earlier, the definition was wide enough to include people of all ages and both sexes. Thus, the early ecclesiastical witch-hunters did not emphasize old age; this emphasis came from those in the general population who thought that witches were basically crazy or senile older women trying to cope with an uncompassionate world (see Bever, 1982).

Prosecution of witches started in the twelfth and thirteenth centuries, but reached its peak in the sixteenth and seventeenth centuries when fear and the reaction to witchcraft reached epidemic proportions. As witch-hunting increased in popularity during this period, older women became a disproportionate share of those identified as witches by both Catholics and Protestants (Kastenbaum & Ross, 1975). Older women were suspected in witchcraft and stood trial as witches more often than other groups. One-half to three-quarters of all accused witches were older women, yet they comprised only about 20 percent of the total population (Bever, 1982). Reay Tannahill (1980) reports that witches in the sixteenth and seventeenth centuries were usually women between 50 and 70 years of age, with distinguishing social characteristics such as their being professional midwifes. Some estimates indicate that 80 percent of those accused of witchcraft were women over 50 years of age (Scarre, 1987). In sixteenth- and seventeenth-century Scotland, witches were mainly middle-aged and older women. As high as 92 percent of those accused of witchcraft were women. Christina Larner (1984) concludes that, in certain periods, being a woman and being a witch were almost interchangeable. Many of those accused were also widows (Scarre, 1987). Many admitted to witchcraft only after being tortured to extract a confession.

There were a few courageous individuals who questioned the existence of witches during this period. In 1563 the physician Johann Weyer suggested that witches were harmless old women who confessed to impossible crimes only because they were tortured. Weyer viewed witchcraft rather as evidence of the follies of old women. Reginald Scott was an Elizabethan skeptic who challenged several of the current premises about witches in his *Discoverie of Witchcraft* (1973/1584). By calling attention to the plight of older women, however, these skeptics may have inadvertently furthered the labeling of older women as witches (Bever, 1982).

There are several reasons why older women were accused of witchcraft. Under the English Poor Laws, local villages were responsible for the care of their sick and poor, including older women. This role may not always have been a welcomed responsibility; some communities simply did not want to take care of their older people. For one thing, the need for care was seen as a sign of human failing and thus was placed in a negative context (Holmes, 1974). The response must have seemed expedient at the time. Label the needy as witches and then condemn them (Bever, 1982). In 1711, Joseph Addison reported that, when an old woman would become dependent on the charity of the parish, she was straightaway labeled a witch and legally terminated (Scot, 1973/1584). The point is that community resources were scarce, indeed. Once a person became dependent on community support, they also became very expendable.

Older women proved to be ideal scapegoats, then, because they were viewed as expendable, weak, defenseless, and poor (Walker, 1985). It was very decidedly the view of just a minority of people, during the sixteenth and seventeenth centuries that witches were only helpless old women in an unhelping world (Kastenbaum & Ross, 1975). Commenting on the 1574 trial of the Windsor witches in England, Ronald Holmes (1974) notes that the trial was an outcome of the extreme poverty in which older women lived. The historian Keith Thomas in *Religion and the Decline of Magic* (1971) also supports this view of witchcraft. Thomas contends that marginal old women were ostracized by their communities; their begging and misfortune would then lead to accusations of witchcraft.

Another explanation is that older women sometimes resorted to magic, sorcery, trickery, and other behaviors defined as witchcraft in order to obtain power within their communities. Such tactics and practices may have provided modest incomes and some support for women judged to be socially unproductive and useless otherwise. Undoubtedly, there were also older women who did believe themselves to be witches and persuaded their neighbors that they were (Ravensdale & Morgan, 1974). After all, there is a long tradition in Western society of older women serving among the people in the often positive roles of the advising crone, the midwife, and the lay physician.

It may be, as Bever (1982) suggests, that witchcraft was indeed widespread among the general population. After 200 years, it could hypothetically have become concentrated with older women, perhaps because senile older women were the only ones willing to risk persecution. In any case, commentaries from the period often refer to older women being identified as witches. A good example is Cotton Mather's *On Witchcraft, Being the Wonders of the Invisible World*

(1950/1692). Mather speaks of witchcraft in Puritan America. He describes a case that was typical of the period:

The most remarkable was an Old Woman named Dayton, of whom it was said, If any in the World were a Witch, she was one, and had been so accounted 30 years. I had the Curiosity to see her tried; she was a decrepit Woman of about 80 years of age, and did not use many words in her own defense. She was accused by about 30 Witnesses; but the matter alleged against her was such as needed little apology, on her part not one passionate word, or immoral action, or evil, was then objected against her for 20 years past, only strange accidents falling out, after some Christian admonition given by her, as saying, God would not prosper them, if they wrong'd the Widow. (Mather 1950/1692: 172)

Witches were the universal scapegoats for societies: Death, poor weather, crop failure, dry wells, illness, infertility, and other undesirable situations were often attributed to witchcraft (Walker, 1985). It is estimated that between 100,000 (Scarre, 1987) and 300,000 (Holmes, 1974) people were put to death after being convicted of witchcraft during this period. Many executions were not recorded, and so the figures differ.

The 1692 Salem witch trials are a classic case of the persecution of women as witches. In Salem, Massachusetts, a group of young girls began to act peculiarly. The theory circulated that witchcraft was the source of their behavior. As a result, a number of people, including older women, were accused of witchcraft and punished. Nineteen were hanged; two died in jail; and one was pressed to death. All of the older women who died had reputations in the community that contributed to their being accused of witchcraft.

Art—the mirror of society—portrayed witches as being both sexes and all ages prior to the sixteenth and seventeenth centuries. After that time, the witch became more and more symbolic rather than real in the popular mind, and older women are found increasingly in the portrayal. By the nineteenth century, the older woman was firmly entrenched as the image of the witch. There are several old witches already present in the art of the seventeenth century. For example, David the Younger Rykaert's painting *The Witch* (1655) shows an old woman in the company of various demons. Frans Francken's *Witches' Sabbath* (1607) includes witches of all ages. In this painting, there is an old woman in the foreground involved in the central ceremony, but she is accompanied by women of all ages. Pennethorne Hughes has written a book on witchcraft (1965) that is a virtual catalog of images of witches from the fourteenth through the twentieth centuries. The fourteenth-century witch from the Lyon Cathedral is ageless. However, the seventeenth-century example—Jennet Dibb and her cat—is clearly of an old woman, although she lacks the dramatic image of the witch with the pointed hat, sharp nose, and wrinkled skin. In that regard, the twentieth-century Disney witch embodies all the features of the stereotype held today. Plate 21 shows a witch on a broomstick from the mid-nineteenth-century fairy-tale book

Plate 21. *The Crone*. 1880. Artist unknown. From *The Water Babies: A Fairy Tale for a Land Baby*, by Charles Kingsley. (New York: Macmillan Publishing Company, 1880; orig. ed. 1863).

by Charles Kingsley titled *The Water Babies* (1880). We see that by this time the old woman is the icon for the witch in Western society.

THE OLD MAN AS TIME

Time has taken many forms over the ages, one of the oldest being the beast with hooves and wings to symbolize its fleeting character. It has also appeared as a winged cherub, the hourglass, the scythe, and other representations. Time the old man, usually with a long beard, has been the most common image, although it was unknown prior to the Renaissance (Quinones, 1972). The ancients did not always link time to the concept of destruction. Medieval art and literature did, however. Time in the late Middle Ages and the Renaissance became the destroyer that leads to decay. During the Renaissance time was also recognized as the revealer of truth. And time would triumph over love only to be itself conquered by eternity.

So during the late Middle Ages and Renaissance, time took on the aspects of old wizened men. Often these would be almost rude old men with wings and winged feet; they were carrying hourglasses, whips, swords, clocks, or scythes—each item endowed with a special meaning associated with time. The scythe or sickle represented the passage of life and death. The winged feet stood for fleeting moments and opportunity. The wings also represented communication between humanity and God (Whittick, 1972), which was a natural association made in regard to older people. After the Renaissance, Baroque artists relied on hourglasses, crutches, and zodiacs to represent time.

A sixteenth-century woodcut by Giovanni Andrea Gilio shows time as an old man with a whip. In Willem Swidden's *Time the Destroyer* (1580), the old man has wings and winged feet; an hourglass and a whip are shown with him. Otho Van Veen's engraving *Time Brings Consolation to Age* (1612), Nicholas Poussin's *Time Saving Truth from Envy and Discord* (1641), and Francois Le Moyne's *Time Revealing Truth* (1737) are a few other examples. The old man as time is also seen in Puritan stonecarving, such as the *Joseph Tapping Stone* (1678) found in the King's Chapel in Boston and the *John Foster Stone* (1681) found in Dorchester, Massachusetts (Tashjian & Tashjian, 1974).

A fine example in the Baroque style is the French artist Simon Voulet's *Time Vanquished by Hope, Love, and Beauty* (1627). The painting shows three figures: Saturn, with an hourglass and scythe; Hope, wearing a wreath of fresh flowers; and Venus, holding Saturn by his hair and threatening him with a spear. Giovanni Battista Tiepolo's *Time Unveiling Truth* (1745–1750), shown in Plate 22, is another painting of time as an old man. It includes the familiar elements of winged feet and a scythe, and also shows a chariot. That time eventually exposes us to the truth is the central theme of this work.

CLOSING THOUGHTS ON OLDER PEOPLE AND SYMBOLS

The aged were selected by their respective societies to represent certain themes and concepts. Older people have symbolized time, the miser, the witch, and other cultural images. They have been linked consistently with certain symbols associated with old age and aging in general—including owls, canes, and goats, for instance. In the abstract, common to all these symbols were the underlying themes of aging, the passage of time, mental and physical decline, growth in spirituality, wisdom, death, God, and contemplation.

There has been a long tradition of associating older people with key religious concepts and figures. Partly due to their advanced years, they have been considered closer to God. What can we conclude about images of older people as religious figures? Clearly, older people have been strongly associated with many religious activities. Artists chose to portray them in contemplation, life review, preparation for death, prayer, and other spiritual practices. There was a strong and enduring emphasis placed on their depth of understanding in spiritual matters. They and only they were viewed as capable of understanding the true meaning of life, God, and the hereafter. Their closeness to God and nearness to death,

Plate 22. *Time Unveiling Truth*. C. 1745–1750. Giovanni Battista Tiepolo. Charles Potter Kling und. Courtesy of the Museum of Fine Arts, Boston.

along with their life's experiences, were thought to provide older people with great insight into the nature of God and heaven.

The themes of contemplation, surrender of worldly possessions, and devotion of God even came to prescribe how older people should respond to the aging process. In this regard, they were expected ideally not to focus on this life and their personal decline, but rather on the promise of heaven and its reward.

Partly because they were perceived as examples to imitate, certain older religious figures such as Saint Jerome were immensely popular subjects in art. Jerome's image was so widespread that he was almost an icon for old age during the sixteenth and seventeenth centuries. Jerome and many of his saintly older counterparts conveyed a sense of serenity, but also intensity. These are images of people at peace with the world, quietly and seriously involved with scholarship and prayer in their last days. The earliest models of this ideal for aging were the likes of Moses, Lot, Abraham, and Joseph. God has always been an old man in the Christian tradition, since He is the father of us all. In art, however, this image of God the Father would become rare as Christianity placed more and more emphasis on the Holy Family, the saints, and the Christ. Today, although we are seldom exposed to the image, it is so ingrained that most Westerners still picture Him as an old man.

In addition to these sacred icons, artists also created secular images of older people. For example, when depicted in human form, avarice was usually an old woman, although older men were often shown as misers. This is a practice that continues today. There may have been some justification for making this association, as older people sometimes needed to be miserly to ensure their survival. We know that wills were often very detailed so as to secure adequate care of older parents and relatives during old age, as will be pointed out in Chapter 4. Some of these provisions and cautions may have been interpreted as evidence of miserly behavior. If so, they would have fueled the perceptions of older people as misers and symbolic of avarice. Actually though, without many of the social support systems present today, older people's miserly behavior was probably a rational response to difficult circumstances.

The pursuit of youth and a prolongation of life has endured throughout Western history. Explanations for how this youth and longevity might be attained never drifted far, however, from what the ancient Greeks proposed. Their notion of bodily humors found a following late into the eighteenth century. The theories were remarkably consistent over the centuries, with little in the way of new ideas creeping in until the eighteenth and nineteenth centuries. The key has always been held to be moderation in all things, so as not to upset the body's balance. Interventions were also proposed from time to time that would purportedly postpone the negative effects of aging, restore youth, or prolong life—the latter always questioned by the Church, which was suspicious of attempts to interfere with God's will.

Reports and rumors of people surviving well into old age have always been welcome news and examined with great interest. This may have been particularly true in the first years of the American Republic and, more generally, the seventeenth and eighteenth centuries in Europe and America. We have never surrendered our desire to extend life and recapture youth. Even today, youth continues to be the ideal for many people. They put on makeup to hide the signs of old age and dye their grey hairs to appear younger. One does not wear makeup to stress old age nor dye the hair grey to appear older.

The contrast between youth and old age served as a springboard for many images of older people. Artists and authors over the centuries have used the contrast to create the themes of their work. The two major negative themes have been the depression associated with lost youth, and envy of youth for its beauty and promise. Some contrasting between youth and old age has been favorably handled, however, as in accentuating when older people share their time with younger people in leisure or learning activities. Older people are then portrayed as the transmitters of wisdom and culture.

Today, one of the symbols we take for granted is the image of the witch as an older woman. This was not always the case, as early witch-hunters were interested in apprehending witches of all ages and sexes. Thus, at the beginning of the fervor over witches, older women stood on an equal footing with others in being accused of witchcraft. Images of witches during this period show them as being all ages and both sexes. During the sixteenth and seventeenth centuries, older women were increasingly the ones accused of witchcraft; and by the eighteenth century, they were firmly entrenched as the archetype of the witch. This image persists today and is widely promoted by popular culture. Why Western society focused on the older woman in this regard is unknown. There is a scattering of evidence that suggests a variety of reasons: self-promotion of the idea for economic survival; community reluctance to aid them under the Poor Laws; and their perceived uselessness to society, to name a few.

During this same period, older men came to represent time. The connection was first made during the Renaissance and continues to the present; it was based on associating physical decline with the passing of time. This decline being visually evident in most older men, they were considered excellent personifications of time.

There are other symbolic images of older people, as well; some have not been included here, but are addressed in other chapters. What is most impressive about almost all of these images is their enduring quality. The old witch, the crone, Old Father Time, God the Father, the mean old miser, and the venerated older scholar are all still with us, although their various meanings and significances may have changed somewhat.

4

IMAGES OF OLDER PEOPLE AND THE FAMILY

The evolution of the modern family has received considerable attention from historians, who have studied the subject along several dimensions. This chapter focuses on the issues that relate to older people. It has been stated in the literature that family life is one of the most important aspects of old age (Dahlin, 1980). However, despite this importance there is still not much scholarly information about the role of older people within the family.

THE FAMILY STRUCTURE

Out of all the study on the development of the family in Western history comes a myriad of ideas on its evolution and structure. One of the key subjects in the literature has been the nuclear versus the extended family structure. For years social scientists and historians operated under the assumption that the multigenerational or extended family—that is, a family with more than two generations living in the same household—was the predominant form in preindustrial Western history. This assumption led to the assertion that, as industrialization and modernization occurred, the extended family was torn apart. Specifically, the change in family structure resulted from the increased demands placed on the extended family unit by industrialization (Burgess, 1960; Parsons, 1942). And as a consequence of the change in structure, the care of and status of older people were thought to have declined. This has been characterized as a disintegration of the family unit (de Beauvoir, 1972). Rosenmayr writes that "processes of industrialization and urbanization lead to the dissolution of the extended or multi-generational family" (1971:87). Some social scientists assert that this decline in the extended family also transferred the care of older people to the larger community.

However, not everyone agrees that industrialization and modernization were responsible for the disintegration of the extended family (Quadagno, 1982). Current historical thought challenges the view that the extended multigenerational family was ever common in the Western societies (Collomp, 1989; Goldthorpe, 1987; Laslett, 1965; Laslett & Wall, 1972). Summarizing the research, Eugene Friedmann (1960) finds a lack of evidence that the extended family ever prevailed in either the United States or Europe. High mortality rates in preindustrial England helped limit the number of large extended families (Hendricks & Hendricks, 1977–1978). Therefore, few families included grandparents in the same household as their grandchildren.

A sampling of studies provides us with an idea of the prevalence of multigenerational families. David Herlihy (1985) found little evidence for this family form in mid-eighth-century Saint Germain, France, because few people survived to old age. Out of 3,044 individuals residing in Saint Germain, only 26 were identified as grandmothers and none were grandfathers. Certainly, the rarity of old age during this period would indeed have severely limited the frequency of the multigenerational family.

This pattern saw no change during the Middle Ages. Contrary to popular stereotype, extended families were generally not so common during this period (Gies & Gies, 1978). The medieval family was seldom large and extended, due in part to late marriages and early deaths. Likewise, Georges Duby (1978) reports that French high society of the twelfth century had a long tradition of two-generation families. The same situation found in late medieval England, where households were neither complex nor extended (Hanawalt, 1986).

The evidence on household size in preindustrial England and early America (Friedmann, 1960; Laslett, 1965; Laslett & Wall, 1972; Shanas et al., 1968; Smith, 1979; Zimmerman, 1980) and preindustrial regions of Western and Central Europe (Mitterauer & Sieder, 1982) indicates that the multigenerational extended family was uncommon everywhere. According to John Demos (1970), the model family in the Plymouth Colony was a married couple plus their children. Similarly, Michael Anderson (1971) found little evidence of extended families in nineteenth-century Lancashire, England. Studies focusing on the nineteenth century found that in urbanized areas there was a higher percentage of older people living with their married children than in rural areas (Anderson, 1971; Chudacoff & Hareven, 1978). Summarizing the history of the family, Richard Wall (1984) concludes that over the past 400 years there has been a decline in the numbers of children living with older people. Edward Shorter (1977), after conducting an extensive review of the evolution of the family, found that no single type of household characterized traditional societies. Diversity was the rule.

Nevertheless, there is some evidence that such families were more common in preindustrial times than they are today (Laslett, 1977). This appears to be true (with certain regional exceptions) not only in the United States, but in Europe as well. And in some areas such as Eastern Europe and in particular

Russia, extended families were widespread in the eighteenth and nineteenth centuries; such was also the case in areas of France as late as the eighteenth century (Collomp, 1989).

In some places, the older couples would move out of the central household to one nearby. This was a traditional practice in certain European countries. The grandparents' cottage helped reduce family tensions, but also reflects a lack of mutual interest and affection between the older and younger generations. Older relatives were close by, but not too close for comfort.

Historically, the living arrangement preferred by older people in the United States—and for that matter, Europe—has been not to live with their adult children (see Shanas, 1977). Multigenerational families within the same household are no less common today than they were in the past (Beresford & Rivlin, 1969). During the fourteenth and fifteenth centuries, older people often expressed a desire to live in their own homes (Hanawalt, 1986). The same was true for colonial America, as most older people did not require assistance and lived independently well into old age (Metress, 1985). In colonial New England, older people lived close to children, but preferred to look after themselves (Demos, 1978). Many continued to live in their own homes even after their children had left, although the children may have lived close by (Demos, 1986). The same was true in preindustrial England. Older people were not much more likely than they are today to be living in the households of their married children (Laslett, 1976).

Countless studies have reaffirmed older people's desire to be independent of their children. The nineteenth-century French demographer Frédéric Le Play found this to be the case among his contemporaries in France (Wall et al., 1983). In pioneer America, primary responsibility for one's living arrangements was considered to rest with the person concerned, given the strong sociocultural value of rugged individualism (Randall, 1965).

Economic Dependence: A Major Reason for Multigenerational Families

Suffice it to say that for the centuries covered by this book, poverty was common. Living conditions for most families were hard to begin with, and full of adverse circumstances (Goldthorpe, 1987; Stone, 1979). There is some evidence that older parents might have felt the difficult living conditions worst of anyone. Hard times meant that every member of the family needed to contribute to its survival. Historically, economic dependence of the generations has been a major reason behind the extended family (Shanas, 1977). Economic cooperation was more important in the survival of the family unit than socializing the young, which is the case in contemporary society (Mitterauer & Sieder, 1982). Young single and married adults would sometimes stay with their parents out of economic necessity, rather than affection. For one thing, the younger adults were often needed to help with farming and light production of goods within the household. This relationship might then become more fixed with the birth of grandchildren. This is not to suggest that the extended family was common, but that economic dependency was. The opposite arrangement was also true: older people living with their children out of economic necessity rather than choice (Quadagno, 1982).

Mutual Support

Over the centuries, older and younger people have had mutually complementary roles within the context of the family. Older women have been commonly occupied with caring for their youngest children and their grandchildren while the other parents work in the fields or factories (Litchfield, 1978). In colonial America, grandparents were sometimes called on to care for orphaned grandchildren (Demos, 1986); and in preindustrial England, widowers might send their children to live with grandparents (Laslett, 1977). Andrew Achenbaum (1978) found that, in the United States during the period from 1790 to 1860, older people's contributions to the home were extolled. Howard Chudacoff and Tamara Hareven (1978) also found that mutual support and assistance between older and younger generations were characteristic of mid- and late-nineteenth-century Essex County, Massachusetts.

Some have suggested that new functions for older people emerged in the context of the family as industrialization spread. In nineteenth-century England, older people—often grandparents—provided child care, housekeeping, and other useful family roles, partly in response to the increase in numbers of women working in the factories (Anderson, 1971). Grandmothers especially played an important economic function in the working-class families of Britain (Anderson, 1971). And it was particularly common for grandparents to provide child care for working parents. Occasionally under these circumstances, grandchildren were even taken in by the grandparents (Quadagno, 1982). Older people benefited from these relationships, as they would receive support and care in return.

THE FAMILY AS PRIMARY CARETAKER

It has been the general duty of children to provide care for their parents when the latter can no longer care for themselves (Ozment, 1983). Biblical teachings such as the story of King David, who cared for his elderly parents, lent early support to the concept of the obligation of children to care for their parents (Ozment, 1983). In addition, the Bible linked honor to family support in old age. Ecclesiastes says that parents must be honored and obeyed, and that their children must aid and support them in old age and illness.

As would be expected then, the family has served historically as a major source of care for older people. The family, according to Leo Simmons (1945), has always been considered the safest haven for older people. And it has sometimes been a legal stipulation, as well, that the primary responsibility for the care of older people rests with the immediate family. For example, the early American poor laws clearly defined the family as the unit of primary responsibility for maintaining the elderly (Zimmerman, 1980). Generally, first-generation off-spring took the lead role, but there have been periods and locations when grand-children also provided care, as in colonial America (Demos, 1986) and in nineteenth-century Lancashire, England (Anderson, 1971).

In the traditional English family, it was the legal duty of the children to provide assistance to parents; but in practice there were limits to how far this assistance would be expected to go (Laslett, 1977). Thus, relying on the family as a source of care could be rather precarious (see Mitterauer & Sieder, 1982). There is clear evidence of this state of affairs. In late medieval England, older parents sometimes had to beg in order to survive, even when their children lived in the same community (Hanawalt, 1986). Among those who could afford it, some older people in medieval England lived as pensioners with families not related to them (Hanawalt, 1986). The precariousness of the family as caretaker stems partially from the economic and social strain of having older people in the household. Although older dependents often contributed to child care as well as directly in the economic activity of the households of their offspring, they also drew on scarce family resources.

Historical research has shown that in seventeenth- and eighteenth-century America (Fischer, 1977) and nineteenth-century England (Robin, 1984) there were married children who stayed with their older parents in order to provide care. In the eighteenth century, both widows and widowers turned to the oldest son for care; but as inheritance decreased in relative importance, daughters were increasingly called on (Stearns, 1980). Society had moved from a property/son-dominated orientation to a daughter-oriented system of family care by the nine-teenth century. It should be noted that in America at least in the eighteenth and nineteenth centuries and perhaps earlier, much of the responsibility rested on the daughter's sense of filial duty to the aging parents (Premo, 1984). Sons gave financial support, while daughters provided actual hands-on care. This was partly due to women being regarded as better suited for the role of domestic caretaker. The earlier sacrifices of aging parents were viewed as needing repayment by the offspring—and in particular, daughters.

There is evidence in the literature that older people were very concerned about the stress and strain they imposed on their offspring. Terri Premo (1984) notes that older women in eighteenth- and nineteenth-century America were often aware of the stress and strain they were placing on younger daughters charged with the responsibility of providing them care. Some of these older women desired an early end to their lives, as opposed to being a burden on their families.

Alternatives to Family Care

The family was not the only form of care available to older people. In feudal Europe, both the landed classes and the Church took some responsibility. Older peasants received a certain amount of protection from destitution from the lords of their manors (Gordon, 1960). Later, craft guilds also provided support for older members (Friedmann, 1960). In Europe generally, institutional care for the needy—including older people—has been traced as far back as the twelfth century (Dieck, 1980). In addition, Ollie Randall (1965) reports that homes for the aged were in existence as early as the fourteenth and fifteenth centuries in Yugoslavia. There is also evidence of local community care in fifteenth- and sixteenth-century Germany (Dieck, 1980).

In spite of these and other efforts, social care for the aged did not reach everyone, nor was it ever adequate enough to have met everyone's needs. With the rise of guilds, some older people found assistance, but again it was not always sufficient to match even the needs of those who qualified (de Beauvoir, 1972). Many older people were simply forced to become beggars which was more widely accepted in the past than it is in contemporary times.

Women also had the option of moving into a convent or nunnery. Women who were widowed, who never married, or who did not marry after the loss of their spouse could opt for the Church. In most periods of Western history including the early and late Middle Ages, women have generally outlived men (Goody, 1983). This meant that widows were common. But mere survivorship and wealth were no guarantee that older widows would be taken care of in their old age. The Church provided on alternative to the dangers of widowhood and old age. Thus, the late medieval Church provided some—albeit sporadic—care for older people (Hanawalt, 1986). Retirement into a convent or nunnery kept a woman within her own social class (Goody, 1983) and protected her from exploitation. In fact, the Church was very interested in attracting wealthy old women, as they represented a viable source of needed income. The Church was considered a very socially acceptable outlet by which these widows might pass on their wealth. In later periods such as seventeenth-century New England—even without the nunnery structure—the Church establishment provided for widows who were incapable of supporting themselves (Faragher, 1976).

Elizabethan Poor Laws

Historians usually trace the English Poor Laws back to the enactment of the Statute of Laborers in 1350. But it was not until the reign of Elizabeth that the principle of taxation for the relief of the poor, including the old, was envisioned and enacted. The Elizabethan Poor Laws of 1601 were an early reflection of the British public's sense of responsibility for the old, the disabled, and the poor. However, the Poor Laws were minimal and rudimentary (Holmes, 1974). At best, they provided minimal support to the needy. Still, these laws helped establish almshouses and gave supplemental support to the old and poor in their own homes; they served as a model for laws over the next 300 years.

The intent of the Poor Laws has been researched in great detail. The current thinking is that the Poor Laws of Elizabeth were punitive and restrictive, offered meager relief, and were designed to be executed at low cost. One has to admire, however, the social consciousness that underpins many of the provisions in these early works of law. In terms of our discussion of family, the Poor Law of 1601 specifically confined responsibility for the relief of older people to their children alone (Laslett, 1977). Thus, the legal foundation for the family's primary responsibility as care givers can be traced to the early Poor Laws.

Under the laws, local villages and communities had some responsibility for the poor, including older people. As discussed in Chapter 3, local communities did not always welcome this responsibility. Older people—and particularly older widows—were at times seen as social parasites because they drew their support from scarce community resources. Regarded as not serving any useful social function, they might consequently be labeled as witches and destroyed.

A number of older people lived in institutions such as those provided under the Poor Laws in seventeenth-century England (Smith, 1979). Others who were living far from their families in colonial New England sometimes appealed to local authorities for assistance, with varying degrees of success (Demos, 1986).

Modern measures toward social insurance were taken by the start of the nineteenth century. In France, public institutions were sometimes called on to provide care (Stearns, 1980); almshouses and asylums operated in parts of France. These institutions usually stripped the old of what they owned as a condition of admission. By the middle of the nineteenth century, U.S. welfare institutions began to provide an increasing amount of care for older people. Poor law provisions provided some care for older women. Even with welfare institutions and the development of pensions, the main source of care remained with the family, at least in Massachusetts (Chudacoff & Hareven, 1978). Some believe that institutional alternatives were still relatively rare in the Western world at the close of the nineteenth century and that families continued to bear the full responsibility for care of their older parents and relatives (Dahlin, 1980).

Detailed Provisions for the Care of Older People

Evidence from preindustrial Central and Eastern Europe, (Mitterauer & Sieder, 1982), late medieval England (Hanawalt, 1986), traditional English society (Laslett, 1977), and early New England (Demos, 1978, 1986; Hareven, 1979) suggests that legal provisions for care of the elderly were often very detailed, implying that social relations between the generations were often strained (Stearns, 1981). For many periods in European history, property rights and ownership were used by older parents to ensure themselves care during old age (Berkner, 1972; Demos, 1970; Greven, 1970; Thomas, 1976). Their security often depended on control over property and wealth, as mentioned in Chapters 2 and 3. Without this bargaining power, their care could not be guaranteed. In colonial America as well, this power of parents over their children by controlling the wealth was present (Demos, 1970; Greven, 1970; Smith, 1973).

But as Chudacoff and Hareven (1978) note, older people remained insecure and anxious about their care in old age. Wills read like legal contracts, spelling out in fine detail the requirement of providing care for the older parents. Summarizing the development of the family, Shorter (1977) notes that there were times when older people knew they would not be treated well once they relinquished control over their property. Indeed, dispossessed fathers and mothers were often treated badly by their heirs, as in the literary case of Shakespeare's King Lear. Thus, older parents might hold onto their wealth for as long as possible—but not for too long, as the children could always move away if the control were delayed too long. Older parents therefore had to balance their control very carefully. Shorter (1977) has likened this to a moral and material calculus.

The existence of affectionate relationships within the family cannot be assumed historically. True affection rarely characterized the medieval nuclear family (Stone, 1977). It follows then that affection toward older relatives was uncommon, as well. Under these conditions, the provision of care might have taken on more of an instrumental tone than one of affection. In fact, Lawrence Stone (1977) suggests that sentimentality toward family relations did not emerge until the middle of the seventeenth century. There is additional evidence that by the eighteenth century new affectionate and loving attitudes toward older family members had developed (Fischer, 1978). Thus, sentimental ties among the generations evolved only slowly. Over the centuries, this evolution dramatically affected how older relatives were treated within the context of the family.

INTERGENERATIONAL CONFLICTS

In preindustrial societies, power, authority, and wealth often rested in the hands of the oldest members of the family. Control of property gave older people a great deal of power within the family (Quadagno, 1982). In traditional societies such as England, this authority was very real (Laslett, 1977), but was occasionally challenged nonetheless (de Beauvoir, 1972). Several studies conducted in Europe during different periods have found patriarchal authority to be a dominant characteristic. The father exercised strong control in the twelfth and thirteenth centuries, while mothers and maternal grandparents had little power over children (Duby et al, 1988). Later on, the existence of powerful old patriarchs with young wives and children created a great deal of tension in fourteenth- and fifteenth-century Tuscany (La Ronciere, 1988). Philip Greven (1970) found that, in seventeenth-century New England, parental control of property provided fathers with considerable family power. In Europe generally, as well as colonial America, patriarchal authority continued well into the eighteenth century (see Collomp, 1989). Despite this authority, most parents were not the restraint on their offspring they could have been (Laslett, 1977). But as George Banzinger (1979) suggests, some older parents—and in particular, fathers—did use the authoritarian arrangement to be tyrannical and interfering in the lives of their children. One must keep in mind that parents choosing their childrens' mates was a strong practice during the Middle Ages and the early modern period (Ozment, 1983).

The predictable result was youthful rebellion. Shakespeare's *Romeo and Juliet* reflects this enduring theme of young lovers rebelling against parental control over their relationship. Such rebellion and resentment occasionally led children even to abuse their older parents (Berkner, 1972; Quadagno, 1982).

In *The Village Betrothal* (1761) by Jean-Baptiste Greuze—reproduced here as Plate 23—the artist shows an older patriarch in the midst of his family (see Gauthier, 1964). Greuze records a scene that must have played over and over again in Western history: the patriarch blessing the betrothal of his daughter. He hands to his future son-in-law a purse containing the dowry. The mother holds her daughter's arm and a younger sister leans against the future bride. The man in a hat who is seated to the right is drawing up the marriage contract. As time progressed, the power of older patriarchs over family matters such as marriages and property diminished to contemporary levels.

At times there has been a strong desire by parents to break the will of the child (Aries, 1962; Stone, 1975). According to Stone (1975), this desire was particularly powerful from 1500 to 1660 and especially with the Puritans, who viewed children as needing discipline and strong parental control. This coercive relationship may have aggravated intergenerational tensions and probably contributed little to a sense of goodwill when children took over responsibility for the care of their older parents.

All in all, the possession of wealth—usually in the form of property—and power have historically caused tension between older people and their heirs. Control over property is thus a key factor to be examined in the study of intergenerational relationships. In his cross-cultural study of older people's relationships, Leo Simmons (1945) found a high correlation between older men's having property rights in a culture and their receiving support from their families during old age.

Intergenerational conflict has surfaced as a recurring theme in Western history and literature. Banzinger (1979) found intergenerational conflicts to be prominent in drama and literature over several centuries. Generally, Banzinger observes, the young are innocent and virtuous while the old folks are portrayed as obstructionist and tyrannical. Older people are dramatized as sterile, conniving, and stubborn, and were in reality often seen as nuisances because of their interference with their offsprings' sexual and economic independence. The net result was bound to be tension between the generations; and as certain researchers have pointed out, the tension was no doubt greater than court records would indicate (see Flandrin, 1979).

Several studies have reported the existence of intergenerational tension over property rights. For example, Barbara Hanawalt (1986) found considerable tension between the young and old in fourteenth- and fifteenth-century England. Both the young couples and their older parents could be tense about security (Shorter, 1977). Literature has many times picked up the theme of passing wealth and power over to the younger generation. During the Middle Ages, the popular and oft-poeticized legend of El Cid spoke of the transfer of power from the old

Plate 23. *The Village Betrothal.* 1761. Jean Baptiste Greuze. Louvre, Paris. Courtesy of Cliché des Musées Nationaux, Paris.

to the young. Shakespeare's *King Lear* involves a father's agony in old age. Lear gives his power and wealth to his ungrateful older daughters, and in the process becomes stripped of his worldly delusions. Anderson (1971) sees the theme in those nineteenth-century works of literature that depict unmarried children enduring substantial hardship to maintain their infirm parents.

As industrialization developed, older people lost power over the economic and matrimonial decisions of their children. This led to a decline in intergenerational tensions. But also, by the nineteenth century older people became increasingly viewed as economically dependent and useless. This too is partly due to the rise of industrialization, which forced a number of older people out of productive social roles. Thus, while the reduction in tension was certainly positive, the change helped to remove older people from the economic power structure virtually altogether.

At this point, we may allow ourselves a few speculations on the overall trends of relationships between older parents and their offspring. Parental control declined with time, as did the emotional weight that parents brought to bear on their children. The result was a lessening of tensions among the generations over property, choice of mates, and other personal decisions. With the lessening of tension, it probably became easier to feel affectionate toward and to romanticize older parents—to view them in more sentimental terms than was possible in the past when they exercised considerable control over the lives of their offspring. Simone de Beauvoir (1972) places this decline of grandparental authority at the close of the eighteenth century. The expansion of industrial jobs allowed young couples to set up independent households. By the time industrialization was in full swing, grandparents lacked authority and control but continued to be respected out of custom. It became easier for grandparents—no longer dominant in the family—to assume new benevolent roles, such as being the benefactors of their grandchildren. Affectionate and sentimental relationships between grandparents and their grandchildren then emerged.

Plate 24, a nineteenth-century print from Currier and Ives, captures this theme of affection between young and old, as does their print on the seasons of life shown as Plate 9 in Chapter 2. The former print depicts three generations on the female side of a family. The sentimentality linking them is obvious, as all smile. The mother breast-feeds her infant daughter. An older granddaughter shows a basket of kittens to her grandmother, while the mother cat tries anxiously to reunite with her litter.

This is the picture of familial harmony. There may be considerable disharmony surrounding the family: The cupboards are flung open; an apple sits outside of its bowl; sewing remains undone; books are not neatly shelved; and a doll lies discarded on the floor. But the four females are ordered along a continuum of generations. There is an affection that unites the group.

The remainder of this chapter will present several other portrayals of the family that include older family members. We will review the grandparental role in

Plate 24. *An Increase in Family*. 19th century. Currier and Ives. Courtesy of the Library of Congress, Washington, D.C.

both its secular and sacred appearances, the images of the Holy Family, Joseph, and Saint Anne, and the rise of family portraiture.

AGE AT MARRIAGE

The differences in age between men and women at marriage varies over the centuries. David Herlihy (1982, 1985) cites evidence of men marrying at a much older age than women in medieval and Renaissance Italy. In Renaissance Florentine Italy, females married at about 17.6 years and males at 34 (Herlihy, 1976). By contemporary standards, this is a major age difference. And in seventeenth-century Connecticut—for instance—the ages were comparatively much closer, as women were 23 and men 28 (Faragher, 1976).

By the end of the Renaissance—according to Herlihy (1985)—age differences had decreased, with males being younger than before and thus closer in age to their mates. Still, more than a third of the women available for marriage were taken by established or elderly men. Rossiaud asserts that "such was the pattern of marriage depicted in stone and on canvas, and which conformed with the way in which a family was traditionally ruled" (1985:82). Women were expected to succumb to marital authority and provide care and service to their husbands in old age.

On the other hand, the feeling that people should marry someone of a similar age has been an enduring concern in Western history. An occurrence of marriage between individuals of widely differing ages would often lead in England and France to the couple's being the target of social ridicule (Shorter, 1977). Ceremonies of harassment and public mockery, known to the French as *charivaris*, would be held by members of the community—most often youths—to lambast marriages between people of vastly different ages or social positions (Fabre, 1989). Such mockeries often followed the marriage of widows or widowers (Fabre, 1989; Stearns, 1976). A *charivaris* might consist of bell-ringing, parading the couple through town, and other commotions. The tormentors would perform these mockeries until they were paid by the couple to cease. The practice was common throughout the period from 1300 to 1800. Thus, unequal marriages were sometimes subject to a form of social blackmail.

There is demonstrative evidence that, in most Western societies, differences in age have actually been fairly small (Laslett, 1977). There is also evidence that a portion of wives were older than their husbands (Laslett, 1977). However, the social acceptability of this latter practice has never been particularly strong in Western history (Bell, 1980). It has been a theme in art and literature from at least the twelfth century onward that love is only lasting between people of similar age (Stewart, 1979).

Age at marriage becomes an important factor in determining the ages at which key life-cycle events take place—such as child rearing and departure; birth of grandchildren; and, most importantly for older people, death of spouse. Married couples of the past tended to bear children much later in life, and often well into their forties. In medieval and Renaissance Italy, many Florentine fathers were past the prime of life when they assumed responsibility for children (Herlihy, 1982). Stone (1979) notes that, in seventeenth-century England, childbearing and rearing occurred much later in the life-span. Women married in their mid-twenties and continued to have children in their late forties. The same was true for colonial American parents, as they also continued to have children until their mid-forties or even later (Kammen, 1980). Therefore, it was common for older people to have children in the home (see Laslett, 1977). Unlike older people today, who expect to spend the final years of their lives alone and without children in what some term the "empty nest," the older people of colonial America spent most of their married lives raising children (Haber, 1983). Even in the nineteenth century, women still bore children relatively late by today's standards. Michel Dahlin (1980) observes that it was not unusual for women in their sixties to have unmarried children at home (Kett, 1971). High fertility, late age at marriage, and prolonged childbearing guaranteed that older people would still have children in the home well into old age. This translates into less dramatic role changes and exits than today. The parental role and authority continued into old age, sometimes until death (see Haber, 1983).

Family portraiture over these earlier centuries reflects this late childrearing pattern. Portraits of older parents with relatively young children are numerous. Frans Hals's *Family Group in a Landscape* (1648) at the National Gallery in London shows a late-middle-aged couple with children ranging from the cradle to young adult. The artist's contemporaries would not have been surprised by this grouping.

THE IDEAL IMAGE: THE HOLY FAMILY

For centuries, the Holy Family served as an ideal image in art. This came about when the Church became very interested in the morals of its families in fourteenth- and fifteenth-century Tuscany. During this period, the Holy Family represented spiritual perfection to the Church. Families were expected to mirror the ideal and also be the foundation of society (La Ronciere, 1988). In any case, apart from these early Florentine images of the Holy Family, we have few artistic references to the family at all prior to the sixteenth and seventeenth centuries. Until this latter period, artists paid little attention to the actual nature of the human family.

Jean-Louis Flandrin (1976) raises the interesting point that the Holy Family was not—in Catholic iconography—the equivalent of the nuclear family, because it so often included Mary's mother Saint Anne and also at times the infant John the Baptist, a kinsman of Jesus. Flandrin observes that, according to medieval thinking, God the Father might also be added to the picture. This is important because it suggests that images of the Holy Family were often expanded to include multiple generations.

The most striking feature about images of the Holy Family must be the difference in age between Joseph and Mary. Joseph is consistently shown as an old man—much older than the young Mary. This age difference can be seen in Simone Martini's painting of *Christ and His Parents* (1342), the Duke de Berry's *Book of Hours* (c. 1410–1413) by the Limbourg brothers, Martin Schongauer's *Adoration of the Shepherds* (1475–1480), Ghirlandaio's *Adoration of the Shepherds* (1485), Giorgione's *Holy Family* (c. 1500), Michelangelo's painting of *The Holy Family* (1504), Pontormo's *Holy Family* (1525), Jacopo da Ponte's *Flight into Egypt* (1540), and Tintoretto's *Flight into Egypt* (1583–1587), among others. Thus, either through Joseph or Saint Anne, images of the Holy Family incorporated the three ages of life. The theme became so familiar that occasionally it survived in artistic imagery within the context of secular families. For example, Le Nain's *Peasant Family* (1642) conveys the three ages-of-life theme: It shows an old woman, a middle-aged man, and children playing instruments (Collomp, 1989). Plate 25, *The Adoration of the Magi* (early 1480s) by the late-fifteenth-century Florentine master Botticelli, is a fine example of the Holy Family iconography. The three ages of life (see Chapter 2) are represented in the three Magi as well as the Holy Family. Notice that the age difference between Joseph and Mary is quite evident, as was typical of the genre.

The old age of Joseph carries symbolic meanings that have been subject to much controversy. On the one hand, his old age symbolizes his role as patron and protector of the Holy Family. It was Joseph who led the Holy Family into Egypt, and it was Joseph who was the great provider. On the other hand, much has been made of Joseph as a powerless old man. He rarely appears in medieval writings and is seldom portrayed outside the context of the Holy Family. When he did make an appearance, he was often called *senex*, the Latin for old man. The historian David Herlihy (1985) notes that the fifteenth-century priest Bernardino de Fettue complained of Joseph's usual portrayal as a powerless old man. Earlier, Jean Gerson, chancellor of the University of Paris, had started a movement to celebrate Joseph. Gerson challenged the prevalent view that Joseph was a feeble old man; he held that Joseph was in his mid-thirties when he married Mary. According to Herlihy, Gerson writes of Joseph, "He wasn't at all old, ugly, ineffectual, feeble, and so to speak, incapable of work" (1985:128). Yet in spite of these and later protestations to the contrary, Joseph remains forever imagined as the old man.

SECULAR FAMILY PORTRAITURE

Art historians have long concluded that portraits reveal a process of emerging individualism in Western history. But to Philippe Aries (1962), the more important trend is that portraiture shows a progression toward the cultural unit of the family. If so, it should then be very revealing to note who is allowed in the portrait, where they are, and what they are doing. With respect to older people, this is certainly the case: Great insights emerge from looking at how older people are displayed in the context of the family portrait.

Plate 25. *The Adoration of the Magi.* Early 1480s. Sandro Botticelli. National Gallery of Art, Washington; Andrew W. Mellon Collection. Courtesy of the National Gallery of Art, Washington, D.C.

As mentioned earlier, images of families other than the Holy Family were relatively rare before the late Middle Ages. The family had traditionally been neglected by artists. It was during the fifteenth century that family portraiture really started, when several commissions for portraits were granted. This was a period when family members, and notably older people, were concerned with passing their images on to future family members. In a sense, they wanted symbolic immortality within the family.

Many portraits were also commissioned because the wealthy sought to capture their good fortune and persona in art. In any case, donors were frequently shown with members of their families (Praz, 1971). There was a definite desire to be portrayed as they would like to be seen and remembered. Many portraits of older men and women at this time characterize the subject in the most favorable and complimentary light. Titian's 1560 painting of the male members of the Cornaro family typifies the portraiture of the period. Noticeably absent are all the female members.

True family portraiture did not really get much of a start until the seventeenth-century work of Dutch and Flemish artists in the Low Countries. This group is famous for its depictions of everyday life, including interiors and families. Andriaen Van Ostade (1610–1685), a Dutch artist and student of Frans Hals, took for his subject an ordinary farmer's household when he created the drawing reproduced as Plate 26. The mother and infant are posed similar to the Virgin and Child, however, and even the father and son look familiar: They could be illustrating a traditional childhood scene from the life of Christ (Maxon, 1970). The older grandmother in the background is shown toying with the family dog. She seems in relative isolation compared to the rest of the figures—alone in her own world, yet still a member of the family. Perhaps she is a widow living with her offspring's family.

Occasionally, older couples have been portrayed by themselves, independent of their offspring and families. Jan Gossart's *Elderly Couple* (1520–1525) at the National Gallery in London is an example of this type of image. Older couples were also popular religious subjects. The story of Tobit and Anna was painted by several artists. Rembrandt's *Anna Accused by Tobit* (1626) at the Rijksmuseum is one version. Spirituality and the continuity of the couple's relationship surface as themes in many of these works.

Plate 27, *Older Couple Reading* by the seventeenth-century French artist Gerard Dou, illustrates the typical content in paintings of the older couple. Usually these paintings show the couple engaged in some joint activity such as reading, repairing, sewing, talking, and other everyday behaviors. In Dou's rendition, the wife reads the passage out loud for both to hear. The couple is surrounded by the trappings of their everyday life. The continuity of the relationship pervades the scene; the two have spent most of a lifetime together.

Family portraiture of the eighteenth century is very formal and structured. The naturalness and realism of the seventeenth-century Dutch artists is no more. Instead, the family members are well posed and often expressionless. Historians

Plate 26. *The Family*. 1647. Adriaen Van Ostade. Courtesy of the Art Institute of Chicago.

find a great deal of interest in reviewing these portraits, however, in terms of the implied status of the family members. For example, David Fischer (1978) observes that, in the eighteenth-century, American family portraiture shows older father figures towering above the other family members. Afterward, family portraits became increasingly horizontal in design. In other words, the patriarch was vertically positioned in the eighteenth century, and horizontally in the nineteenth century. If height in portraiture is any indication of status within the

Plate 27. *Older Couple Reading*. 17th century. Gerard Dou. Louvre, Paris. Courtesy of Cliché des Musées Nationaux, Paris.

family, then we might be tempted to conclude the older members experienced a leveling of their status in Western culture at the beginning of the nineteenth century (see Barash, 1983).

Another important observation about family relationships in portraiture was made by Aries (1962). He notes that the only person ever seated in the early paintings is the older father—a custom that was later dropped. Aries cites a seventeenth-century painting by Jan Steen as an example of the seated father. Other examples exist in Western art well beyond the seventeenth century. In many family photographs from the nineteenth century, the patriarch and occasionally the family matriarch are shown seated. The seated position is always in front and center—the place of honor and respect.

THE AWARENESS OF GRANDPARENTAL ROLES

An awareness of grandparental social roles within the family predates the Middle Ages (Herlihy, 1985). Yet this awareness developed in the context of being comparatively rare, as grandparents were not so common as they are today. One could not expect to survive long enough to know one's grandchildren. In fact, this was generally the situation up until the advent of industrialization (Laslett, 1984). Compared with other historical periods, today's youth are much more likely to know and associate with their grandparents; sometimes they get to know their great-grandparents.

However, in the sixteenth and seventeenth centuries, European court records indicate that grandparents and grandchildren were well aware of each other, regardless of living arrangement (Farge, 1989). Commenting on colonial America, Demos (1978) notes that we know very little about relations between grandparents and grandchildren at that time. Probate records from early New England suggest that grandchildren were often the benefactors of their grandparents' good wishes. In addition, grandparents were sometimes requested by court order to provide care for their grandchildren—and vice versa. Demos concludes from his review that grandparental ties were potentially very close and relatively widespread in colonial America (Demos, 1986).

Terms of Grandparenthood

Terminology provides a valuable source of information regarding perceptions about older people within the context of the family (see Goody, 1969, 1983). The concept of grandparent has existed for a long time in Western thought. Many words have been developed in the English language to represent grandparental roles. "Grandparents," "grandfather," "grandmother," and other related terms used to describe the parent of one's father or mother can be traced back to the early thirteenth century. Two early forms were "grandame" and "grandsire," which have been traced back to 1225. At first, both had meanings and functions similar to the words we use today. Later on—by 1550—"grandame" would come to mean an old woman who was a gossip, and "grandsire" lost way to "grandfather" by the year 1424.

Early related and other forms of "grandfather" were "grauntefader," "grautefadyr," "graunfadre"—and in French, *grandpère*. By 1651 the "great" was added to "grandfather" to reflect an even older generation and its set of familial relationships. These definitions were basically the same as they are today. In 1525 "grandmother" was sometimes used in a general sense to represent female ancestors, possibly even those without any direct parental connection. When John Calvin was writing on Genesis in 1587, he used the expression "great graunde graund father" to denote the second degree removed in descent of a relationship. These sixteenth-century terms were developed and used in a context where grandfathers were symbolic of the family.

"Grandsire" and "grandame" found new uses at the end of the sixteenth century. "Grandsire" was used in 1596 to represent a man of an age befitting a grandfather or an old man. "Grandame" was used in 1620 to refer to an ancestress of Eve. About this same time, grandchildren began to be acknowledged in the vernacular by such terms as "grandchild" (1587) and "grandson" (1586). Several other words have been derived from "grandfather" and "grandmother," as well. In 1663, the English dramatist John Dryden used "granny" and "grannie" in a contemptuous manner to represent grandmother. "Granny" at that time also meant an old woman who was a gossip. Later, by 1794, a "granny" could be a nurse or a midwife. Other forms of modifications of "grandmother" were "grandmamma" (1763), "grandma," and "grandmammy." The late-nineteenth-century expression, "teach one's grandmother to suck eggs," meant to give advice to an older person in their area of expertise. In the eighteenth century, "beldam" was used to mean grandmother, but later the meaning changed to that of hag (see Fischer, 1978).

"Grandfather" would also take various forms. Some of these were colloquial substitutes such as "grandada" and "grandaddy" (1698), "grand papa" (1753), "grandpa," and "grandad," which in 1819 was considered a term of affection. By the nineteenth century, elaborations on "grandfather" and "grandmother" were appearing in the language: "grandparent" (1830), "grandmotherhood" (1846), "grandmotherly" (1846), and "grandparental" (1844). Not all terms were complimentary. In 1887 "granny" could mean a stupid old woman. "Gramps" has also been used—possibly since the nineteenth century—with negative connotations, but also at times with affection.

The usages of most terms found in the nineteenth century are similar to their meanings today. However, certain situations in which they were used may not be familiar to us. In 1897, "grandfather" was the name of a country dance. A "grandfather's beard" referred to a type of chair in the late 1800s. A "granny bonnet" (1894) referred to a muff. Certain other expressions—such as "grandfather clock" (named after a popular song of 1880 and later used to describe a high-standing eight-day clock), "granny knot" (1867), and "grandaddy long legs" (late 1800s)—are still used in contemporary society.

Thus we see that the words used to characterize grandparents derived originally from affection and respect. This changed over time and the terms became increasingly derogatory when used in reference to nonrelatives. In addition, as Jack Goody (1976) observes, the terminology regarding grandparents has always emphasized age and the developmental aspects of kinship roles, rather than lineage differentiation. Whether one's grandparents are on the mother's or the father's side is less important than age and the degree of descent. This appears to be true for all terms related to grandparental roles in the Western tradition.

Images of Grandparents

Grandparenthood has certainly been a common—if not the most common—relational role played by older people, and is very important to their perceived value in society as well as to their self-perception. It was first and perhaps best personified by the master Florentine fresco painter Domenico Ghirlandaio (c. 1448–1494). Ghirlandaio's 1475 portrait of a grandfather and his grandson that has been reproduced here as Plate 28 is a classic view of the differences and connections between the two generations. One sees a high degree of empathy in the grandfather's face, looking down at the grandson with his future before him. Patrick McKee and Heta Kauppinen (1987) characterize this painting as one of wisdom and spiritual fulfillment.

Other examples of artistically interpreted grandfathers are Henry Raeburn's *John Tait and His Grandson* (1793) and John Roger's (1790–1860) statue of a family with grandparents. Countless family photographs from the nineteenth century incorporate grandparents, who usually occupy positions of honor and respect in the group.

Secular images of grandmothers were rare in Western art until the time of the Dutch masters of the seventeenth century; but by the nineteenth century, they had become more common. Saint Anne is the one exception to the absence of grandmothers in the early art. Her image as the mother of Mary generally conveys a message of wisdom, kindly old age, and oversight. She is a major figure in the Holy Family scene, but fades into the background after the infancy of Christ. Examples include the Flemish artist Rogier Van der Weyden's *Visitation* (1425), Leonardo da Vinci's *Virgin and the Child* (c. 1500–1507), and the Florentine artist Pontormo's *Holy Family* (1525). In this latter work, Anne is shown accompanied by an angel as she leans on a cane and gazes at the Christ child.

Another Florentine artist, Piero di Cosimo (1462–c.1521), provides an image of Saint Elizabeth in the painting reproduced as Plate 29. Saint Elizabeth is always, as here, shown in a solemn pose. She holds hands with the Virgin Mary. In the background mothers and babies are being assaulted and wrenched apart by Herod's men. In the foreground, two saints are shown in the scholarly activities of reading and writing.

Plate 28. *An Old Man and His Grandson*. 1475. Domenico Ghirlandaio. Louvre, Paris. Courtesy of Cliché des Musées Nationaux, Paris.

Plate 29. *The Visitation with Saint Nicholas and Saint Anthony Abbot.* 1490. Piero di Cosimo. National Gallery of Art, Washington, D.C. Samuel H. Kress Collection.

WIDOWS AND WIDOWERS

Historically, older women who survive their husbands have been in limbo. Generally, Western culture has not provided old women with a sense of purpose or usefulness once their child bearing and rearing is done (Walker, 1985). Much of the value and position of women has been linked to their marital status. And widowhood has too often brought on a collapse in social standing. After the loss of their spouses, some older women were actually excluded from their homes in preindustrial Britain (Laslett, 1984). Older women have also been highly dependent on the graces of their offspring for care in old age. Widowhood, as Peter Stearns writes, "has never been a treasured state" (1980:50). Furthermore,

Barbara Walker (1985) suggests that societies have historically been ambivalent about caring for older people and especially older women (see also Chapter 3 and earlier in this chapter). However, special provisions for widows were available in the nineteenth century (Stearns, 1980).

Some say that widowhood was not common in earlier times, as people married late and died young in the period from the sixteenth to the eighteenth centuries (Collomp, 1989). In fourteenth- and fifteenth-century Tuscany, 46 percent of the older women age 60 and over were widows; by age 65, 53 percent; and by age 70, 75 percent (Duby et al., 1988). In a sampling of figures on widowhood, Peter Laslett (1977) found that in 1599 in Ealing, England, 67 percent of males and females of age 65 and over were widowed. Using another English sample from 1695, Laslett (1977) cites the figures 19 percent and 77 percent for men and women, respectively. And a sample from England in 1796 turned up 25 percent widowed for males, and 36 percent for females. Finally, a sample from France taken in 1778 showed that 22 percent of males and 69 percent of females age 65 and over were widowed. From evidence gathered for the period between 1574 and 1821, Jon Hendricks and C. Davis Hendricks (1977–78) report that 5 percent of households were headed by widowers, and twice that many by widows. We may gather from all of this that widowhood was indeed reasonably common in Western society, so far as the spot samples have allowed us to see, anyway. Other researchers have reported only slightly different figures.

Older women have paid the higher price for their old age and widowhood. Widowhood could lead to extreme poverty (Anderson, 1971; Walker, 1987) and dependence (Stearns, 1980). Herlihy (1985) reports that late medieval Florence is known to have had several widows who were dependent on charitable institutions. It is true that some widows took over their husbands' businesses, but those who did this faced opposition from the community. Another consequence of their dependency is one we have discussed before: According to Keith Thomas (1971) widows on relief were most often listed or labeled as witches. Furthermore, in preindustrial Eastern Europe, a widow might sometimes find that the family farm was being turned over to successors (Mitterauer & Sieder, 1982).

Actually, the evidence indicates that community support of widows varied. According to one researcher, widows' and widowers' status did not change much in seventeenth-century England, and in fact they often remained the heads of their households (Smith, 1979). Thus, for some people widowhood may have caused relatively little change in their circumstances. Other fortunate widows did find an adequate support system within their communities (Faragher, 1976). Yet for the most part, widows prior to the nineteenth century did not have the pensions or supportive institutions that they have today (Carlton, 1978).

Widowers have generally had higher likelihood of remarrying than widows have. In seventeenth-century Connecticut, for example, widowers remarried more than twice as frequently as widows. However, after the age of 50, it was rare for either to marry (Faragher, 1976). This pattern of relatively scarce remarriage predates the seventeenth-century (Laslett, 1984). And even in later periods, such as nineteenth-century France, older people were not really expected to remarry (Stearns, 1976).

In regard to this issue of remarriage, one popular theme in sixteenth- and seventeenth-century literature was that widows would often be targets of young men who married them for their wealth rather than for their love (Carlton, 1978). This theme may have been an aspect of the unequal-lovers theme noted by Alison Stewart (1979), which portrays young men and women in pursuit of older women's and men's wealth. In any case, widows—and in particular, rich widows— were viewed as very likely marks for potential opportunists. It is a matter of historical fact that the European systems of dowry and dower resulted in considerable property sometimes ending up in the hands of women (Goody, 1983; Leyser, 1979). Thus, certain women from the propertied classes may indeed have been attractive targets for young men seeking their (or someone else's) fortune.

The courting of older widows has been a popular and enduring theme in Western art and literature. Old widows married to young men were perceived as being couched in selfish gain, rather than needing affection or companionship (Ozment, 1983; Stewart, 1979). British artist William Hogarth used this perception to satirical ends in a series of prints known as *The Rake's Progress* (1735). In the segment *Married to an Old Maid*, Hogarth shows Tom the Rake marrying an old one-eyed heiress. Tom does so just to handle his gaming debts. His eyes are focused on the bride's lady-in-waiting. Two dogs mimic the ceremony on a smaller scale. But the old maid's vanity makes her foolishly believe that he marries her for love and not her purse. Plate 30 is a print from *The Rake's Progress* executed by an unknown eighteenth-century artist, but along the same lines as Hogarth's.

Another curious theme related to widows is that in the sixteenth and seventeenth centuries they were viewed as sexual maniacs (Carlton, 1978). Freed from marital ties, they were almost expected to have strong sexual appetites. There developed the spirited widow's tale, in which they were characterized as fun, highly sexed, and very much courted by younger men (Carlton, 1978).

Inherent in this attitude toward widows must have been a wide streak of sexual jealousy. It may be—as Carlton (1978) proposes—that widows, including older ones, were seen as sexual predators. Husbands were threatened by the prospect of their wives remaining sexually active after their deaths. Charles Carlton likens the situation to being posthumously cuckolded. Victorian men, too, feared that their widows would become sexually active after the husband's death (Smith-Rosenberg, 1983).

The evidence indicates that this popular image of widows was not based in fact, however, as older widows seldom remarried and loneliness was common. Probably much more true to life than the widow's tale, Oliver Goldsmith's eighteenth-century poem *The Deserted Village* characterizes an old widow's life as solitary, wretched, poor, and desperate (Charles, 1977).

To repair his Fortune He Marries a Rich old Woman.

Plate 30. *Marriage to an Old Maid*. C. 1735. William Hogarth. Courtesy of the British Library, London.

CLOSING THOUGHTS ON IMAGES OF OLDER PEOPLE AND THE FAMILY

It had been a contemporary assumption for some time that, as modernization and industrialization took over, older people were abandoned by their families. The nuclear family was said to have replaced the extended family—which resulted in older relatives spending their waning years in meaningless involuntary isolation. On this point, historians now increasingly agree that the extended family was never the predominant form in the Western world. The major implication in this new conclusion is that older relatives were never actually expelled from their families because of modernization, urbanization, or industrialization. Rather, if they could afford and were able to, they preferred to live independently of their offspring and grandchildren. Much of aging is in fact a balancing act between independent living and maintaining ties to the family. Independence, when affordable, is the preferred way of life among older people.

The provision of care to older relatives is a useful focus in understanding older people and their families throughout history. In sum, the family has always held primary responsibility in caring for older relatives. This responsibility has not always been welcomed or embraced by the younger generations. Research suggests that in the late Middle Ages the security of older family members was often very tenuous. This was also true in earlier centuries. In general, as the centuries unfolded, the provision of care became more humane, and there was a slow evolution from the attitude of a contractual relationship being arranged between older parents and their offspring to the concepts of filial duty and sentimental affection. This shift might be linked to the erosion of older people's authority and control over the disposition of property and family members' lives.

In other words, this erosion may have paved the way for a shift in the provision of care, because family tensions may have decreased. Moreover, while it is true that other nonfamilial providers of care were also evolving into their current capacities, they have never been present in sufficient quantity to supplant the family as the primary care-giver. Besides, until quite recently, the rise in alternative sources of care may have affected only a few. It actually became necessary for more humanitarian motives in family care to emerge. And as the tension between generations in all likelihood declined with the loosening of parental control, it probably was easier for family members to love one another. Intergenerational conflicts, while still present, did not take on the significance that they had when property and every significant decision rested with the older members. The tyrannical power of older parents—and in particular, grandfathers and fathers—dissolved over the centuries.

But in the old days—because the provision of care was tenuous—older parents had to protect themselves from destitution and desertion by their families. This protection involved maintaining control over property and offspring. Such control contributed to tension and conflict with younger family members. It should come as no surprise, then, that miserly behavior and avarice were symbolized by older figures (see Chapter 3), for such characteristics may have been necessary adaptations to guarantee survival in old age. In some instances, older people had to be self-preserving to a fault, or run the risk of destitution.

For centuries, parents played a dominant role in the selection of the marriage partners of their children. This influence undoubtedly also led to tensions between the generations. Again, this and other types of parental control did little to endear older parents to their offspring. As time passed and history moved on, however, offspring had more freedom to select their own mates.

Overall, we can speculate that there has been a general reduction in the tension between older people and their children. While no one would deny that such tensions continue—as older parents are still abused, neglected, and mistreated by family members—it is probably true that the frequency and strength of such occurrences have toned down compared to the past. In any case, as the sources of tension diminished, it became easier to develop sentimental attitudes toward older parents and grandparents.

Western artists of portraiture have emphasized certain features of older people and family life that are worth noting. For instance, family relationships in the eighteenth century were rather formal and structured, and this is reflected in portraiture. By the nineteenth century, artists were free to show some of the more human aspects of relationships between older people and their families. Apparently, artists were simply capturing the change in attitudes and perceptions between families and their older members. They were illustrating the shift toward more sentimentality and affection.

While reducing tension and stress is certainly desirable, there might nevertheless have been an important down-side for older people. When they had more control over their offspring, they were at least involved—for better or worse—in the family decision-making process. As they lost control and power, it became easier for the younger members to isolate and ignore them. Thus, from being a force to be reckoned with, older parents became sentimentalized isolates and not always true factors in the family.

Care for the old would eventually tend to shift from the family to the community. But regardless of whether it might be a community or a family responsibility, there is a negative connotation attached to needing care, which has traditionally been viewed as a mark of personal failure and unworthiness. This is particularly true in the American context, where independence, self-determination, freedom of thought, and economic self-sufficiency are so highly valued.

The circumstances under which older people could remarry or get married have historically been subject to public scrutiny and—more importantly—public ridicule. Older people were subjected to some fairly rigid social restrictions over whom they could marry and how they were to conduct themselves within the marriage. Western preindustrial societies responded especially to marriages between people of unequal age with ceremonies of public mockery that are rare and possibly unrivaled in modern times. The general context, then, has been one in which the marriage of older persons was not well received.

Society's ridicule and rejection of older people marrying younger partners are also witnessed when it comes to sexual relations between older and younger people, as will be discussed in Chapter 5. The rejection of these "unnatural" relationships has been enduring and continues today. Married or not, older people have not been permitted to have normal sex lives, whether in real life, art, or literature.

Portrayals of older widows, specifically, have run the gamut from religious reverence to mockery. When widows tried to maintain normal lives through remarrying, they were mocked by the artists and writers. When they were willing to surrender to their fate of isolation, they were shown as pious, asexual, and reserved. When they became impoverished, they were often branded as evil and occasionally as witches. The positive, independent, and socially adept widow is just about absent from the realm of art. Rather, the widow was characterized as always up to something or—at the other extreme—as a secular nun with only one dimension to her life, and that being her devotion to God.

Images of grandparents were relatively rare in Western art until the eighteenth and nineteenth centuries, although the English language has several very old expressions that refer to grandparents. They were occasionally painted, however, and early family images incorporated older people. These early portraits are not sentimental in the slightest sense. The late Middle Ages and Renaissance artists chose to show older relatives in a very structured and formal manner. The nineteenth-century Currier and Ives images of older family members are dramatically different from the Renaissance artist Titian's portraits of upper-middle-class Italian families. While the fifteenth through eighteenth centuries emphasized the formality of family relationships, the nineteenth century stressed affection.

5

OLDER PEOPLE AND SEXUAL IMAGES

It is difficult for most people to picture older persons as sexual beings. The thought of them having sexual relations even strikes some people as repulsive and unnatural. Generally, we have come to view older people, and especially our grandparents and older relatives, as void of sexual desire and behavior. It is assumed that all sexual urges have long since departed. Yet much of how we are judged and how we judge others is based on sex and sexuality. Therefore, it is critical to our understanding of older people in history to review the perceptions of their sexual attitudes and behaviors.

Recently, human sexuality has been the subject of several good historical reviews (see Aries & Bejin, 1985; Stone, 1979; Tannahill, 1980). However, the treatment of older people and their sexuality has been rare in both contemporary and historical literature. There are a few historical references to the sexual behavior of older people (see Covey, 1989a; Spisak, 1978; Weg, 1983), but—as Bernard Starr (1985) has observed—treatment to date has been marginal. Yet there is considerable evidence that sexual activity among older people may (at least in contemporary times) be more common than was once assumed (see Masters & Johnson, 1966; Pfeiffer et al., 1969).

Ambiguity characterizes most Western perceptions of older people. Even the process of aging and old age itself have a perceived element of inherent ambiguity, as discussed in Chapter 2. The sexuality of older people, however, has been perceived with not a trace of ambiguity in Western history. On the contrary, it has been the topic of some fairly strong opinions and ageist attitudes. Summarizing the literature, Starr writes, "If ageism typifies the history of attitudes toward older people, then nowhere is this prejudice more apparent than in the area of sexuality" (1985:97).

The sexuality of older people has been the object of strong cultural stereotyping (Hotvedt, 1983). Some of these stereotypes have resulted in sexual desires and activities on the part of older people being considered taboo and hence not open to discussion. Thus, the stereotypes have a negative effect on the sexual attitudes and behaviors of older people themselves (Corby & Zarit, 1983; Weg, 1983). Mostly, the negative effect has been a repression of desire, which then leads to an unhealthy agreement with the attitude that sex is unnatural and immoral in old age.

In any case, since at least the Middle Ages, Western culture has held that the sex drive disappears with old age, that sex is perverse during old age, and that those older people who attempt it only practice self-deception. In addition, all the traditional concepts related to sexuality—such as beauty, attractiveness, sexual potency, and female orgasm—have never referred to older people, but rather excluded them.

This chapter reviews some of the main themes about sexuality of older people ranging from the Middle Ages to the nineteenth century, with emphasis on the eighteenth and nineteenth centuries. The nineteenth-century Victorian era is one of the more interesting times in which to study the sexuality of people of all ages, including those of advanced years. Like the other chapters, this one also draws on historical observations, art, and literature to identify social attitudes. However, it is important to realize that whatever historical information, art, and literature concerning sexuality have survived from one century to the next are bound to be strongly influenced by the dominant social groups of the era. And as research has shown, what the dominant group defines as being proper may not necessarily correspond with the actual behavior of its time (Degler, 1974; Stone, 1979; Taylor, 1970).

Two major dimensions of Western thought were used here to examine the information. First, the ages-of-life theme was taken to be a conceptual basis for some of the notions on sexuality involving older people. It seems that, for several of the early centuries at least, sexuality among older persons did not fit Western notions about what was appropriate behavior during the later ages of life. The ages-of-life schemes developed as a social, moral, and scientific guide to appropriate behavior. Second, religious teachings were also used to organize society's thinking about the sexuality of older persons. Nevertheless, the sexuality of older people did not necessarily fit the moral prescriptions and teachings of the Church.

THE AGES OF LIFE AND SEXUALITY

The idea that the life-span can be divided into distinct stages or ages has a very old tradition in Western European thought, as described in Chapter 2. Old age has usually been viewed as the one stage of the life-span that is very different from the rest—particularly when thinking about sexuality—because it was associated with decay and viewed as a reversal of the growth process (Burrow, 1986; Kammen, 1980; Smith, 1976). Youth, on the other hand, was very often associated with sexual activity and reproduction (Smith, 1976).

Thus, linkages were often made between the ages of life and sexuality. The extent to which older people of the Middle Ages actually adhered to the prescriptions of the ages-of-life models—or, for that matter, the teachings of the Church—is unknown. There might have been very little correspondence between the rhetoric and actual behavior; but then again, the correspondence might have been great. We do know that, in medieval works on the ages of life, a common theme was that sexual behavior is inappropriate for old people (Burrow, 1986). Those who departed from their age-appropriate behavior and engaged in any sexual activity were subject to a variety of negative social responses. For example, medieval writings indicated that older women who behave like younger women deserve to be publicly ridiculed (Burrow, 1986).

By the seventeenth century, old age was largely viewed as the decline of the other ages. It was associated with decay, a reversal of the growth process (Burrow, 1986; Kammen, 1980; Smith, 1976). Youth—on the other hand—was often depicted in association with lechery, sexual activity, and reproduction (Kammen, 1980; Smith, 1976). In the seventeenth century, male impotency was linked to the coldness and dryness of older men's bodies (Smith, 1976). In the eighteenth century, some people thought that sexual excess would shorten life itself (Stone, 1979). This latter notion carried over into the time of the Victorians, who connected sexual excesses with decline, debility, and even premature aging.

Even the related concept of romantic love has been defined as age inappropriate for older people, though literary reference is occasionally made to love among the old. Romance itself has been traced to about the year 1100 (see de Rougemont, 1974; Tannahill, 1980). In the centuries preceding the twelfth, women were portrayed in literature either as sex objects or as noble and virtuous wives and mothers who encouraged their offspring to be brave and follow in the footsteps of their slain fathers (Bullough, 1976a). Some medieval moralists such as Peter Lombard reduced all love to simple desire, even within the bounds of marriage. Too ardent a love of one's spouse was viewed as sinful (Spisak, 1978)—a sin that was, according to Lombard, worse than adultery. In the beginning of the twelfth century, a school of poets called troubadours developed the concept of courtly love (see Stone, 1979; Tannahill, 1980; Taylor, 1970). This was designed to be an unhappy love, as it was one of unconsummated passion (de Rougemont, 1974). Initially, sexual encounters were never linked to romantic love. This would soon change as the concept developed.

When medieval scholars were writing on the ages of life, they generally viewed older people as incapable of romantic love (Burrow, 1986), although there are some exceptions found in the literature. In any case, when the concept of love was refined and developed in the fourteenth and fifteenth centuries, it did not include the old (Hotvedt, 1983). Love and sex continued to be viewed as inappropriate or impossible for older people. Even when romantic love was popularized in the eighteenth century, it carried on this tradition of excluding older people (Hotvedt, 1983). From the Middle Ages to the nineteenth century portrayals of the life-span showed plenty of young courting couples involved in romantic love, but not older ones (Kammen, 1980).

SEX FOR PROCREATION ONLY

Perceptions regarding the life-span and age-appropriate behavior affected the sexuality of older people in a variety of ways. Regardless of what model was used, the ages of life never located procreation in the latter part of the life-span. Childbearing was appropriately placed only in the first half of life. It is a known fact, however, that childrearing often went on well into the life-span because women were bearing children late in life. And procreation has naturally always been associated with the childrearing years. This may belie a discrepancy between rhetoric and reality. In any case, childrearing, childbearing, the ages of life, and sexuality all became parts of the same issue, particularly for women (Maoz & Landau, 1983).

The absence of a link between old age and sex is partly due to the very old binding association of sex with procreation. Christianity emphasized procreation as the sole purpose of sexual activity and said that anything else is unnatural (Bullough & Bullough, 1977; Flandrin, 1975). In the fourth century, Saint Augustine—who set the moral tone for the Church for many centuries afterward—considered sex a necessary evil for the perpetuation of the human race (Benedek, 1978; Weg, 1983), and regarded virginity and celibacy as more virtuous. This perspective was echoed much later by the medieval theologians Albertus Magnus (1206–1280) and his pupil Thomas Aquinas (1225–1274). The strong moral association made by the Catholic Church between sex and procreation sent the message to men and women that sex for any purpose other than making babies was improper (Pfeiffer, 1977). This may have contributed to the neglect of the sexual needs of the old—especially women, because they could no longer conceive (Mitterauer & Sieder, 1982).

Older couples who were sterile posed a unique problem for the moralists of the Middle Ages, as their sexual relations did not result in offspring. As with other instances sterility, older couples were permitted to remain married and have sexual relations. If impotence was involved with the older couple, the theologians and moralists either ignored the problem, failed to reach a conclusion, or concluded that impotent older persons should be able to copulate through other means (Noonan, 1986). Some moral experts argued that, for married couples beyond the years of procreation, the answer—based on Augustine's writings—was to abstain from sexual activity. Therefore, couples should decrease sexual relations with the advance of age (Noonan, 1986). Others held that sex among the sterile aged was acceptable, as it promoted fidelity and offered symbolic stability to the marriage.

Historical evidence indicates that homosexuality has had a long tradition in Western society (see Boswell, 1980; Bullough, 1976b, 1979). Such relationships were common in the Middle Ages (Boswell, 1980). During the eleventh and twelfth centuries, in fact, homosexuality was tolerated by society and the Church. Only later in the fourteenth and fifteenth centuries did the practice fall victim to increasing suppression (Boswell, 1980). Apart from these general observations, historians have done little work on homosexuality among older people in periods such as the Middle Ages. In all likelihood, older homosexuals faced the same increasing intolerance that younger ones did which often resulted in negative social sanctions and even persecution.

THE HISTORICAL CONTEXTS OF SEXUALITY

In order to understand attitudes toward the sexuality of older people, it is important to examine the general context in which sexuality itself has been seen over the centuries. A comprehensive review of all that is known about sex in Western History is not possible within the confines of this chapter, but we may attempt at least a cursory highlighting of the major conditions and changes in which older people found themselves.

The Middle Ages was a time of great interest in morality and concern with modifying morals and sexual behavior. The medieval Church played a dominant role in defining appropriate sexual behavior. The Church claimed all matters concerning morals to be within its purview, and increasingly exercised its control. And, as mentioned above, it was the basic conviction of the Church that the sex act was to be avoided, except for the purpose of procreation (Bullough & Brundage, 1982; Taylor, 1970).

Early medieval writers looked to the Bible for ideas on sex. Surely—they assumed—the Bible will guide us; but the Bible proved to be ambiguous (Bullough & Brundage, 1982). To address this ambiguity, early scholars such as Saint Jerome (342–420) and Saint Augustine (354–430) wrote about sex. Augustine's works dominated attitudes and teachings about sex even up until the nineteenth century (see Flandrin, 1975; Waldemar, 1960). During Augustine's time and later in the Middle Ages, the Church defined most sexual activities as deviant and regarded them as sins against nature. They were sins against nature because of the pleasure derived from their occurrence. Only sex for the purpose of procreation was not a sin against nature, and then only if the couple did not experience any pleasure from the experience. Sexual activity on the part of older people—by virtue of its nonprocreative nature—would therefore have to be considered a sin against nature, according to most Church experts. This point will be taken up again later in the chapter.

Basically, there was considerable effort on the part of the Church to repress sex during the early Middle Ages. The Church attempted to dictate sexual mores and customs. Its control was never absolute before the fourteenth century, however, and most of the medieval period was actually characterized as being rather sexually open. This sexual freedom reached an apex in the fourteenth century. In the centuries prior to that, it was a commonly held belief that life was mechanical and predetermined. By the late Middle Ages, however, people began to believe that they were free to act as they wished. This contradicted the perspective of the Church, which was trying to impose a strong set of rules backed by divine authority (Taylor, 1970). Believing in individual freedom, some people took great liberties in acting out their sexual desires.

The sexual openness witnessed in the fourteenth century declined rapidly with the advent of the Black Plague. The plague killed a large portion of Europe's population—perhaps as much as a third. And people asked themselves why the plague had occurred and why so many people were dying. Many concluded that God must be punishing them for their liberal and sinful sexual practices and that sin should be repressed. This new attitude led to increased efforts by the Church and the public itself to repress sexual activity, which was viewed as a major source of sin. During this and later periods the concept of guilt over sexual thoughts and activities developed and served as a primary mechanism for restricting the sexual practices of all people, including older ones (Maier, 1984).

By the late fifteenth century, a major effort had been undertaken by the Church to eliminate heresy and witchcraft, as described in Chapter 3. In 1484, Pope Innocent VIII issued his famous papal bull that approved the persecution of people who were suspected of forming liaisons with the devil (Mullins, 1985). Two years later, the manual on witch-hunting called *Malleus Maleficarum*, or *The Witches' Hammer*, was published. This manual emphasized that certain sexual acts were to be seen as evidence of witchcraft (Bullough, 1982; Bullough & Bullough, 1977; Maier, 1984; Taylor, 1970). And witchcraft was blamed with regard to many other problems relating to sex, such as miscarriage, failure to conceive, and male impotency (Bullough, 1976b). All witchcraft, according to *The Witches' Hammer*, must be due to carnal lust (Mullins, 1985; Stone, 1979), which for women was said to be insatiable (see Taylor, 1970).

The rise of witchcraft persecution in the late fifteenth and sixteenth centuries paralleled a belief that women are more sexually avid than men (Thomas, 1971). Overall, the concern over witchcraft and evil had a negative effect on sex and on older women in general. The connection between sex and evil would become more firmly entrenched in the Western psyche. And because women were more frequently linked to witchcraft, they would also be linked more often than men to evil sexual practices and sexual liaisons with the Devil.

Actually, society in the late Middle Ages found itself to be sometimes at odds about sexuality (Spisak, 1978). There were two divergent forces working to shape opinion—one inhibiting and sex-denying; and the other, self-indulgent and permissive (Taylor, 1970). As the Middle Ages came to a close, many people—especially within the Church—were pushing hard to institutionalize attitudes toward sexuality and to punish deviant ideas and practices (Boswell, 1980; Bullough, 1976a). And yet, a range of sexual activity persisted throughout the period. In sum, the Middle Ages were full of contradictions. The official Church stance was that sex is sinful and the work of the Devil. Actual behavior appears to have departed from this ideal, as this was an age characterized by active sex, prostitution, erotic love, and other "deviant" sexual behavior (see Bullough, 1976b).

At the close of the Middle Ages, the Renaissance would stand in distinct contradiction to traditional medieval ideas and thoughts, which it took great exception to. The Renaissance artist and writer saw the human body as an object of beauty. Unlike the medieval mind, which equated nudity with sin, the Renaissance mind considered nudity to be perfectly natural (see Mullins, 1985). Sexual attitudes and practices became more liberal. Sexual expression—while still influenced by the Church—was relatively open compared to the greater part of the Middle Ages.

In the sixteenth century, attitudes and practices toward sex were very much a reaction to the liberal ideas of the Renaissance. This was a period of great hostility toward sex, although its hostility was mitigated to some extent by the Protestant rejection of virginity as an ideal state (Stone, 1979). With the sixteenth century came the religious reform movements led by Martin Luther and John Calvin. A basic tenet of these Protestant reformers was that people should try to overcome their sexual impulses. Yet, Luther also viewed chastity as actively dangerous and celibacy as an evil that results in perverted practices (Waldemar, 1960). Some of the issues of the Reformation focused directly on sexual issues, such as clerical celibacy, vows of continence, and marriage of the clergy (Lewinsohn, 1956).

From 1545 through 1563, the Council of Trent convened and made several decisions leading to the Counter-Reformation. The Council of Trent and the Counter-Reformation gave rise to a new Catholic morality in response to the Protestant reforms. The Counter-Reformation attempted to restore the sanctity of marriage, eliminate prostitution, and banish sex. The Council reaffirmed the state of virginity as being closer to God than the state of marriage (Mullins, 1985). This led to a preoccupation with virginity and the Virgin Mary witnessed in art, literature, and architecture of the period.

Even sex within the confines of marriage was restricted, according to the recommendations in marriage manuals of the sixteenth century. Intercourse was forbidden when conception was not possible (Stone, 1979). Extramarital sexual activity was disapproved—at least in theory, if not in practice. And in the centuries that followed, sexual restrictions were still the norm. Matrimonial chastity remained in vogue from the sixteenth through seventeenth centuries and hung on through the nineteenth century (Stone, 1979).

Aristotle's *Masterpiece, or The Secrets of Generation* was a popular reference book during the sixteenth century. Aristotle notes in this work that sexual activity begins at age 16–17 for males, increases to the age of 45–55, and then dies away. For females, it begins at age 14–15 and disappears with menopause at about the age of 44 (Stone, 1979). Thus, Aristotle suggests that sexual desire and ability decline quicker for women than men. This common Western notion is therefore traceable as far back as the ancient Greeks. Aristotle and his readers over the following centuries believed that older people should experience a decline in sexual desire and activity for both biological and moral reasons. Whenever sexual behavior on the part of older people was observed, it was viewed as abnormal by those sharing Aristotle's perspective.

Sexual practices during the seventeenth century were a mixed bag of attitudes and behaviors. Aristotle continued to be the most widely read authority on sex and reproduction (Bullough, 1976a). But following the Restoration, there was a liberalization of sexual attitudes. Some people saw no need for secrecy, and performed sexual acts with little in the way of public concealment (Foucault, 1978). On the other hand, Puritanism was a dominant and conservative force in England and America. Its dominance in England continued until the restoration of King Charles II to the throne, and persisted to a lesser degree in the centuries that followed.

Although small in numbers, the Puritans would have a lasting influence on future attitudes toward sexuality. They viewed sin as inherited, and went to great lengths to regulate sexual conduct (Bullough, 1976a). However, the Puritans have a reputation for prudery that may not be accurate. They were probably not so squeamish about sexuality as once was thought. In fact, according to Peter Gay (1986), the Puritans were not puritanical in their view of love. They regarded joy and pleasure during sex as normal within the confines of marriage (Maier, 1984; Morgan, 1983); an active sex life was perceived as essential to good marriage. And the early American colonists were informed by Aristotle's *Masterpiece* that sex is a blessing (Bullough, 1973).

Colonial families often produced offspring on into their forties and even later; consequently, the youngest child sometimes did not leave home until the mother was in her sixties (see Demos, 1986; Kammen, 1980). What effect the presence of children had on the sexual practices of older parents is unknown, but it is clear that privacy—let alone sexual privacy—was a luxury in the American colonies (Thompson, 1986). In all likelihood, the lack of privacy may have had a dampening effect on older people's sexual practices.

In contrast to sex within the family, the Puritans viewed sexual behavior outside marriage with great hostility. Adultery could be punished by death. Even in light of the rather harsh penalties, however, court records indicate that sexual offenses were more common than might be expected in the Puritan settlements (Morgan, 1983; Oaks, 1978; Thompson, 1986). Evidently older men were at times cuckolded by their younger Puritan wives (Thompson, 1986).

Mortality rates for women were very high in the colonies, and men greatly outnumbered women. The result was that men had to find outlets for their sexual needs other than the traditional family, and some men committed sex offenses (see Morgan, 1983; Oaks, 1978). There is no evidence that older people were any different from other Puritans in their views on sexuality. If anything, older people were expected to set and maintain higher moral and sexual standards for the community. The older people were the custodians of the moral order and were expected to conform to the established sexual mores of the community.

The eighteenth century was the Age of the Enlightenment and the Age of

Reason. It was the time of Voltaire, Haydn, Mozart, and Rousseau. Generally, the Enlightenment encouraged the free play of sexual practices. After all, some people were arguing that the state of nature is the highest ideal. But as the eighteenth century progressed, the scientific and intellectual community that had initially favored fewer inhibitions toward sex found itself wanting more regulations over sexual behavior. Scientific evidence of the period increasingly reported sexual activity to be dangerous and said that it could even lead to physical and mental decline and insanity (Bullough, 1976a). This emerging view served as a highly credentialed foundation for the attitudes of the nineteenth-century Victorians.

During the eighteenth century, interest grew in all aspects of sexual behavior, and advice books were widely read (Pearsall, 1976). In 1727 Daniel Defoe published a typical pamphlet warning that sexual excesses would lead to impotence and disease in old age (Stone, 1979). It was also a century of scandal and a time when lovemaking was viewed as sport—best personified in the adventurous Casanova.

However, not everyone viewed sexuality as sport. Ben Franklin's *Reflections on Courtship and Marriage* served as a behavioral guide in some quarters. Franklin proposed that couples should be modest and reserved in marriage and that people should act in public as if they were virgins. Displays of affection ought never to occur in public places. Ironically, Franklin himself is reported not to have practiced what he preached and supposedly had love affairs well into old age. And in a listing of virtues that Franklin drew up, he put chastity in the twelfth place out of thirteen. This strikes at least one social historian as a low priority (Nissenbaum, 1980).

It was also during the eighteenth century that notions about the delicacy of the female sex developed (Johns, 1982). This was the elegant century: the era of consorts, lovers, partners in pleasure and sensuality (Taylor, 1970). This romanticized view of love was geared to the young and the middle-aged, and not to older people. It did not pointedly exclude older people, but it also did not actively seek their participation. Importantly, this was a period of heavy makeup and clothing designed to accent sexual differences, at least among the well-to-do classes. One product of this emphasis on appearance was the attempt to conceal one's age. Thus, old age was pushed further outside the circumscribed realm of sexual attractiveness. Even with this handicap, older people were not totally prevented from exciting passion in the beholder. For example, the German Romantic poet Goethe is reported to have made a deep impression on women during his old age (Waldemar, 1960). But Goethe was the exception, rather than the rule.

In the late eighteenth-century, sexual behavior was becoming increasingly a police matter (Foucault, 1978). The public had moved to extend the legal purview of decency to cover almost anything, including sex (Pearsall, 1976). By the early nineteenth century, an elaborate set of sexual and public attitudes called Victorianism arose. It was assumed under this perspective that men are subject to animalistic drives but women do not need sensation from sex because they are passionless (Altherr, 1983).

The Victorian era was filled with sexual contradictions (Degler, 1974; Smith-Rosenberg, 1983). Certainly, the Victorians rejected the Enlightenment's liberal attitudes and practices. They viewed the sensuality of the previous century as materialistic and sinful, and were influenced in their notions of love and sex by the Romantic poets. These poets idealized love and, in particular, women. Writers such as Lord Byron, Henry Thoreau, Ralph Waldo Emerson, and Louisa May Alcott tended to elevate women and emphasize passion; they focused on man's romantic quest of woman. Chivalry was the vehicle men were to use in courting women.

During this period, many changes in attitudes were made within the general context of the movement toward social purity. Sexual behavior became viewed as bestial and disgusting. There are a variety of reasons why the Victorians were bent on taking the fun out of sex, and older people may have played a major role. Perhaps the old folks knew only how to restrict the sexual attitudes and activities of younger generations, since they themselves had grown up under restrictive circumstances. Pearsall (1976) proposes that the people who set the standards for morality were too old to indulge in young love and did not see why the young should have pleasures which their elders were denied.

The Victorians developed various new attitudes about women. Unlike their predecessors who regarded women as the source of sin, the Victorians often thought of women as pure and sexless (Taylor, 1970). Victorian women were considered to be more spiritual than men (Maier, 1984).

In the physiological theories of earlier periods such as the Middle Ages, women were said to be capable of more sexual pleasure than men (Cott, 1983; Degler, 1980). The Victorian woman was a different creature altogether: She was viewed as delicate and chaste. It was assumed that she did not enjoy sex, but passively submitted to her husband's wishes out of a sense of duty. Women were expected to repress their sexual feelings (Bever, 1982; Degler, 1980), if it was ever even admitted that they had any. Coupled with ignorance about sex, such attitudes served to pin middle-class women to their homes (Tannahill, 1980)—Victorian homes, in which prudery was common and women were expected to have a natural distaste for sex.

The Victorians attached not only shame to sex, but religious medical stigma as well (Bullough & Bullough, 1977). This may be best illustrated by citing their most prevalent theory about sperm. Certain medical authorities held the view that wastefulness of sperm during the life-span would result prematurely in physical and mental decay—in other words, old age. Wastefulness of sperm included frequent sex, masturbation, and homosexual relations. This theory had been earlier proposed by Sinibaldi, whose *Geneanthropeia* (1642) argued that gout, constipation, hunched back, bad breath, and other forms of decline were the result of a wasting of sperm. The late eighteenth-century physician Samuel Tissot's work *Advice to the People on Their Health* (1762) held similar views that found favor in the Victorian era. The theme resurfaced in the teachings of Ellen White (1827–1915), founder of the Seventh-day Adventists Church, who thought that the waste of sperm could turn a man into a cripple and imbecile. The loss of sperm was considered to be a loss of the vital energy that is life itself (Barker-Benfield, 1983). It was then logical to conclude that, the more sexually active a man is, the sooner will the decline and characteristics of old age occur.

The nineteenth century had no shortage of writers on the virtues of abstention, two of its American advocates being the nutritionist Sylvester Graham (1794–1851) (see Nissenbaum, 1980) and the physician Benjamin Rush (1745–1813). Sylvester Graham believed that certain foods intensify the sex drive, including that of older people. And the influential Dr. Rush believed that all disease can be traced to physiological situations in which nervous energy is increased and then lost, leading to debility. Because sex can be said to cause this kind of loss, Rush believed that sexual activity leads to debility (Degler, 1980). Vital life forces were thought to be depleted with excessive sex (Smith-Rosenberg, 1983). Another supporter of this perspective was the British physician William Acton (1814–1875), a chief spokesperson of the Victorian movement. He was one of those who claimed that women are asexual (Freedman, 1982).

An immensely popular expert in the United States was Dr. John Harvey Kellogg (1852–1943). In 1881, Kellogg wrote his main work titled *Plain Facts for Young and Old*, which sold more than 300,000 copies by 1910 (Degler, 1974). In this work, he warned about the dangers of masturbation, which he believed would lead to general debility, a weak back, mental decline, and nervous shock (see Bullough, 1976a).

Dr. Kellogg made several observations that are directly related to the sexuality of older people. On the sexual activity of women after menopause, Kellogg instructed:

As with childhood, old age is a period in which the reproductive functions are quiescent unless unnaturally stimulated. Sexual life begins with puberty, and in the female, ends at about the age of forty-five years, the period known as menopause, or turn in life. At this period, according to the plainest indications of nature, all functional activity should cease. If this law is disregarded, disease, premature decay, possibly local degenerations, will be sure to result. Nature cannot be abused with impunity. (Kellogg, 1881: 123)

The doctor also had some thoughts about sexual activity on the part of older men:

The generative power of the male is retained somewhat longer than that of the female, and by stimulation may be indulged at quite an advanced age, but only at the expense of shortening life, and running the risk of death. . . . Some learned physicians place the proper limit of man's functional activity at fifty years, if he would not render himself guilty of shortening his day by sensuality. (1881: 124)

Kellogg later spoke of the physical decline of older men:

In old age the seminal fluid becomes greatly deteriorated. Even at the best, its component elements could only represent decrepitude and infirmity, degeneration and senility. (1881: 134)

On marriage between older men and younger women, he issued a warning:

There are old men who marry young wives, and who pay the penalty by becoming martyrs to paralysis, softening of the brain, and driveling idiocy. (1881: 137)

The observations of Kellogg are representative of a number of medical and scientific thinkers in the Victorian period. They were sending the message, first of all, that one should avoid sexual activity or face premature aging. Another of their messages was that sexual activity is neither healthy nor appropriate during old age. From our own perspective here, the most important message from these and other works of the period may be that the negative effects of sexual activity mirror the characteristics attributed to old age and older people. Thus, older people wind up having more in common with those who are sexually active than they do with other groups.

SEX SELDOM ASSOCIATED WITH OLDER PEOPLE

In contemporary society, when we think of old age we seldom think of sexual behavior. We are more likely to link sex with youth (Christensen & Gagnon, 1965). The mystique of sex in old age pales in comparison to our cultural fascination with sex in the younger years (see Starr, 1985). This is a fairly old way of thinking in the Western world. The ancients too generally associated sexuality with youth, the essence of life, and even immortality (Weg, 1983). There are exceptions to this way of thinking, but they are relatively rare. For example, the Old Testament tells the stories of patriarchs such as Adam, Methuselah, and Abraham along with his elderly wife Sarah—all of them producing children at very advanced ages (Fowler et al., 1982).

In fact, the cultural marketing of youth as an ideal has come to mean that sexuality is seldom linked to the elderly. In contemporary times, it is routine to value youth above age and to equate youth with sexuality (Robinson, 1983). The mass-media images of sexuality promote this perception by linking it only to youth, and seldom older people (Smith, 1979; Starr, 1985). Those who do remain sexually active in old age are accused of acting too young and are treated with scorn or ridicule (Loughman, 1980). Moreover, the elderly often buy into the association of sexuality with youth and view themselves as unattractive and unacceptable sexual partners. In effect they deny their sexuality, their sexual needs and desires.

As mentioned above, the association between youth and sexuality can be traced to the ancient Greeks and Romans, who were both fairly open about their practices of sex and thought little of displaying it in their art. Much of this erotic art has been surveyed by historians (see Johns, 1982; Tannahill, 1980), but very little of it addresses the sexual activity of older people. Sexuality as portrayed by the Greeks and the Romans was essentially a function of middle age and youth. Plato's *Republic*—for one—treated the elderly as sexless (Loughman, 1980). Almost all representations of sexual behavior neglected the aged. The erotic art shows middle-aged humans and youths performing acts of sex, as well as men and beasts, humans and gods, and humans and semihuman creatures—satyrs, maenads, nymphs, and others. And the classic image of the nymph is of a youthful divine maiden. There were exceptions to the absence of older participants from all this sexual activity, but they were few. We see a clear and early bias toward youth.

THE LIFE-SPAN OF WOMEN

The timing of the ages of life and the perceived appropriate behaviors from each age form one basis for understanding women and men in terms of their sexuality. Old age has been perceived as beginning much earlier in the female than in the male, regardless of the individual's physiology and health (Roebuck & Slaughter, 1979; Stearns, 1980). The medieval scholars, for example, thought that women's life-spans are shorter than men's and that women age sooner (Dove, 1986). Consequently, sexual decline has been perceived as occurring much earlier in life for women.

Many of the medieval anatomic and physiological ideas came from the fourth-century B.C. works of Hippocrates and the second-century A.D. writings of Claudius Galen. For example, for several centuries the factors of body temperature and moistness were considered to have an important influence on and represent changes in the stages of life (Burrow, 1986). Also, Aristotle's *Masterpiece* was very popular during the Middle Ages and the centuries that immediately followed. The *Masterpiece*—a guide for understanding procreation, sex, and the life-span—proposed that sexual activity ends for women at menopause around age 44, and for men somewhere between the ages of 45 and 55 (Stone, 1979).

The perception of women aging much faster than men continued from the Middle Ages through the nineteenth century and is present even in contemporary times. The historian Michael Kammen (1980) found nineteenth-century portrayals of the ages of life that place the zenith of a woman's life 20 years before that of a man. Western societies have traditionally pinned much of a woman's social worth on her sexuality and sexual atractiveness. When these decline, the worth of the woman is also perceived as declining, at least in the judgment of men.

That older women and older men experience different factors affecting their sexual behavior is well established (Robinson, 1983). In fact, the differences are dramatic (Pfeiffer, 1977). Throughout the ages-of-life models, women have had more restrictions on what is considered the appropriate attitude for them to have, whereas men are confronted with more physiological limitations to continued sexual behavior in old age.

In general, women have bought into the notion of their earlier decline. The emphasis on sexuality and attractiveness has traditionally been stronger and more influential for women than for men. Authors such as Daniel Defoe picked up this theme in their work. In Defoe's *Moll Flanders*, written in 1721, the single woman Noll is continually assessing her sexual marketability throughout her life-span (Sokoloff, 1986). In general, older women are more concerned about the importance of physical attractiveness than older men are. The development of the cosmetics industry in the nineteenth century was based on this reality. The historian Peter Stearns (1980) notes that women are less prepared culturally for the results of aging than men tend to be.

Women have to contend with the strong restrictions attached by the popular mind to the biological passage of menopause, even though they are capable of sexual relations throughout old age (Hotvedt, 1983; Skultans, 1970). Medieval physiological theories held that, before old age, women are capable of more sexual pleasure than men (Degler, 1980). Menopause was thought to mark the end of sexual desire and desirability. Male decline was seen as less dramatic and was thought to occur 15–20 years later (Stearns, 1980).

Clearly, then, men's sexual decline—being considered more gradual—does not carry the cultural weight of female menopause (Skultans, 1970), even though there is evidence that men do experience some form of climacteric (Weg, 1983). Menopause serves as a convenient marker of old age for women (Roebuck & Slaughter, 1979). For men, old age has traditionally been associated with withdrawal from work; and for women, with loss of the ability to bear children. Once a woman was unable to reproduce, it was as if she no longer existed (Weg, 1975). According to Eric Pfeiffer (1977), the nineteenth-century medical establishment supported this notion. As Peter Stearns (1980) notes, medical science of the nineteenth century definitely considered women to be old after menopause.

Sexual desires, feelings, and behaviors among older women are seldom seen in art. Where they are found, it is usually with negative connotations such as folly, witchcraft, or evil. Postmenopausal sexual feelings and behaviors among older women have not been much recognized in Western culture, and particularly not in art.

Occasionally the sexual feelings of older women have been lampooned by authors. For example, William Congreve's *The Way of the World* (1700) has a character, Lady Wishford, who expressed an extraordinary sexual desire at the advanced old age of 45 (Freedman, 1978). Of course, there have been exceptions to this negative attitude toward older women, such as Thomas Hersey's *Midwife's Practical Directory or Woman's Confidential Friend* (1836). In this book, Hersey noted that productivity ends with menopause but passion increases (see Degler, 1980).

Most people, however, ascribed to the view that sexual desire ends with menopause. As Barbara Walker (1985) puts it, women have been permitted to be sexual only at a certain time of life. Any display of sexuality on the part of postmenopausal and older women has been perceived as grotesque, threatening, and inappropriate. Furthermore, in earlier centuries, postmenopausal sexual desires were thought to be unhealthy and disgusting (Bever, 1982). The Church certainly frowned on postmenopausal sex, as it would not lead to procreation (Noonan, 1986). By the nineteenth century and much of the twentieth, all women—regardless of age—were expected to be passive, asexual, and submissive to the wishes of men.

Women were expected to be passionless to begin with and then to have sexual relations only to bear children or to perform a duty for their husbands. After menopause, women of the nineteenth century presumably would have had no reason for sexual behavior other than duty. In the rare instance of literary plot, say, when a sexual theme involved an older woman, she was often depicted as striving to conceal her old age in the pursuit of a (younger) man (Fowler et al., 1982).

Historically, the sex life of older men has been treated in drama and literature as a source of humorous mishap. When an older woman was featured, however, the handling has been very different. Her sexual activity was not humorous, but evil. Control over the sex partner—and especially a younger partner—has been commonly attributed to the older female. And whereas sex with a younger partner was sometimes regarded as leading to virility or prolonged life for older men, older women having sex with young partners were granted no such beneficial effect on their life-span. Sexually interested older men were seen as practicing ridiculous self-deception, due to their actual inability to attract and perform. On the other hand, sexually active older women were portrayed as the deceivers of others—practicing trickery and control in order to meet their own unnatural needs. Older men might access sex through their purchasing power and social status, but older women gained access through their seductive evil powers over men. All in all, older men were the fools and buffoons of sex, whereas older women were seen as its evil and sinister sorceresses.

Marital status has been a key determinant in the sex lives of older people, and for women more so than men (Burnside, 1975; Corby & Zarit, 1983). In general, from the Middle Ages to the nineteenth century, sex within marriage itself was restricted (see Stone, 1979). Sexual relations with one's spouse in old age were neither common or expected. It is very likely that, even when sex between older married couples did occur, it was viewed as an affront to human dignity. Furthermore, since women have generally outlived men, the majority of widowed sexually stranded older people have been women (see Pfeiffer, 1977). Remarriage after 50 was always relatively rare (Stearns, 1980), and anyway—because of the differences in life expectancies—there were consistently fewer older males than older females (Corby & Zarit, 1983; Starr, 1985). Given the strong social norms against marriage to younger men, older women's opportunities for sexual expression have been limited indeed. Bever (1982) characterized older women in the sixteenth and seventeenth centuries as sexually frustrated because marital opportunities were so uncommon. These limitations on remarriage, and social sanctions against any sexual behavior on the part of older women, continued into later centuries.

SEXUAL INDIFFERENCE

Commenting on their review of literature involving older people, David Fowler, Lois Fowler, and Lois Lamdin (1982) observed that the bulk of writings prior to the nineteenth century assume the fact of sexual indifference in old age for both sexes. The moralistic and religious ideal of the dignified older person no longer interested in sex is an enduring image in Western thought (de Beauvoir, 1972). For example, the seventeenth-century French scholar Simon Goulart suggested that old age frees people from sexual lusts and desires (Smith, 1976). This was tied to the idea that sexual desires represent a kind of shackles— shackles that hold older people to this world.

Older people have been often referred to as desexed (Sommers, 1978) and sometimes as sexual eunuchs (Loughman, 1980). Viewing the old this way in effect lessens them as sexual competitors not just perceptually, but also actually— since we humans are so affected by the perceptions of others (see Barash, 1983; Pfeiffer, 1977). This may in fact have been a motive for doing so. By promoting the image of older people as asexual, the younger section of the population effectively reduced the competition.

SEX AS A NEGATIVE ACT

Whenever the subject of sex and older people has been written about or portrayed in art, it has most often been lodged within a negative context. As mentioned earlier, sexual activity on the part of old men was portrayed as either disgusting, humorous, or impossible. Sexual behavior on the part of postmenopausal women has been seen as grossly inappropriate—if not evil—by artists, writers, and moralists. The notion of healthy, natural sex among older people does seem not to have existed.

The negative treatment of sex in old age can be clearly seen in the biblical Apocrypha story of Susanna and the elders. This was a popular, enduring, and not at all humorous story written between 167 and 164 B.C. about a young, virtuous woman who unwittingly arouses the sexual desire of two evil old men. The old men watch her as she bathes in a stream, and decide to seduce her right then and there. They accost her at her bath and threaten to accuse her publicly of adultery if she does not submit to their wishes. She refuses and they do as threatened. Susanna is then brought to trial where the wise judge Daniel uncovers the old men's deception by obtaining contradictory testimony from them. The old men are condemned to death.

Plate 31 shows a typical rendition of Susanna and the elders, this one made by Jan Metsys in 1564. Susanna is in the center of the painting in order to draw attention to her beauty. She is not yet aware of the two elders watching her from behind the wall. Other versions were created by Tintoretto in 1555 and Lucas van Leyden in 1508, as well as other artists. Lucas van Leyden places the old men in the foreground, which in effect adds emphasis to their social status and power over Susanna.

Other popular Bible stories also link sex and old age in a negative manner. One of the most commonly translated into art was the story of Lot and his daughters (Gen. 19). Several of the artists who painted this story include Guido Reni (1575–1642) and Albrecht Altdorfer (1480–1538), whose nude version was created in 1537. In Plate 32—the reproduction of a 1633 painting by French artist Simon Voulet—Lot is shown clothed, along with his two daughters. The daughters attempt to seduce Lot into fathering their children, since the three are exiled and living in a cave and the daughters' husbands stayed behind in the destroyed city of Sodom. The daughters have gotten Lot drunk with wine to weaken his resistance. That temptation can overcome even an old man is evident here. Lot is always shown as a very old man. The dark theme of incest is also very clear, giving sexual activity in this and other renderings of the story a decidedly negative context.

OLD MEN AS LUSTFUL FOOLS

Plates 31 and 32 notwithstanding, sexuality among old men has been mostly the subject of ribald humor throughout Western history. The Greek comedies of Aristophanes provide us with an ancient example of the mockery that has been directed toward sexual behavior in old age. Aristophanes chose to characterize older people as lecherous and impotent, and thus plain disgusting. In his *Ecclesiazusae*, or Women in Parliament, older women seize power and change all sexual relations, giving themselves the dominant position when it comes to sexual rights and then imposing themselves on young men everywhere. Two humorous themes that have endured the test of time are these: (1) he thinks he can, but is unable; and (2) no one thinks he can, but he does anyway.

Whereas older women had few avenues for sexual expression, older men of wealth and power could attract younger women (Hotvedt, 1983). Thus, the old man with a younger woman has long served as fertile ground for humor and ridicule. As mentioned earlier, older men were famous for being portrayed as victims of their own self-deception, believing that they were sexually attractive and capable of holding the interest of younger partners.

Geoffrey Chaucer managed to create vivid stories of sexuality, deception, and old men as fools even within the bounds of marriage and the proprieties of the fourteenth century. In his *Canterbury Tales*, Chaucer likes to chronicle the humorous misfortunes of rich old men who make use of their wealth and status

Plate 31. *Susanna and the Elders*. 1564. Jan Metsys. Courtesy of the Royaux des Beaux Arts, Brussels.

Plate 32. *Lot and His Daughters*. 1633. Simon Voulet. Courtesy of the Musée des Beaux-Arts, Strasbourg.

to marry younger women. These old men then fail to perform sexually and are often mocked and betrayed by their younger partners.

The Merchant's Tale, for instance, tells of a 60-year-old knight named January who decides to marry a young woman. It is important to January that this wife be young so that she will satisfy his enormous sexual appetite. January states his preference for a young and not an older woman when he states,

Flesh should be young though fish should be mature;
As pike, not pickerel, makes the tastier meal,
Old beef is not so good as tender veal.
I'll have no woman thirty years of age;
That's only fodder, bean-straw for a cage.

Although he wants an heir to his fortune, January is more interested in meeting his sexual needs. This priority would have been viewed as sinful in Chaucer's day, when people were not to enjoy sex or love too ardently. To Saint Jerome and other Church scholars influential during the Middle Ages, too ardent a love would be sinful, and therefore January was committing a sin (Field, 1970). January himself professes just the opposite, however, when he declares,

And blessed be the yoke that we are in
For nothing we can do will count as sin.
A man is not a sinner with his wife,
He cannot hurt himself with his own knife.

January is warned that he will be cuckolded if he takes a younger bride, but he is persistent nonetheless and finds a young bride named May. Prior to his consummation of the marriage, January makes this bold statement of his sexual potency:

I may seem hoary, but I'm like a tree
That blossoms white before the fruit can be;
Blossoming trees are neither dry nor dead
And I am only hoary on my head.
My heart and all my members are as green
As laurel is; all the year round, I mean.

Then, despite consuming large amounts of various potions to enhance his sexual powers, January's performance is well below both his own claims and also May's needs. Later, a young male servant named Damian falls in love with May. Damian and May plot to have a secret love affair, so that May will not lose her inheritance from January. Eventually, January becomes blind and cannot even see their courtship. One day out in the garden, the blind January is tricked into helping May make love with Damian in a pear tree. As the two are making love, January suddenly regains his eyesight and discovers them. May spends the rest of the tale convincing January that he has imagined the incident and should take her back. January winds up apologizing and is reunited with his young wife. Thus, Chaucer has made a connection between senility and sexuality of old age (Berger, 1982; Burrow, 1986; Field, 1970).

The important moral theme in *The Merchant's Tale* would have been immediately evident to the medieval mind. January is interested in satisfying his large sexual appetite, but only with a young woman. From the start, this attitude pits him against the teachings of Saint Augustine, as January commits the venial sin of wanting sex for reasons other than procreation (Spisak, 1978). Although physically guilty only of being unable to perform adequately, old men were still considered sinful for their thoughts. Their interest in sex involved sin because they could not always sexually perform or reproduce. This association between old men and impotency was referred to as *senex amans non potens* (Spisak, 1978).

William Langland's *Piers Plowman* describes in less humorous terms the assault of old age on male potency (see Palmer, 1978). But in fact, both English tales and French *fabliaux* of the medieval period told of the lusty but half-impotent man whose younger and more lustful wife finds a young lover to meet her needs (Berger, 1982). Chaucer's works indicate that the fear of being cuckolded was a major concern in medieval sexuality. Named after the cuckoo bird that lays its eggs in other birds' nests, men were cuckolds when other men made love to their wives. Being cuckolded would destroy a man's honor (Flandrin, 1975; Stone, 1979). Chaucer's tales include two cuckolds: January in *The Merchant's Tale*, and John the Carpenter in *The Miller's Tale*. The latter character has such an excessive fear of being cuckolded that it dooms him from the start. January—we have seen—was doomed because he was so boastful of his sexual potency (see Berger, 1982).

The theme of the older cuckold lived past the Middle Ages. The character was standard stock in many of the novelle of Renaissance Italy (Herlihy, 1976). Cuckoldry was also a common theme during the sixteenth and seventeenth centuries (Carlton, 1978). And cuckolds were usually older men. For example, William Shakespeare's *Sack Full of Newes* depicts a young woman who makes a cuckold of her older husband. Another example is in William Congreve's late seventeenth-century comedy *Love for Love*, whose main character is an older cuckold. The cuckold was also the subject of artists in the sixteenth century. Old men were frequently shown with younger wives and their young lovers (see Stewart, 1979). Treatment of the theme in the seventeenth century can best be described as pornographic: It had become aggressive, disgusting, and cynical, encouraging the audience to laugh much and often at "old goats," "cuckolds," and the "impotent." However, the derision fit right into the tradition of making older people's sexuality the target of humor (Covey, 1989a). In seventeenth- and eighteenth-century France, cuckolds were subjected to *charivari*—the public ceremonies of humiliation also experienced by wedding couples of unequal age (Shorter, 1977).

There is historical evidence that the January–May themes developed from actual practice (Herlihy, 1967). Plague, climatic catastrophes, death during childbirth, and other factors affecting the mortality rates in the Middle Ages resulted in a disproportionate number of older widowers who remarried younger women in haste and later regretted their decision.

A spin-off from the cuckoldry theme was simply the old fool and the young maiden. Sexual liaisons between old men and young women were deplored by medieval and later moralists, even within the confines of marriage (Burrow, 1986). Yet, in sixteenth-century Germany, unions of older people and youth were common (Coupe, 1967)—partly due to the population disparities mentioned above. These relationships mocked the ideal of marriage, as people of similar ages were expected to marry. Thus, the older husbands were automatically characterized in the popular mind by jealousy, lechery, and lack of sexual prowess; and their younger women partners were often branded by reflex as adulteresses and liars.

The theme of love and sex between old and young people—sometimes referred to as unequal couples—was present in art and literature even in antiquity (Stewart, 1979), reached its height of popularity during the late Middle Ages and the sixteenth century, and can be found right on up to contemporary culture (as in the movie *Harold and Maude*). Regardless of century, the theme's basic assumption has been the same: that sexual relationships between people of different ages are unnatural and immoral.

The unequal lovers might be an older man and younger woman, or an older woman and a young man. In art, the old man is often wearing a fool's cap,and has his arm around the younger woman or his hand on her breast—to convey a sense of blind lust. The younger partner almost always has her (or his) hand in the older person's purse. Such an image undoubtedly arises from the attitude that lust is unbecoming for older people, especially in iight of the wisdom expected to come with old age (Stewart, 1979).

Erasmus in his *Praise of Folly* (1511) writes about unequal lovers. Erasmus notes that it is more acceptable for an older man to have a young partner than for an older woman to have one. In the late seventeenth century, William Wycherley's work *The Country Wife* and the comedies of William Congreve played with the complications of unequal relationships.

As for the theme in art, an early-sixteenth-century woodcut by Hans Wandereisen shows a young woman and her older husband. The old man declares,

> My love is young, and I am old,
> She is very hot, and I am cold,
> Her hair is yellow, and mine is gray,
> Her cheeks are red, mine are blue, . . .
> For that reason, we quarrel the entire day.

Other examples include Hans Baldung's *Unequal Lovers* (1507), Lucas van Leyden's *The Fool and the Young Woman* (1520), Albrecht Dürer's *Ill-assorted Couple* (1495), and Quinten Massys' *Ill-matched Lovers* (c. 1515/1525). One common thread present in all these works is that an old man can only gain the favors of a young woman by buying them (Coupe, 1967). They all have overtones of lust, sexual inadequacy, and prostitution.

Plate 33, Flemish artist Quinten Massys' *Ill-matched Lovers* from the National Gallery in Washington, is a typical rendition of the old fool and the young

Plate 33. *Ill-matched Lovers.* C. 1515/1525. Quinten Massys. Courtesy of the National Gallery of Art, Washington, D.C.

maiden. In this tavern painting, Massys gives us a low-life genre scene of an old man attempting to seduce a young woman. Massys' old man wears the fool's cap, and his hand is resting on the woman's breast. The woman has already taken his purse and is handing it to her partner in the background, who also dons a fool's garb. It is clear within the painting's narration that, without the purse, she would have no interest in her would-be suitor. There are cards on the table in the bottom left-hand corner of the scene, symbolizing the game of love between the sexes (Stewart, 1979).

This humor and mockery surrounding the sexual desire of old men for young women can also be found in the popular legend of Aristotle and Phyllis. During the thirteenth century, a cleric named Jacques de Vitry used the legend to discredit what he saw as an overreliance on classical philosophy. As the story goes, Aristotle was complaining that his male student—sometimes taken to be Alexander the Great—was spending too much time with his wife Phyllis and neglecting his studies. Hearing of Aristotle's criticism, the student's wife arouses Aristotle in the garden and persuades him to disrobe and give her a ride on his back in exchange for her sexual favors. "Alexander" is off to the side, watching as the master makes a fool of himself.

Plate 34 shows a print by Hans Baldung titled *Aristotle and Phyllis* (1513). Baldung's Alexander watches from a roof ledge above the couple. Phyllis rides on the philosopher's back and whips him in the rump. She leads him by way of a bit in his mouth. Aristotle is clearly being humiliated. The tree stump ahead of him is symbolic of impotence.

Several themes intertwine in these works of old-fool art. One idea that consistently surfaces is that the old men do not have enough sense to realize they are being taken advantage of by the other actors. Another theme is the power of women over men, which was a popular apprehension from the thirteenth to the sixteenth centuries. Ambition also shows its face: The younger partners always have some material motive for their actions, whether they marry the old fools or not.

While older women who express a sexual desire for younger men are less common, there are a few such stories. In fact, many of the ill-matched couples in paintings and prints that were popular during the late Middle Ages portray older women with younger partners. Like the older men, the older women in these works are full of lust and folly. Their relationships often provoked the ridicule of society (Sommers, 1978). However, as discussed previously, old women seeking liaisons with younger partners were not considered humorous, but evil.

Plate 35 is a reproduction of *Old Woman, Young Man, and a Demon* (1515), a pen drawing by Niklaus Manuel-Deutsch. In it, an older woman sits with her young lover. The purse she holds is decorated with an ass's ear, symbolic of her foolishness. Furthermore, a demon sticks an ass's ear on her hat. The demon is pumping a bellows—a symbol for foolishness, evil, and lust. Since they are used to incite fire, the bellows are an apt metaphor here for passion. The young

Plate 34. *Aristotle and Phyllis*. 1513. Hans Baldung Grien. Courtesy of the Staatliche Museer Preussischer Kulturbesitz (Berlin-Dalheim Museum).

Plate 35. *Old Woman, Young Man, and a Demon*. 1515. Niklaus Manuel-Deutsch. Kunstmuseum, Basel. Courtesy of Öffentliche Kunstsammlung, Kupferstichkabinett, Basel.

man opens his purse to collect the money the old woman offers him for his attention.

YOUNGER PARTNERS ASSUMED TO PROLONG LIFE

The search for sexual potency and enhanced performance is an old tradition in Western culture (Weg, 1983). A variety of potions and methods have been touted. In addition to all the pharmaceutical enhancements moreover, the practice of having sexual relations with younger partners has also been thought to prolong life and sexual ability. It has even been perceived as a prescription for immortality. For example, when the Israelites were worried about King David's old age and illness, they encouraged him to practice what is now called "Shunamitism," after King David's young partner Abishag the Sunamite. The practice calls for the ailing old man to sleep with a young woman—and does not necessarily involve sexual relations. Rembrandt's *Departure of the Shunamite Wife* (1640) at London's Victoria Albert Museum draws on this tradition.

Shunamitism is only one of many ways that have been attempted in combating old age. Other Near Eastern as well as Far Eastern cultures are full of testimonials for the belief that a man absorbs virtue and youth from women (see Comfort, 1965). And the notion is not so unknown in the West, either. During the fourteenth century, the French poet Guillaume de Marchaut wrote of rejuvenation resulting from the beauty of a young mistress (Burrow, 1986). It was believed that the energies coming from a chaste young woman activate the aura of men—and in particular, older men.

As mentioned in Chapter 3, in the eighteenth century, it was thought that the lives of older men could be prolonged if only they would breast-feed. To this end, wet nurses were employed. Since human milk was regarded as the elixir of human life, the practice may have been common throughout Europe (Waldemar, 1960). There is evidence that it may have been particularly popular among the wealthy older men of Paris (Waldemar, 1960).

In any case, the sexual desire of older men for younger women has been a lasting theme in Western art and literature. The desire of older men was seldom—if ever—directed toward older women. As for the older women themselves, they were never thought to achieve greater sexual powers or prolonged life through sexual relations with younger partners. And as for the younger women, they generally did not show sexual desire for older men so much as an attraction to the older men's wealth, status, and power.

SEX AS TEMPTATION FOR OLDER PEOPLE

As the foregoing sections indicate, sex has often been portrayed as a temptation for older people and especially for older men. The Duke de Berry's *Book of Hours* contains an illustration of the temptation of Saint Jerome. After his conversion to Christianity, Jerome regarded sex to be unclean (Stone, 1979). He is always shown as being quite old in his celibacy (see Chapter 3), yet still he remains subject to memories of tempting young maidens (Tannahill, 1980). Importantly, we find here another acknowledgment of sexual desire among older people—in this case, even a celibate saint.

A related theme is that sexual desires restrain people—particularly older people. Some early scholars assumed that old age would free people from such restraints. Petrarch—for one—hoped and believed that old age would free him from lust (Folts, 1980). In his *Secretum*, Petrarch likens sexual desire to shackles (Burrow, 1986), as mentioned earlier. Sexual desires were sometimes even viewed as hampering the transition from this life to the next.

OLDER WOMEN AS SEXUAL PREDATORS

Generally, the medieval Church treated women as the source of all sexual evil (Mullins, 1985; Taylor, 1970). On those occasions when older women were portrayed as having any sexual desire at all, they were shown as being predatory toward men—sexually powerful though foolish and morally weak, and often the tool of evil forces (Stewart, 1979; Walker, 1985). Throughout the Middle Ages there was a conflicted ambivalence toward women: They were simultaneously placed on a pedestal and judged as the incarnation of evil (Gies & Gies, 1978).

The view that women—especially those judged to be beautiful— are deadly and dangerous is among the oldest in Western civilization (Mullins, 1985). According to ancient Greek mythology, the goddess Gaea (Mother Earth) persuaded her youngest son Cronus (Saturn) to castrate his father Uranus with a sickle. Cronus did so, and threw his father's genitals into the sea. From the foam that spewed up hotly arose Aprodite (Venus).

A medieval idea popular in the twelfth century was that of woman as temptress. This was based in part on the Old Testament story of Adam and Eve (Palmer, 1978). The ability of women to control men through sexual power was an often repeated topic. The legend of Aristotle and Phyllis mentioned earlier is one example. Others include the biblical tales of Samson and Delilah, and David and Bathsheba. This idea of women controlling men persisted over the centuries. The theme can be found in Titian's *Diana and Actaeon* and *Death of Actaeon* and Caravaggio's *Judith and Holofernes* in the sixteenth century, as well as Jacque Louis David's *Death of Marat* in the eighteenth century.

Witchcraft also affected perceptions of the sexuality of older women (see Chapter 3). The rise in witchcraft persecution that occurred in the fifteenth and sixteenth centuries corresponded with the advent of the notion that women are more sexually avid than men (Thomas, 1971). Concern over witchcraft reached its height in 1600 and declined by the middle of the eighteenth century. The witch has historically been viewed as erotic (Waldemar, 1960) and associated with sexual deviance (Bullough, 1982). According to *The Witches' Hammer*, a witch-hunting guide written in 1486, women's sexual appetites are insatiable (Taylor, 1970). All witchcraft was said to arise from carnal lust (Stone, 1979).

The underlying fear of witches was not only a fear of sexual lust, but also of women themselves (see Bullough, 1976b; Walker, 1985).

Initially, the definition of witchcraft was applied to a variety of people of all ages and walks of life, as discussed in Chapter 3. As the perceptions of witchcraft evolved and narrowed, it is unclear whether the association between witchcraft and sexual lust remained. We do know that, during the sixteenth and seventeenth centuries, widows were frequently accused of witchcraft (Carlton, 1978). The jealousy of husbands contemplating their wives' possible remarriage may have contributed to the negative connotations placed on sexuality during widowhood. To such husbands it was as if they would be posthumously cuckolded. In nineteenth-century Victorian times, men still sometimes feared that their widows would become more sexually active after their deaths (Smith-Rosenberg, 1983).

CLOSING THOUGHTS ON IMAGES OF SEX AND OLD AGE

Very little is actually known about the sexual behavior of older people. Several contemporary experts have commented that one of the most enduring themes involving the aged is the taboos on the topic of their sexual activity (Loughman, 1980; Pfeiffer, 1977). This taboo has resulted in an absence of information from earlier periods. Even the historical texts on sex that are written today fail consistently to acknowledge the sexual desires and activities of older people.

One useful framework for our understanding is to structure people's attitudes and expectations about sex into two very different levels—the level that has applied to everyone, regardless of age; and the level that has applied only to older people. There have been two sets of rules governing sexuality, when it comes to age. How this dual standard was perceived, enforced, and reacted to by older people themselves as well as younger people is of great interest here.

Sexual activity in old age has been viewed as immoral, inappropriate, and negative, although the actual sexual behavior of the older population may always have departed from the social and religious prescriptions of the times. There has certainly been an awareness on the part of artists and writers that some older persons try to maintain their sex lives even when the popular wisdom judges them to be immoral and inappropriate, as well as doomed to failure.

Western views on the ages of life have never associated sexual behavior with old age, although sexual desire was sometimes recognized. When acknowledged, the desire was always considered a negative characteristic, however. Older men have suffered ridicule and been the targets of humor about their lust, being cuckolded, and their inability to perform sexually. Older women have been scorned and even persecuted as predatory and evil. This was partly due to their being tainted by the Church as the source of original sin. Menopause was long perceived as the end of a woman's normal sex life.

The prescriptions of the Church worked against sexual activity in general, but especially against activity by older people. This is because it regarded sexually active older persons as lustful and not able or willing to procreate, which to the

Church was the main—if not sole—justification for sexual activity in the first place.

Thus, Western society has never accommodated nor encouraged sexual behavior on the part of older people. This fact has been consistent. Yet, in spite of the centuries of ridicule and degradation, interest in sexual activity has not disappeared from old age. This is an important observation, for the activity and desire have persisted regardless of social repression and some fairly inhospitable circumstances.

It is only in the latter half of the twentieth century that the natural fact of sexual relations involving older people has begun to be acknowledged. However, today's researchers and writers—though occasionally positive and encouraging—are still more often negative and defensive about the subject (Starr, 1985). Thus, even in contemporary Western societies, there is often a negative context that ropes off all sexual activity among the aged. One can only wonder what the future will hold, should Western society ever acknowledge and truly accept its reality.

6

IMAGES OF OLDER
PEOPLE AND DEATH

The meanings attached to death have changed over the centuries (Aries, 1974a, 1985; Markson, 1980; Marshall, 1980). It has been romanticized—as in Victorian times, and minimized—as in contemporary times (Markson, 1980), seen as a release, and viewed as a swift and capricious force (see Marshall, 1980). Death and dying have also taken on different meanings for older people over time. The subject is receiving some attention from contemporary scientists (see Kalish, 1985; Kastenbaum, 1969a, 1969b, 1979; Marshall, 1980; Riley, 1970; Smith, 1978; Van Tassel 1979); but overall, little historical attention has been paid to what death may mean to older people—both actually and as a societal perception. As John Demos (1986:178) concludes, the matter of attitudes toward death, and especially death and the elderly, is a major "lacuna" in our knowledge.

The purpose of this chapter is to identify and describe some of the major meanings and themes regarding death and older people. As before, information was drawn from the works of historians and from the 500 or so years of literature produced in the late Middle Ages through the nineteenth century. Art has proven to be a particularly good index of social attitudes toward death and dying (see Aries, 1974a, 1974b, 1985; Chew, 1962; Goody, 1974; Kamen, 1976; Tashjian & Tashjian, 1974; Tristram, 1976).

Any review of the meanings of death and older people must acknowledge the dramatic changes in life-span expectancy at birth that have occurred over the centuries. It is safe to say that, for the greater part of Western history, life expectancy at birth was relatively short for most people (Dublin, 1965; Kastenbaum, 1979; Thomlinson, 1976). For example, during the Roman Empire, the average life expectancy at birth was between 20 and 30 years (Preston, 1977). From the thirteenth to the seventeenth centuries, life expectancy is estimated to have been between 20 and 40 years (Goldscheider, 1971; Smith, 1978). Later it rose to between 33 and 40 years during the eighteenth century in Europe and the United States (Goldscheider, 1971). After studying British records from the period 1550–1600, historian Henry Kamen (1976) observed that life was generally short then; only a small portion of the population made it to old age. Consequently, youth of the period did not plan for old age. They did not expect to live that long.

In spite of the short life expectancies at birth, there is evidence that some people did indeed live to be old. If one managed to survive the early years of childhood, and then—for women—the childbearing years, one's chances of reaching old age were quite favorable. Thus, older people may have been more common in earlier societies than we once thought. For example, Peter Stearns (1976) reports that massive declines in infant mortality in preindustrial times allowed many to live to old age (see also Thomlinson, 1976). Philip Greven's (1970) study of seventeenth-century colonial Andover, Massachusetts, found that those who survived to adulthood could anticipate long healthy lives. The same has been true for other regional populations over the centuries.

DEATH AND DYING FROM THE MIDDLE AGES TO THE NINETEENTH CENTURY

To understand the images that artists have made of older people and death, it is important to realize the general context in which death and dying were viewed from the Middle Ages through the nineteenth century. During the Middle Ages, death was everpresent. Simply put, the era was tough on everybody, regardless of age. Mortality rates were exceptionally high compared to later periods. Thus, in the Middle Ages death was viewed as the great equalizer: It triumphed over all living things (Aries, 1974a, 1974b). Death could come unexpectedly and often did. Given these circumstances, it should be no surprise that death and dying were major preoccupations of the people living then (Stannard, 1977; Huizinga, 1952). Life was understood to be transitory—a temporary state leading to heaven or to hell. The preoccupation with death is witnessed in cultural artifacts of the period: several popular manuals on how to prepare for death, called *artes moriendi* (see Choron, 1963; de Beauvoir, 1972); soul and body poems (Hendricks & Hendricks, 1977); and other *mementos mori* (Aries, 1985; Choron, 1963). The art of the Middle Ages, too, displays a keen awareness of the passage of time and the approach of death (Herlihy, 1982). Older people derived meaning and direction from these cultural instruments.

The preoccupation with death brought with it, during the Middle Ages, a fear and horror that transcended all other emotions (Choron, 1963; Douglas, 1974; Stannard, 1977; Warthin, 1931). The agony of dying was a commonly witnessed occurrence. It would be centuries before medical technology was able to reduce some of its pain and suffering. In addition, some of the horror of dying can be attributed to the medieval fear of going to hell. In any case, the horror of death and dying was often dramatized by artists, such as in the bizarre works of Hieronymus Bosch (Choron, 1963). Furthermore, death was viewed by many people as a ghastly visitation on the human body. The physical ravaging of decay and decomposition became a focal point of thought in the late Middle Ages (Stannard, 1977). This emphasis on the morbid aspects of death declined as the Middle Ages drew to a close, and death then become less of a preoccupation.

The beginning of the Renaissance marked a revolutionary change in attitudes, as the focus turned to life in this world rather than in the next. As Jacques Choron (1963) notes, this and other attitudinal changes deeply influenced the Renaissance person's view of death. Significant though it remained, death was no longer the primary focus of the living as it had been during the Middle Ages. As far as citizens of the Renaissance were concerned, death could wait. Public mourning of the dead was still important, however, and was becoming increasingly ritualized (Aries, 1974b). The concept of the afterlife underwent significant modifications during the Renaissance and the role of purgatory developed. Purgatory became an increasingly popular subject for artists (see Stannard, 1977). The question was no longer whether one would be going to heaven or hell—as in the Middle Ages—but rather, how long one would have to spend in purgatory before entering heaven. With this device, the Renaissance mind was able to mitigate the horrors of hell much more effectively than individuals from the Middle Ages had been able to do.

In the centuries following the Renaissance, it became more common to challenge the established thinking and to want reasoned justification for religious and other teachings about death and the afterlife. The circumstances surrounding death and dying changed fundamentally during the seventeenth century, according to Philippe Aries (1974b, 1985). The individual surrendered control over his or her death to other people, such as members of the immediate family. Before this, the dying individual had orchestrated the conditions and terms of his or her own death and dying. This was no longer the case by the seventeenth century, as a variety of interested actors now made decisions about the person's death.

The eighteenth century witnessed a preoccupation with what follows death (Choron, 1963). Relative to other periods, religious texts of the seventeenth and eighteenth centuries emphasized that older people should turn away from this world and prepare for the next, but they also encouraged older people to stay alive in order to help guide future generations (Troyansky, 1982).

John McManner's 1981 study of attitudes toward death in eighteenth-century France found that a shift toward more private expressions of dying and mourning had occurred. He attributes this shift to the growth of the nuclear family as an emotional center as well as to the widespread experience of greater longevity. Longer periods of marriage allowed relationships to develop more fully than in prior centuries. Emotions became more focused within the immediate family. These and other factors promoted a more private and less public form of dying and death.

Aries (1974a, 1974b, 1985) suggests that in the eighteenth century death also became more erotic in tone. Artistic renditions of Death assaulting the living were fairly commonplace. One familiar image in this period was that of death embracing a young and beautiful virgin. And later in the eighteenth century Death itself became a thing of beauty, garlanded with bouquets surrounded by cherubim and full-fledged angels in supporting roles.

By the nineteenth century, death had been clearly romanticized (Cannadine, 1981; Markson, 1980). Dying was more of an emotional and theatrical event than ever before. In fact, says Geoffrey Gorer (1965), death was an obsession in the nineteenth century. Furthermore, mourning received a great deal of emphasis, and the living were increasingly likely to show an impassioned grief for the dead (Aries, 1974b). This mourning was particularly evident, given the relatively high death rate in that era (Cannadine, 1981).

As this overview has been meant to suggest, the social conditions of death and dying have shifted over the centuries. At times, the individual has had considerable control over the process of dying—and at other times, very little control. Dying has sometimes been a public ritual, and sometimes one of great solitude. It has been a romantic embrace, and a morbid visitation. All the while, older people have been experiencing death and dying within these shifting contexts.

OLD AGE ASSOCIATED WITH DEATH

In contemporary society's art and literature, old age is associated with death and dying more than any other period of life. Some historians have suggested, though, that death's strong association with old age is a relatively recent phenomenon (Marshall, 1980; Van Tassel, 1979). This is supported by the fact that death more generally touched people of all ages in earlier centuries. Lawrence Stone (1979), for instance, notes that death was a normal occurrence in all ages and was not something that happened mainly to older people. Other scholars find, however, that the association with old age has existed for some time (see Fischer, 1977). In fact, there have been historical periods when the association between death and old age was very common, and others when it was not. And the trend over the centuries has been toward an increasing association of old age with death. This association developed overall even though the risk of dying remained high for people of all ages (Kastenbaum, 1979). For a while at least, periods of high mortality rates for infants, childbearing women, and men fighting in wars would cause death to be connected with all ages of life. A case in point in early New England: Morbidity was not associated with any particular age, and therefore was not used to distinguish older people from other ages of the life-span (Demos, 1986).

That death associates with people regardless of age is important. Medieval illustrations of the dance of death enlist the participation of people of all ages, including older people. Late in the fourteenth century, the dance of death occupied a prominent place in art and thinking (Choron, 1963; Huizinga, 1952). An anonymous work from the early fifteenth century found at the Cemetery of the Innocents in Paris is claimed to be the original *Dance of Death*. It shows people from all walks of life dressed in appropriate clothing and carrying symbols of their position in medieval French society. Every one of these figures is being grasped by the skeletons of Death. This early work served as a model for later artists.

Lithography made the image of the dance of death a popular item, and prints were mass produced throughout Europe. Their popularity may be attributed to the high mortality rates in the fourteenth and fifteenth centuries and to a public fascination with the needs of departing souls (Thomlinson, 1976). Three main points were made by the various depictions. First, death was regarded to be powerful and inevitable, a perspective not always held in ancient times (Choron, 1964). And Death's will to take whomever it wished could not be overcome by any individual or even the collective will.

Second, death was shown as treating all people equally—regardless of age, rank, or position in society. Death would call them all, including older people (Warthin, 1931). In a sense, it must be oblivious to one's position. During the fifteenth century and for several centuries afterward, many factors contributed to high mortality rates throughout society—factors such as poor sanitation, plague, epidemic, malnutrition, and famine (see Kamen, 1976; Thomlinson, 1976). David Stannard (1977) notes that, from the early sixteenth to the middle of the seventeenth century, London was free from plague for barely a decade.

Third, the dance of death reminded people of the frailty and vanity of earthly things (Huizinga, 1952). One's focus was supposed to be on the afterlife, and not on the possessions and concerns of earthly existence. This is one of the strongest themes in the linking of older people to life and death in Western history. The dance of death proclaimed for all to see that one should not focus on worldly pleasures.

In that they were equally touched by the dance of death, older people were viewed no differently from the other ages (Brandon, 1975). However, they did receive some special emphasis, often being represented by artists as a separate group in the dance. Old age was a distinct image, comparable to—say—the child, the soldier, the king, and so on. For example, in Hans Holbein's *Dance of Death* (1538)—perhaps the most famous of all the renditions—he includes two separate older figures: a man and a woman.

As can be seen in Plate 36, Holbein's *Old Woman* trudges along a rocky road accompanied by two dancing skeletons, one of them playing a flute. The old woman leans on a cane and focuses her attention on the rosary in her left hand (Clark, 1950). The physical signs of her old age are obvious: the wrinkled face, and her bent posture like that of the skeleton leading the procession. The second dancing skeleton stands in sharp contrast to the old woman: It conveys a sense of merriment and gaiety. This dancer seems to view the old woman's inpending death with a great deal of pleasure. It steps lightly in the procession, wearing a crown of twisted leaves. And it taunts and teases the old woman during her journey to death.

Plate 36. *Dance of Death—The Old Woman*.
1538. Hans Holbein. Courtesy of the Bibliothèque
Nationale, Paris.

Holbein's *Old Man*—reproduced here as Plate 37—contains both similar and different symbols from *The Old Woman*. The cane is again present, along with the poor posture and other signs of physical decline. The old man walks arm-in-arm with a skeleton who is plucking on a zither. Holbein includes an hourglass in the background—symbolizing the passage of time—and an open grave. In fact, the old man already has—as we say—one foot in the grave. He seems to step toward his grave with a sense of haste and relief, while turning toward his keen companion Death.

A key distinction between the old man and woman and the other figures in Holbein's *Dance of Death* is their stance or attitude. The old man and woman are shown accepting death, whereas the others resist it (see Tristram, 1976). The message comes across that the older people are not reluctant, but resigned. They are weary from their life's journey and prepared for the grave. In a sense, they almost seek the grave. Peter Stearns (1976) suggests that the welcoming of death in extreme old age was a theme present even as early as Hippocrates. This theme may have been influential when Holbein created his popular series of prints.

Over the centuries, as renditions of the dance of death continued to be created,

Plate 37. *Dance of Death—The Old Man*. 1538.
Hans Holbein. Courtesy of the Bibliothèque Nationale, Paris.

they became more and more macabre. This was reflective of the growing medieval
fascination with the physical texture of death (Stannard, 1977). Artists became
progressively morbid in their portrayals. Not content with the simple use of
skeletons, they draped their figures of death with rotting flesh in various stages
of decomposition. The ugliness of the death images contrasted sharply with the
illusion of the body as something beautiful. Simone de Beauvoir (1972) has
pointed out that the connection between bodily decay and death was the major
message in these later works. More importantly, she observed that the old person
and this new image of death eventually became one and the same. In a sense,
the old people themselves began to represent a walking Death. This was a
dramatic departure from the original dance of death that showed it to be im-
partial—escorting people of every age all to the same end.

Reasons for Associating Death with Old Age

Historically, there have been many reasons why old age would be associated
with death. As John Hinton (1967) suggests, one reason may be that death during
old age has been viewed as timely death. For example, writing during the

Renaissance, the Italian scholar Giorgio Vasari felt that anyone who had not lived a full life-span was the victim of an untimely death (Gilbert, 1967). The appropriate timing for dying and death was sometimes explicitly linked to the later ages of the life-span. For example, when artists of the Middle Ages and the Renaissance—such as Titian—portrayed the ages of life, they often showed elderly men anticipating and contemplating death (see Plate 5 in Chapter 2). In fact, dying and preparing for death are activities that were often reserved for older people in the ages-of-life genre (see Burrow, 1986; Chew, 1962). Certainly, one of the boundaries of old age has always been death (Bever, 1982; Chew, 1962). Thus, at the most basic level, death was associated with old age because it marked the end of old age.

The implications of the basic association extend beyond it, however. Over the centuries, aging has been seen as part of the process of dying (Kastenbaum, 1979). Since the ancient Greeks and especially Aristotle, Western thought has linked dying to a decline in physical and mental functioning. The notion of decay was a major motif in the Middle Ages (Choron, 1963; Huizinga, 1952). As mentioned earlier, this motif was often expressed in the art of the period. Many tombs of the Middle Ages were covered with illustrations of the deceased in advanced stages of decay (Aries, 1985; Stannard, 1977). During the fifteenth and sixteenth centuries, this decomposition was interpreted as a sign and result of human failure (Aries, 1974b). Aging was linked to decay, and decay to death; therefore, death and aging were one and the same.

It should be noted that there has been a continuing ambivalence toward older people in this regard. Old age has been viewed as a preferred alternative to death, but an unattractive one because of its corresponding physical and mental decline (Kastenbaum & Ross, 1975). One is both happy to survive to old age and unhappy with the concomitant decline.

By the nineteenth century, old age and death were strongly locked together. For example, medical books recommended that older people prepare themselves for a better life beyond the grave (Haber, 1983). Old age had become medically defined as a disease of decay, decline, and eventual death. In fact, old age was frequently listed as a cause of death—which, according to Carole Haber (1983), indicated a lack of precision in medical diagnosis. Thus, as these historical examples indicate, the association between death and old age was due in part to the association between old age and decay.

There have also been other reasons why it developed. For example, the elderly have traditionally been regarded as intercessors between this world and the next. By virtue of their wisdom, age, and generational ties, they are often felt to have a special link with their ancestors (Kastenbaum, 1979). This special link contributed to their being associated with death and dying.

There is a very old belief—traceable to the Anglo-Saxons—that older people are morally and spiritually superior to the young (Burrow, 1986). Therefore, older people may be looked on as the only members of society capable of fully understanding the meaning of death and dying. Evidence of this perception can be found not only among the Anglo-Saxons, but also much later. Andrew Achenbaum (1978) reports that American writers between 1830 and 1860 thought that only the old could truly understand life and death, and that only they had the life experience to die correctly. This perception of older people's special wisdom disappeared after the Civil War (Achenbaum, 1978).

Finally, and perhaps most importantly, there was an overall decline in some of the factors affecting mortality rates in the nonelderly population—a lessening in the ravages of plague, famine, disease, and poor sanitation (Thomlinson, 1976). This gradual improvement in living conditions increased the probability that death would occur in the later ages of life, thus also increasing the likelihood that death and dying would be associated with the advanced years. For these and perhaps other reasons, death would become—at least symbolically—the sole province of the old by the nineteenth century, and it remains so today (Douglas, 1974; Haber, 1983; Stannard, 1977; Van Tassel, 1979).

Old Age as the Image of Death

The association between old age and death has been so strong that old age is occasionally used to represent death itself. Images of old age as death were common in the late Middle Ages and the Renaissance, one of the most ancient of these images being that of Saturn and the crone, who is Death. In fact, the pictorial image of Saturn and the crone has been traced back to antiquity (Walker, 1985). Saturn himself has long symbolized death in mythology, art, and astrology. He is portrayed as a morose, sickly, scrubby old man who occasionally holds a scythe, pick, crutch, or some other symbol of death and the passage of time. Saturn has also been characterized as sluggish and with a gloomy temperament. Of the seven planets known to the Middle Ages, Saturn was the slowest and has long been associated with poverty, hardship, and death (Panofsky, 1939). In classical mythology, Saturn was emasculated by Jupiter. The old man is sometimes pictured devouring children, as for instance in Plate 38—Goya's nineteenth-century rendition of the myth. This eating of his own children could very well signify that time devours what it has created (Panofsky, 1939).

Death images have also taken form as females, such as the crone mentioned above. The image of the crone as the bringer of death is much older than the Middle Ages (Walker, 1985). Judeo-Christian belief contributed to much of the symbolism relating to death, in that Eve's disobedience to God brought about God's creation of death.

Another remarkable example of old age as death is the northern Renaissance–style painting by Lucas Furtenagel titled *The Burgkmaier Spouses* (1529), reproduced as Plate 39. In this gloomy painting, an older couple see their skulls when they look into a hand-held mirror. Aries writes, "The scene combines two illusions—that of old age and that of the reflection; but the reflection is truer than reality" (1985:193). Paul Zucker (1963) links this paint-

Plate 38. *Saturn Devouring One of His Children*. 1821–1822. Francisco de Goya y Lucientes. Courtesy of the Prado, Madrid.

Plate 39. *The Burgkmaier Spouses*. 1529. Lucas Furtenagel. Courtesy of the Kunsthistorische Museum, Vienna.

ing to the medieval dance of death and to a consciousness of the brevity of life.

ABSENCE OF OLD AGE IN FUNERARY ART

At times, the association between old age and death seems to be curiously absent, at least in funerary death art. Effigies made in the Middle Ages and the immediately following periods provide us with numerous death images that contain no reference at all to old age. In fact, the death effigies of the rich and powerful are very revealing about how old age and death were perceived. During the Middle Ages, adulthood and—less frequently—childhood were dominant in effigies, to the exclusion of old age (Martindale, 1979). Such statues were highly symbolic, and certain gestures or bodily features on Christian tombs of the medieval period indicate the function and status of the departed within (Aries, 1985). Kings have their crowns and scepters, bishops their croziers, and knights their swords. Initially, the entire emphasis was on characterizing the deceased only in terms of his or her station in life, rather than as an individual. Many people were not afforded effigies—or, for that matter, identifiable tombs. Charnel houses, catacombs, and mass graves were the general rule for the majority of society. But among those who rated at least a modicum of remembrance, often the location of the corpse in the burial ground denoted position and rank in society (Aries, 1985).

The artists of the period often preferred to depict the deceased in the prime of life, which was never considered to be old age. Even though many people did live a long time, youth and power are ceremoniously conveyed in their death art. Many examples of this practice have survived to our day, such as the eleventh-century recumbent figure of Saint Victor in the Abbé-Isam in Marseilles. In later tombs and effigies, the absence of old age and its characteristics is even more evident. From the looks of the thirteenth-century effigy of Henry III in Westminster Abbey, one would never guess that he died at the age of 65. The lines in the face are smooth, and there is very little attention of any sort paid to the effects of time on the appearance of a human being. The fourteenth-century recumbent figure on the tomb of Charles V at the Louvre is yet another example of the absence of old age.

Youthful portrayals of the deceased can be observed in many of the other tombs at Westminster Abbey, as well—besides that of Henry III. But by the fifteenth century, old age does begin to be recognized, along with other individual characteristics. This marks a clear change and historical precedent in the portrayal of old age and death. For example, the tomb of Elizabeth I—who lived to be 70—acknowledges the effects of old age in the queen's effigy. Another fine example is the tomb of Lady Margaret Beaufort, who died at age 66 in 1509. The effigy shows clear signs of her advanced years.

By the sixteenth century, funerary masks were being used to make the artwork on tombs. These plaster casts of the deceased captured a true likeness. Therefore, the portrayal of old age was an inevitable product of the artistic technique. By the last half of the seventeenth century, the symbolic functions of the effigy were greatly diminished; instead, the idea was to be as lifelike as possible (Fritz, 1981). Still later, however, we find a return to the youth and middle-age bias in death-related art. For example, in Westminster Abbey there is an eighteenth-century monument to Sir Isaac Newton, who lived to be 85. The artist obviously chose to portray Newton as middle-aged rather than old. One possible reason for this decision may be that most of Newton's scientific work was accomplished when he was a young man.

The predominance of youth reflected in most funerary and memorial effigies in Western society is quite striking, therefore. The image of the deceased was supposed to be projected as one of youth, strength, virility, and power. Smooth skin and strong bodies were the clearly preferred human form. And so, even though the technology existed to incorporate old age into the art, up until the late Middle Ages it was excluded. Furthermore, this practice recurs from time to time in later centuries.

Denial of the physical characteristics of old age surfaces in art other than effigies, also. Neoclassical paintings of the late eighteenth and early nineteenth centuries consistently show dying old men with strong young bodies. Images of the deaths of Socrates and Cato—popular subjects at the time—often depict these two old men, who lived into their seventies and eighties, as having muscular and healthy bodies. Their old age is acknowledged only through certain traditional symbols: robes, gray hair, and lined, bearded faces.

Jacques Louis David's *Death of Socrates* (1787) and Pierre Guerin's *Death of Cato of Utica* (1797) both display older men with youthful bodies and represent the absence of old age. These works also depict a popular thematic interest among artists of the eighteenth century: the death of the sage. Socrates, Cato, and Seneca were all sages of ancient times whose deaths symbolize the demise of free thinking and secular knowledge. The old sage's role relative to death was also interpreted in the context of the wisdom of life experience.

Plate 40 shows David's *Death of Socrates*, the sage reaching with one hand for the chalice of poison and pointing to the heavens with the other. The symbolic lamp of wisdom sits in the background. Although old, Socrates is rendered in very good and youthful physical condition by David.

All of this may indicate a basic societal bias toward middle age and youth. Aries (1962) contends that centuries have had their privileged ages: In the seventeenth century, it was youth; in the nineteenth, childhood; and in the twentieth, adolescence. However, older people have never had their privileged period. In terms of death and memorial art, the emphasis on youthful features—and the absence of old age—may be due to a variety of reasons. First, a more youthful state may have been seen as powerful and attractive. Few people wanted to be remembered with the characteristics of old age. Second, many of the accomplishments of the deceased occurred at a younger age; thus they wanted to be remembered and symbolized in that condition. Perhaps some even went so far

Plate 40. *The Death of Socrates*. 1787. Jacques Louis David. Courtesy of the Metropolitan Museum of Art, New York, Wolfe Fund, 1931. Catharine Lorillard Wolfe Collection.

as to assume that their funerary image would follow them to the afterlife. Third, the emphasis was on symbolism and not on individual characteristics (Aries, 1985). Individuals were recognized symbolically and not realistically; hence, the characteristics of their old age were ignored or perhaps simply considered not at all important.

THEMATIC CONNECTION BETWEEN OLD AGE AND DEATH IN ART

The Contemplation of Death

Since the late Middle Ages or perhaps earlier, older people have spent time preparing for death. Preparation for death during the Middle Ages was very formalized, and several manuals known as *ars moriendi* provided short instructions on the subject—even though the vast majority of people could not read, nor did they have the resources available to plan for their death. We know also that older people in medieval England were preoccupied with death preparation and the fate of their souls (Hanawalt, 1986). This preoccupation extended to other European countries as well.

One way to prepare was through contemplation. Since the late Middle Ages, the theme of older people contemplating life and death has been illustrated by many artists (see Chapters 2 and 3). Symbols of death such as the human skull were often included in these images. Life review was an expected and common practice, sometimes performed in order to weigh one's deeds and discover one's chances of making it into heaven. Patrick McKee and Heta Kauppinen (1987) note that reminiscence in old age has been frequently represented in art. For example, Rembrandt portrays older people absorbed in contemplation and life review. At times, the practice of contemplation might finally reveal meaning in an otherwise unrelated series of events. It would also tend to make older people aware of certain goals in their life that had not been accomplished (Leming & Dickinson, 1985). Which of these two themes was the intent of the artist is not always known, but both were commonly implied. In any case, contemplation does have an adaptive function, as well. The anticipation of death helps to smooth over the event when it occurs.

Life review and contemplation were sometimes incorporated into the art works of the ages-of-life genre, such as in the sixteenth-century artist Titian's *Three Ages of Man* (see Plate 5 in Chapter 2) and the seventeenth-century artist Van Dyck's *Four Ages of Man* (Plate 8 in Chapter 2). Usually, the older person, who is always a male in this case, is accompanied by a skull, an hourglass, or a candle. Often the old man focuses trancelike on these symbolic objects. Usually the implication is that he is deep in thought. This pose has been interpreted as evidence of senility by some observers, and by others as evidence of serenity and growth. Death and contemplation were also shown in a religious context.

Saint Jerome, a favorite subject of artists, was often shown in deep contemplation with some symbol of death—such as a human skull—in the foreground.

The Deathbed Scene

The deathbed scene has been one of the most enduring artistic images over the centuries. Aries (1985) notes that, regardless of century, the various versions of the deathbed always incorporate certain characteristics in common. For example, as Aries says, the atmosphere of the scene acts something like a vacuum in that figures are always drawn to the side of the bed. In addition, these figures are predominantly either secular or sacred—never a mixed crowd. The illustrations have often involved older people, either as the dying person or among the observers at the bedside.

Artists' portrayals of the deathbed scene changed in function over the years from the late Middle Ages through the nineteenth century. The romanticized Victorian view of the loving family overseeing the soon-to-be departed is dramatically different—in intent as well as composition—from Hieronymus Bosch's medieval vision of the deathbed as a test of the dying's judgment.

According to Aries (1974a), at about the fifteenth century, dying—and especially the death of old men—began to be depicted as a struggle. Frequently it was portrayed as a battle between the forces of good and evil (Choron, 1963). Therefore, spirits and other mystical and religious phenomena were often present in deathbed scenes. Evil and good were thought to be fighting for possession of the dying man's soul. In fact, fifteenth-century artists sometimes chose to place the image of God in the background as overseer. God was there to judge how the dying old man conducted himself, in light of the temptations and myriad events whirling around him. Dying was thus a test of moral character. As mentioned above, men were the primary subjects of this art in the medieval period.

The Death of the Miser (1485–1490) by Hieronymus Bosch—reproduced here as plate 41—provides us with a dramatic example of the medieval perception of death as a moral test. Unlike the funerary art of the same period—which served a different purpose and was, as we have seen, characterized by age denial—Bosch's deathbed scene acknowledges and emphasizes old age, showing an old man on his deathbed surrounded by his earthly possessions. There is clearly a test going on here. The old man is caught at the moment of deciding whether to side with his earthly possessions or to opt for a moral path by letting go of them.

In addition to the old man who is dying, there is another old man standing at the foot of the deathbed. This secondary figure carries the full signs of his old age in stature, clothing, and action: He is shown in a crooked stance bent over a trunk. Soon, he too will no doubt be on his deathbed. He holds a walking stick—a common appendage to the old of the time—and a guilder, symbolic of his accumulation of wealth. Bosch makes a strong connection here between old

Plate 41. *The Death of the Miser*. 1485–
1490. Hieronymous Bosch. National Gallery of Art. Washington; Samuel H. Kress
Collection. Courtesy of the National Gallery of Art, Washington, D.C.

age and the role of the miser—a theme discussed in Chapter 3. Both old men are shown with the material wealth they have accumulated over their lifetimes. And Bosch purposely leaves us with a question as to which way the dying old man will decide. This work is not at all atypical of how people viewed old men and death in the fifteenth century.

There may have been some very good reasons why deathbed scenes from this period would be full of spirits, messengers, and strange illusions. Poor medical care perhaps contributed to dying people's illusionary perceptions. There is also evidence, however, that illusions and claims of visions in the Middle Ages may have been exaggerated (Finucane, 1981).

The deathbeds of colonial Puritans in the seventeenth century form a very different scene of death and dying. The Puritans lived under extremely harsh conditions, which influenced their attitudes toward life and death (Tashjian & Tashjian, 1974). The Puritan deathbed was one of intense grief, prayer, and family involvement in overseeing the dying (Tashjian & Tashjian, 1974). It was a place of preparation for the rise to heaven or descent into hell (Leming & Dickinson, 1985). The rituals surrounding death called for significant amounts of time in preparation, review of life, and the giving of final instructions. Therefore, the way in which one died was very important.

To the Puritans, death was a tangible expression of God's benevolent order (Haber, 1983). They believed that life's mission culminates in death (Davidson, 1971), and they looked forward to spiritual metamorphosis—a shedding of the body and rise of the soul. Therefore, they were taught to welcome death (Smith, 1978). However, even while it was regarded as a blessing and a reward, it was also considered a punishment (Stannard, 1977). The Puritans had an intense fear of death, but were compelled to face it with restraint (Davidson, 1971). Death was known to them as the king of terrors (Stannard, 1977).

The deathbed, though, was a place where the dying Puritan could receive help from visitors for his or her imminent journey (Leming & Dickinson, 1985). If the Puritan had lived well, he or she would die well (Davidson, 1971). Thus, after a long life, an older person—though sometimes plagued by terror—was hopefully surrounded by a sense of calm at the time of death.

Will Writing and Bringing Life to Closure

Concern for finalizing the affairs of this world has had a long tradition. This was certainly the case when the widow would require continued support. Thus, it has been of paramount importance to many older people that they make provision for those left behind. Some scholars have connected the degree of detail in wills to the quality of family relationships—a topic that was discussed in Chapter 4.

In any case, after the Middle Ages and the Renaissance, older people were often portrayed in the process of bringing their lives to closure. Such concerns as disposing of property, seeking forgiveness, making arrangements for the care of dependents, and will writing became popular subjects of art. The nineteenth-century artist John Quidor's painting *Wofert's Will* is a typical rendition of the subject. It shows an old man on his deathbed, writing his last will and testament.

Old women have seldom been shown conveying their last wishes or writing wills. We know that they did hold property rights and power in Western society, however. As widows, they were in a position to dispose of property and wealth, and they did many times over the centuries. Perhaps it was a matter of artistic bias or possibly a cultural failure to connect old women with wealth that led to this neglect.

Death as Slumber

The portrayal of death as a moral test did not survive much beyond the Middle Ages and the early Renaissance. The conveyance of last wishes decreases as a subject of art by the twentieth century. But one very old theme that resurfaced in the early nineteenth century is worthy of note, and that is old age and death as slumber.

This theme can be traced back to the early Christian view of death as virtually a long period of sleep while awaiting the final resurrection of all the dead. Centuries later in the Middle Ages, there were many renderings of death as slumber. For one thing, death effigies were usually recumbent—that is, at rest. The sleep idea survived over the centuries following the Middle Ages. For example, the Puritan John Dutton in the seventeenth century drew an analogy between death and sleep (Smith, 1978a).

However, there is no solid continuous line between these early images and those created in the nineteenth century. All we can conclude is that for some reason—perhaps linked to outward appearances—death and slumber have long been associated, even within widely different cultural contexts. The key difference between the images of the Middle Ages and those of the nineteenth century, however, is a strong association with old age in the latter period. Death, old age, and slumber were linked in the nineteenth century to convey the image of a calm and undramatic passing on. One example is E. Heinemann's wood engraving titled *Death's Slumber* (n.d.), of an old woman sitting in a chair in a peaceful and restful state. From the picture alone, one cannot tell whether she is at rest or has died. The message is probably the familiar one that death is similar to slumber. But there may be another message we can interpret from this work: that the old in slumber are indistinguishable from death.

CLOSING THOUGHTS ON DEATH AND OLDER PEOPLE

This chapter has covered some of the historically important themes related to older people and death. Both artistic and historical evidence suggest that older people have at times been strongly associated with death, and at other times not. Initially, death was not perceived to be connected with any particular age because it was so widespread and unpredictable. But as time progressed, older people became increasingly associated with death and dying, and the association continues today.

Some contemporary scholars have suggested that death's association with old age is a relatively recent phenomenon (Marshall, 1980). The evidence is not completely supportive of this conclusion. The times when the association was not made, as well as the times when it was, have occurred throughout history. What fluctuates is the strength of the association. Over the period covered by this book, the strength of the association between old age and death has increased. And today, the association is a major interest and concern among older people themselves and the society in general (Van Tassel, 1979).

At times, the linking of older people with death has been so strong that they have been virtually one and the same. There is a long tradition of characterizing death as an old man or an old woman. However, this image declined over the centuries. Older people once had to share the dubious honor of representing death with other forms such as skeletons, skulls, and morbid ghouls and cadavers. Proximity with these creatures was not at all complimentary to the public image of older people. In all likelihood, then, their strong association with death simply by virtue of their many years has never been a desired position.

There have been times when artists seemed to be ignoring old age. For instance, the characteristics of old age are often absent from the tombs and effigies of older deceased people. This may or may not be significant in understanding how older people were perceived in those eras. A temporary change occurred in the latter half of the Middle Ages when, for a while, there was some recognition of old age in the effigies. Whether any meaning can be derived from this change requires additional study.

More than any other age group, the elderly have always been expected to prepare for death and the afterlife. In the seventeenth century—Smith (1978a) concludes—death preparation was perceived as part of the natural flow of the life cycle. What is so striking about the images of older people in this era is their great sense of serenity and resolve. They do not seem to be so fearful— but rather, face their deaths solemnly.

The theme of the contemplation of death can be observed in art over the centuries. In fact, this has been one of the most powerful themes linking older people to death and dying. With the exception of biblical figures and war heroes— who are sometimes shown reflecting on their fate as martyrs—the contemplation of death has been fairly age specific. It is traditionally depicted in art as the sole province of older people.

Certainly, the concern for one's remaining time has always become more salient with old age. The subject has been illustrated by several artists over the centuries. Older people are shown deep in thought, life review, and contemplation over their lives and the future. This contemplation and life review were sometimes used to weigh one's deeds on earth and one's chances of making it into heaven. Life review also implies a realization that certain goals in life will not be realized

(Leming & Dickinson, 1985). Therefore, whether pursued for secular or sacred motives, life review seems always to have been a highly significant endeavor on the part of older people.

In its most simple terms, aging has often been seen as the passage of time that propels life toward death. Time itself is even depicted as a close ally of Death (see de Beauvoir, 1972). Time's passage manifests most unmistakably in the form of physical decay and decline in older people. Aging is also sometimes equated with the process of dying. Artists have picked up this theme and often use it to make images of older people.

Much has been written about the stages of dying in contemporary society. One of the most widely accepted models is that proposed by Elizabeth Kubler-Ross (1969), who identified five distinct and progressive stages in the dying process: denial, anger, bargaining, depression, and acceptance. In the Western tradition of art, older people have not generally been associated with the early stages of the Kubler-Ross model. Usually they are not involved with denial, anger, or bargaining, but are certainly associated with the final stages of depression and acceptance. In art there is a resolve, resignation, and determination evident among the images of older people in death and dying. This has in fact been a long tradition in Western art and literature, both. Furthermore, much of the art and literature involving older people and death focuses not on *when* the older person will die, as might be expected, but on *how* he or she will die. The activities that surround dying—such as preparation, contemplation, will writing—are the focus in most of the art.

Whether, in the past, these activities and the approach to death were major preoccupations in old age is unknown. The art and literature seems to suggest so. However, research among contemporary older people has not found death to be a major preoccupation (Marshall, 1980). On this point, there may be a sharp distinction between older people in the contemporary context and those in the past.

Deathbed scenes—often including older people—served as popular subjects for the artists of the late Middle Ages and the centuries thereafter. According to Philippe Aries and others, the deathbed scene in the late Middle Ages was depicted as a moral test when it was an older people who was dying. As the centuries progressed, older people experienced their deathbeds less as a moral test and more as a preparing for the next world and a finishing of one's business in this one. Thus, over time, the moral questions of death and dying changed from whether one would make it to heaven, to how best to arrange the circumstances of one's death.

In summary, the art of earlier centuries can provide insight into how our own notions of death, dying, and old age came about. Some of the ideas held today parallel those in earlier times. More research will need to be done, however, on the linking of older people to death in earlier centuries if we are ever fully to understand death, dying, and older people in the contemporary context.

7

CONCLUSION

Western art and literature have not been indifferent toward older people. Ever since at least the Middle Ages, artists have been providing us with various insights into how older people were perceived in their respective societies. The images displayed and discussed in the previous six chapters convey a sense that old age was neither without norms nor without roles. If art and literature are any indication, then older people during the period covered by this book seem to have understood their various roles and positions in society very well.

Traditionally, though, Western scholars have not shown any particular interest in the subject of old age. Consequently, we know very little about the experience of it in earlier periods. We are left to our speculations. In recent years, however, social historians have started to investigate the lives of older people in the past. Their work is uncovering important new perspectives into the nature of aging and old age, some of which may prove meaningful to today's growing population of older people.

Given the artistic and literary images we have reviewed, it would seem only reasonable to conclude that the majority of perceptions regarding older people have been more negative than positive. There have certainly been exceptions—such as in the eighteenth and early nineteenth centuries when older people were venerated and sought out for their wisdom, survival skills, and experience—but positive perceptions are not the rule. Most characteristics of old age—all but wisdom, in fact—have been generally interpreted as negative. One might argue that old age was romanticized and seen in a favorable light in the late nineteenth century—a point raised in Chapter 4. Again, though, this romanticizing was a relatively recent phenomenon. The gold in one's golden years was actually dependent more on one's socioeconomic status and health than on old age, per se. When older persons aged gracefully and went into retirement, it was due more to what they had acquired than to any reverence due them by mere virtue of their old age. True, religious teachings did say that older people should be respected, but this teaching was in practice not always carried out. Life was simply too hard for most—let alone, older—people to afford much extravagance based on old age. The comfortable old age is thus a modern invention. And therefore, it is quite natural that historically the majority of images of old age would denote its more negative aspects. Besides, it is far easier (and more visually interesting, perhaps) for the artist to portray physical decline than mental or spiritual growth.

Twentieth-century attitudes toward older people are well documented. Basically, these attitudes are included in, but not limited to, the following summation: Older people are devalued by society and thus are thought of as being less important than young and middle-aged people. Interestingly, many older people themselves have bought into this idea. They depreciate their own self-worth as much as contemporary society does, and believe that their old age is inherently undesirable.

How did this notion of old age and older people come about? Are there historical antecedents that gave rise to our current ideas and attitudes toward old age? Has Western culture always devalued the old, used them as the target of humor, and viewed old age as the least desirable stage of life? Or are these and other contemporary attitudes relatively new? Is our current perception a product of modern society or an enduring position in Western history?

To answer these questions, we must identify those images and themes that have remained fairly consistent over the centuries, as well as those that have changed. With this in mind, some images that relate to the basic attitudes are covered in the first sections of this concluding chapter. Those related to the specific chapters then follow.

OLDER PEOPLE AS THE OBJECT OF HUMOR

Old age and older people have been the butt of jokes for many centuries. The old fool and granny images common in contemporary society were also present in earlier times. In fact, these stereotypes have a very long tradition in Western history. Older people have run up against them whether, for example, they attempted to have an active sex life—which has caused them no end of ridicule and humiliation. One of the most recurring of images is the old fool. Older people's physical decline and occasional loss of wit have been favorite topics of the artist and humorist since at least the Middle Ages.

As with other realities oddities that we do not handle well, humor may be the Western world's dubious way of coping with the difficulties of old age; and in this, the twentieth century is no exception. We often see older people and old age as a problem. We do not envision them as problem solvers so much as problems in their own right (see Achenbaum & Kusnerz, 1978). Western society—with a few notable exceptions, such as in antiquity and in the early years of the American Republic—has tended to minimize the contributions that older people make. People are valued for what they actively contribute to the runnings of society; when they are no longer so active, their worth diminishes.

THE BIAS TOWARD YOUTH

The orientation toward youth has been a major tendency throughout Western history and its works of art. Whenever historians take snapshots of particular societies, they almost always find that the desired state of being is any age other than old age. The development of our most basic social institutions—such as the various structures designed for education, and the family itself—have focused on the needs of youth, sometimes at the expense of older people. Ironically, it is only recently that youth have begun to wield any real power in society. As noted above, there have been a few periods in history when older people were admired for their longevity and wisdom. The mere fact of having survived to old age was then considered an accomplishment in its own right. But these eras have definitely been the exception, not the rule.

One can almost hear a great subconscious sigh of relief among younger people that they are not older. Even when positive perceptions about older people are acknowledged, they do not seem to negate the overall assessment that old age is less than desirable. Throughout history, old age has been regarded as something to be postponed, although—ironically—people have often believed that only with aging can one fully understand and appreciate the true meaning of life.

THE AGES OF LIFE

The various ages-of-life models from the late Middle Ages to the nineteenth century were reviewed in Chapter 2. These models can provide us with valuable insights into how aging and old age were perceived in earlier times. Several themes related to old age emerge from our review—themes such as ambivalence, decay, and age-appropriate behavior. And what comes through most clearly is the consistency—regardless of model—in what was defined as age-appropriate behavior for older people. The ages-of-life genre positively characterizes old age as a time for contemplation, spiritual restoration, repentance, and wisdom. On the negative side, however, it was perceived as a time of decay, miserly behavior, lust, foolishness, childishness, dementia, infirmity, and poor health.

The age-appropriate behavior for older people has always been more restrictive than permissive. However, although Western society has been almost dictatorial in what it expects of older people, we can find many examples of famous older people who have broken its dictates. As mentioned in Chapter 2, Michelangelo painted the Sistine Chapel during old age, and continued to work afterward; Verdi composed *Falstaff* at 80; Titian painted *Christ Crowned with Thorns* at 95; Victor Hugo wrote well into his old age; Voltaire was writing even at the time of his death at 84; and Claude Monet painted the *Water Lilies* series at 83. There is some evidence from contemporary society that creativity may actually increase with age (Edel, 1977–78; Woodward, 1978). Besides, many less famous older people throughout history also continued to function as full members of society, often out of economic necessity. Thus, while the ages-of-life models did serve as guides to the human life-span and age-appropriate behavior, older people never did not fully adhere to their social prescriptions.

Contemplation was one of the most common and enduring of the age-appropriate behaviors for older people in the past. In fact, it appears to have been a major activity in old age during the entire period from the medieval to the Victorian eras. Nowadays, however, the emphasis is on staying physically active as long as possible. In the contemporary context, old age is a time for continued engagement—and not necessarily a time for contemplation, which implies a retreat from social interests. Thus, people from the late Middle Ages to the seventeenth century must have had a very different view of aging and what was appropriate for old age (Moody, 1986).

Other expected and appropriate behaviors in the ages-of-life genre were repentance, preparation for death, acting like a miser, resting, and being cold, wise, childlike, pious, religious, solemn, and disengaged. Sexual activity and romance were never viewed as appropriate, but their existence nonetheless was acknowledged by quite a few authors and artists.

In structuring the ages of life, analogies were often made between the human life-span and medieval perceptions of the spiritual and natural world. Thus the seasons, the planets, or the tribes of Israel might be reflected in the number of ages. Also, aging during the latter half of the life-span, and in particular old age, was characterized by physical decay. This was counterbalanced by recognition of an intellectual and spiritual growth over time. As mentioned earlier, some even held that the true meaning of life could only be understood by someone with the experience and wisdom of a long life. There was thus an ambivalence to the interpretation of old age. It was fraught with a sense of duality, as the individual was said to be ascending and descending simultaneously.

Some of the ages-of-life representations of older people closely parallel our own views on older people. In the contemporary context, older people are still generally considered to be declining, and for the most part are expected to behave a certain way. They are still viewed with ambivalence. Therefore, many of today's perceptions of aging and older people run deep in Western history.

SYMBOLIC IMAGES OF OLDER PEOPLE

Artists and authors have long been selecting older people to represent certain themes and concepts. As a result, old age has come to be the standard symbol even in our day for time, the miser, and the witch. There have been other uses for the image of old age, however, and their meanings varied from time to time. With regard to portraiture, older people were very often the subject—possibly because many of them had acquired enough wealth to commission works. It may also be that artists found them to be visually interesting. In any case, numerous portraits of older people were created by Western artists, once there arose in the Western world a sense of individuality and individual characteristics.

Artists also placed within their works a number of accessory symbols that had become traditionally associated with old age and aging in general—which served to reinforce the tradition. A sampling of these symbols would include the robe, the owl, the cane, and the goat. In the abstract, all such symbols were vested with the underlying themes of aging: the passage of time, mental and physical decline, winter, devotion, wisdom, counsel, infirmity, evil, growth in spirituality, and contemplation. Older people were often accompanied by their symbols within a context of social respect. This is evident in, say, the continued wearing of robes by older persons in works painted long after this was an everyday fashion.

There has been a long tradition of associating older people with key religious figures and with religious practices and teachings. Due to their advanced years, they have often been viewed as being closer to God than the rest of the population. Contemplation, life review, preparation for death, prayer, biblical scholarship, and personal piety have all been illustrated using older figures. These illustrations strongly emphasize the wisdom and understanding that come with old age.

Certain older religious figures were immensely popular images. The image of Saint Jerome was so widespread that one could say he became an icon for old age during the seventeenth century. The saintly themes of contemplation, surrendering worldly possessions, and devotion to God were considered models that older people would do well to imitate, in that they should not be focused on this life and their decline, but rather on the promise of heaven.

Older people were also used as the symbol for secular concepts such as avarice. Avarice was strongly associated with older people, and usually appeared in the form of an older women. There may have been some very good reasons why this association was made, as older people probably needed to be a bit miserly to ensure their survival. In any case, this perception of older people has endured to this day.

The pursuit of youth and the prolongation of life are familiar themes throughout Western history. Still, the explanations for how this might come about have never drifted far from what the ancient Greeks suggested. In fact, very few new ideas crept into the thinking until the eighteenth and nineteenth centuries. The classical notion was always to practice moderation in all things, so as not to upset the body's balance. From time to time, therapeutic interventions were also proposed, however—claiming to postpone the negative effects of aging, restore youth, or prolong life. These interventions were usually questioned by the Church, which was suspicious of any attempt to interfere with God's will.

If old age is as undesirable as Western society would make it seem, then why do people desire to prolong life? Is it a question of desiring life in old age, or of avoiding death? The image of the fountain of youth sidesteps and yet may provide the best solution to the dilemma—if only in fantasy.

Nevertheless, rumors and reports of people surviving well into old age have always been welcomed and viewed with interest. This may have been particularly true in the first years of the American Republic, and more generally in the seventeenth and eighteenth centuries. Even today, we have certainly not surrendered our desire to extend life and recapture youth. And as advertising art clearly seems to indicate, youth is still the desired state of being for many people.

In fact, the contrast between youth and old age has served as a springboard for many artworks that deal directly with the perception of age. In most of these works, youth represents the baseline from which aging and old age are to be judged. Older people emulate youth, but youth never seem to emulate older people. On the other hand, beauty must not be nurtured by older people, for this would be vain and ridiculously inappropriate. Also, youthful pursuits such as sex, romance, and adventure are never pictured as being appropriate for older people.

Other perceptions of older people symbolically reflected in art and literature were more positive, such as their being venerated and admired for their wisdom. Wisdom has been a fairly persistent attribute of older people in Western thought. Yet the veneration of older people has changed somewhat over the years and tends to fluctuate. As some historians have suggested, its presence may have been strong in colonial America and then declined after the Civil War. Veneration is a difficult concept to measure because of the difference between what people say and what they actually do. Although people have generally been instructed to venerate older people since ancient times, we know that their actual practice may have been something else.

Certain images evolved radically during the period covered by this book. Initially, for example, older women were no more associated with witchcraft than any other age group. Nevertheless, over the centuries, they became the archetypical image of the witch. The reasons for this connection between older women and witchcraft are subject to much debate. The behavior of older women and especially older widows, their powerlessness, the community need for scapegoats, and community resistance to supporting them may all have contributed to their being labeled as witches in the public and artists' imagination. Now they completely dominate our image of the witch.

Another image that has evolved is that of time itself. Time became an old man in the Renaissance; older men had not been used to characterize it before then. Perhaps the medieval linkages among time, old age, physical decay, and death formed a background from which the old man emerged the ideal candidate for the artistic rendering of time.

IMAGES OF OLDER PEOPLE AND THE FAMILY

Conclusions about older people and their families are difficult to draw over time, as no other area of social history provides so many mixed messages about aging and older people. Information about the family in Western history is overwhelmingly complex and often contradictory. One area of contradiction—for example—is the contemporary assumption that, as modernization and industrialization occurred, older relatives were abandoned by their families. As the nuclear family replaced the extended family—the argument goes—older relatives wound up spending their waning years in meaningless involuntary isolation. On this point, historians are increasingly in agreement that the extended family has never been the predominant form of the family in Western society. The implication then becomes that, mostly, older relatives have *not* been expelled from their families because of modernization, urbanization, or industrialization. Rather, if they could afford and were able to, they *preferred* to live independently of their offspring and grandchildren.

The provision of care to older relatives has proven to be a useful historical measure in attempting to understand older people relative to their families. The family has always held the primary responsibility to care for older relatives—a role it has not always welcomed. Consequently, in more than one era, older parents have had to protect themselves from desertion and destitution. Maintaining this protection meant controlling the family property and thus the offspring, regardless of any tension this might cause. It should come as no real surprise that miserly behavior and avarice would come to symbolize older people (see Chapters 3 and 4), for such characteristics may have been necessary adaptations on the part of older people to guarantee their very survival.

As Western history evolved, parental control over property and offspring diminished—partly due to increased urbanization, the decline of primogeniture, and the advent of industrialization. In addition, the growth of institutional and social care organizations played a role in diminishing tensions among the generations, as some older relatives could now expect to receive care from outside the family. However, one should never lose sight of the fact that the main burden of care has always rested with the family. The rise of alternative arrangements may actually have affected only a few.

It may be that the loss of control and power on the part of older people opened the way for the provision of care based on more affectionate rather than coercive circumstances. In any case, there was a slow evolution to notions and values of filial duty and sentimental care, from the earlier attitude of a virtual contract between parents and their offspring. This shift may be linked to the erosion of older people's control over the disposition of property and family members' lives.

In fact, this erosion may have paved the way for both the attitudinal and institutional shifts in the provision of care. As feudalism faded and democratization prospered, nonfamilial providers of care evolved into their current presence, although these providers have never been present in sufficient quantity to supplant the family as the primary care-giver. However, as mentioned above, in an atmosphere of reduced tension it became easier for more humanitarian motives to emerge even within the family. Intergenerational conflicts—while still present—were generally no longer so significant as when property and family decisions rested with the older members of the family unit. The tyrannical power of older parents and grandparents dissolved.

As with so many other aspects of culture, these features of older people in their family life seem to be mirrored in the art of the various periods. In early portraiture, family groupings were rather formal and structured. As the centuries progressed, artists were free to give us a glimpse of the more human side of relationships between older people and their families. Whether this is reflective of a major shift in the artist–client arrangement is unknown. Quite possibly the artists were simply capturing the changes in attitudes involving older people. Thus, the development of sentimental and affectionate relationships among the generations can be seen in family portraiture over time.

With all the economic and attitudinal changes in the past two centuries, care for the old has shifted at least partially from the family to community. Regardless of whether it be a community or a family responsibility, however, there has always been a negative connotation attached to needing care. It has traditionally been viewed as a mark of personal failure and unworthiness. This is particularly true in the United States, where the values of independence, self-determination, freedom of thought, and economic self-sufficiency are so strongly emphasized.

And while reducing intergenerational tension and stress is certainly desirable for all parties, it might have involved an important down-side for older people. When they had more control over family matters, for better or worse, they were at least involved in its decision-making processes. As they lost control and power, it became easier to isolate and ignore them. Thus, older parents evolved from being a major societal force to being sentimentalized isolates within their families.

Furthermore, the marriage or remarriage of older people has historically been a matter for public scrutiny and—more importantly—public ridicule. Older people were subjected to some fairly rigid social restrictions on whom they could marry and how they were to conduct themselves within the marriage. The literature indicates that Western society has done little to accommodate the marital desires of older people and has in fact consciously worked against them until contemporary times.

Yet older widows have had an especially hard time in Western society. Their portraits run the gamut of artistic treatment, from religious reverence to mockery. When widows tried to reestablish normal lives through remarrying, they were mocked by the artists and writers. When they were willing to surrender to their fate, they were shown as pious, asexual, and reserved. When they became impoverished, they were often branded as evil and occasionally as witches. The positive, independent, and socially adept widow is relatively absent from the artistic images. Rather, she is characterized either as always being up to something or else as a personification of the social outcast who has only her devotion to God to give her comfort in her old age.

Images of grandparents were relatively rare in Western art until the eighteenth and nineteenth centuries, although terminology denoting grandparental status is very old. Grandparents were occasionally painted, however, and early family groupings often incorporate the oldest generation. These early images of older relatives are not in the least sentimental: Late Middle Ages and Renaissance artists chose to show older relatives in a structured and formal pose, as was the custom in all family portraiture at the time. But over the centuries we witness an evolution to a more sentimental image of the grandparent. The nineteenth-century Currier and Ives prints of older family members are dramatically different from Titian's Renaissance paintings of upper-middle-class Italian families. All in all, while the fifteenth through the eighteenth centuries emphasized the formality of family relationships, by the nineteenth century affection was being stressed.

OLDER PEOPLE AND SEXUAL IMAGES

One of the most enduring themes involving the aged has been that sexual activity is taboo (Loughman, 1980; Pfeiffer, 1977). Some authorities suggest that current sexual taboos are left over from the Victorian era (Comfort, 1976). Victorian attitudes do seem to have influenced today's older people; however, sexual taboos regarding older people are much older than the nineteenth century. There is evidence that they had existed throughout most of Western history. Actually, it is not strictly correct to use the term "taboo" in this context for the centuries prior to the Victorians. People wrote about and painted older people involved in sexual activities and having sexual desires. Thus, the topic was anything but taboo. Rather, it was always raised in a negative context, with malicious connotations. The taboo aspect emerged in the Victorian era, and for a variety of reasons older people had a hard time shedding it. For one thing, treating it as taboo was probably a more tolerable and comfortable way to deal with their sexuality than viewing it as evil, humorous, lustful, and abnormal— as was the case prior to the nineteenth century.

One basic premise to the discussion in Chapter 5 is that sexual behavior among older people has never actually matched the historical Western notions about what is appropriate during old age. The perception of inappropriateness was due to physical limitations (real or imagined) and—more importantly—to moral dictates, as sex with older people would not usually lead to procreation.

In contemporary society, we seldom associate older people with sexual behavior. We are much more likely to link sex with youth. The mass media certainly promote this perception (Smith, 1979; Starr, 1985). Elderly people who remain sexually active are accused of acting too young and are still treated with scorn or ridicule (Loughman, 1980). Oftentimes older people buy into the association of sexuality with youth and view themselves as unattractive and unacceptable sexual partners. This equation of youth and sex is a fairly old way of thinking. Even the ancients generally associated sexuality with youth, the essence of life, and immortality (Weg, 1983). And exceptions to this general attitude have been relatively rare all through Western history.

In fact, most writings prior to the nineteenth century assumed sexual indifference in old age for both sexes (Fowler et al. 1982). The moralistic and religious ideal of the dignified older person who is naturally no longer interested in sex endured for many centuries in Western thought (de Beauvoir, 1972). One seventeenth-century scholar suggested that old age frees older people from sexual lusts and desires (Smith, 1976). This thought was a reformulation of the earlier idea that sexual desires act like shackles in old age—shackles that hold older people to this world. The elderly are often spoken of in ways that imply they are regarded as desexed (Sommers, 1978), and sometimes as sexual eunuchs (Loughman, 1980).

The cultural materials examined here do not support the conclusion that older people were ever sexually indifferent. In fact, they were depicted as something else altogether. The one exception to this is the period from the Victorian era to modern times. Up until then, older people were seen as fools for love, or lustful, or evil—but clearly not indifferent. True, many people in earlier times believed that sexual interest declines in a women at menopause. Sexual desires, feelings, and behaviors on the part of older women were seldom shown in art. Thus, a woman could be sexual only at a certain (the reproductive) time of life. Yet there were many contradictions even to this belief in art and literature, and the perception was not universally applied. Men, in contrast, did not have to face the connotations of finality that accompany menopause and were viewed as having sexual desires till death. However—like older women—the desires of old men were considered nonetheless unnatural and inappropriate.

Elderly sexual impotence and inability was a lasting theme for many centuries. Although images of impotency have not been common since the nineteenth century and remain rare today, the idea continues to be with us. Thus, older women and men were viewed as not capable of normal sex lives. From this attitude came the perception of sexually active older men as sinful, humorous, and lustful; they were ridiculed for their futile desires. Older women were viewed as evil and were penalized—even sometimes linked with the devil and labeled as witches. On those rare occasions when older women have been portrayed with sexual desires, they were shown as being predatory toward men, sexually powerful, morally weak, and often the tool of evil forces (Walker, 1985).

It is only in the latter half of the twentieth century that the naturalness of sexual relations involving older people has started to be acknowledged. But even contemporary researchers—occasionally positive and encouraging—are still more often negative and defensive on this topic (Starr, 1985). Therefore, sexual activity among the aged often continues to be viewed within a negative context. In fact, it is only in the latter half of the twentieth century that the sexual feelings and needs of women in general have started to be recognized as natural. And—although society is indeed becoming more open in regard to women—it may still be some time before we publicly acknowledge and accept the sexual needs and desires of older women and men.

At least the image of sex among older people is not so disagreeable to society today as it was in the past. We know that, in spite of all the harassment and persecution throughout history, sexual activity did and does occur in old age. There are signs that, among older people themselves, their sexual activity is now becoming more open. Acknowledgement of sexual behavior among the old in contemporary Western culture—though still rare—is beginning to surface. Celeste Loughman (1980) has observed that old myths about the aged are being attacked by contemporary writers of drama and fiction. Advice books on aging increasingly admit the existence of sexual desires in old age and are becoming more tolerant—if not helpful—in the matter of sexual behavior among older people (Arluke et al., 1984).

According to Lawrence Stone (1979), sexual activity in general is at a much higher level in the twentieth century, compared to earlier centuries. Stone provides ample evidence that poor sanitation, disease, inadequate personal hygiene, and restrictive moral perceptions—among other factors—contributed to the dearth of sexual behavior in early modern times. Consequently, sexual activity among older people may have increased recently due to improvements in the sexual conditions and opportunities available.

In any case, contemporary research has found that sexual activity among the old is more common than was traditionally supposed. Apparently it does decline (Kinsey et al., 1948; Masters & Johnson, 1966; Riley & Foner, 1968), but does not disappear altogether. In some cases, older people may actually increase their sexual activity (Pfeiffer et al., 1969). The assumption that older people—especially women—automatically become asexual after childrearing is more likely than ever to be challenged by practice in contemporary times (Mitterauer & Sieder, 1982).

Therefore, the scorecard is currently mixed. While sex among older people remains a relatively taboo topic, society is becoming more open to its existence. There is a growing awareness that the life-span can afford the individual more flexibility than was imagined in earlier centuries. Sexual activity, as research shows, can and does occur throughout the latter half of life. Romantic love is increasingly considered possible in old age, also. Furthermore, sex for reasons other than procreation is more acceptable today than in prior centuries. Moral and religious precepts are permissive compared to the past. Many people no longer regard sexual desire as an impediment in the transition to heaven or salvation.

However, these changes must be viewed in light of the enduring perceptions about sex and about older people. For example, as mentioned above, sexuality is still viewed as the domain of the young. Beauty and sexual attractiveness are still ascribed to the young. The media in general continue to communicate and reinforce this perception (Bishop & Krause, 1984; Smith, 1979; Starr, 1985). Until society expands its definition of sexuality to include the old, the emphasis will remain on the young and on maintaining the illusion of youth. In addition, many negative perceptions about sex and older people persist also. Sexual activity on the part of older people continues to be seen as dirty and negative. Old men are still viewed as fools and are the targets of stage and street humor. Old women remain in a double bind as their age and gender both act to restrict their sexual options. Menopause and its sociopsychological meaning still operate to hamper the sex lives and perceptions of older women. Widowhood, along with its cultural baggage, is still a significant concern for old people: Men continue to marry younger women who outlive them by seven to ten years.

Generally, then, sexual activity among older people continues to be viewed as perverse. Desire is thought to leave with old age. When an older person does express sexual desires, people figure that he or she is indulging in self-deception. Yet after centuries of derogation, ridicule, social pressure, restriction, and taboo, older people's sexual interest—though usually diminished—remains a fact. And this poses many cultural difficulties for older people. Any change will require a major shift in both societal and personal acceptance and attitudes.

As mentioned above, this change may come slowly. Considerable time may pass before sexual behavior on the part of older people is fully acknowledged and accepted by society. Although there is some evidence that more permissive attitudes are emerging (Arluke et al., 1984), significant changes have not occurred. Socially accepted sexual outlets for older people are still scarce, particularly for older women. Scholarly observers have referred to the current situation of older people as anomic: they are encouraged to maintain their sexuality, but are provided no socially accepted means of doing so (Arluke et al., 1984).

IMAGES OF OLDER PEOPLE AND DEATH

Death and dying have been regarded many different ways in Western society—and not necessarily, at first, with any particular age. But increasingly since the late Middle Ages—and certainly to the present generation of old and young alike—death, as the final completion of being, has become closely associated with old age (Van Tassel, 1979). This association is the result of greater life expectancy at birth, which is due in turn to generally lower infant mortality rates and better living conditions.

The associating of death with old age has done little to liberate older people. Certain gerontologists have recently asserted that the negative evolution of older people in contemporary Western society may stem from the very fact that we do associate them with death (Kalish, 1985; Streib, 1976). Their value as contributors to and actors in society is hence undermined, and they are avoided socially. If we hope to do anything about alleviating the situation, we must first recognize that this association has had a long tradition in Western history and has increased over time, as reflected in art and literature.

For a time, there was also a tradition of actually characterizing death in the form of an old man or old woman. However, this image has declined over the centuries. Older people have also had to share their place in works of art with items such as skeletons and skulls. Nowadays we rarely find images of death in the popular culture; and when we do, they tend to be devoid of age and asexual.

The theme of the elderly in contemplation of death can be observed in art over the centuries. Some contend that the prominence of life review in the older person's mind serves to defend the self against the negative feelings of not reaching all of life's goals (Butler, 1975). This may have been as true in the past as it is today, but one can only speculate. Others suggest that looking back on positive accomplishments can bring on a sense of wholeness even though time is running out (see Erikson, 1963). Whatever the motive or its consequences for the individual, the life review we witness in older people today also occurred in earlier historical periods. There may have been more social acceptance of contemplation in the past, however, along with a greater expectation that contemplation should occur during old age. We do know that the review of life— whether cast in moral terms or simply an attempt to attach meaning to life— was of treat value to older people in earlier times (Butler, 1975).

Familiarity with death and the act of dying has also changed over the centuries. For most of Western history, death was more socially familiar than it is today (Aries, 1974a, 1974b, 1985). It frequently occurred in the public realm, often in the presence of the family. For example, most Puritan deaths occurred within the home (Stannard, 1977; Tashjian & Tashjian, 1974). Today, however, the dying are insulated from the living. Death occurs in institutional settings, such as hospitals and nursing homes. Rarely does it take place in alternative settings, such as the home (Aries, 1974a). Thus, as Philippe Aries (1974a, 1985) has observed, death is more mysterious and unfamiliar than it ever was in the past (see Goody, 1974).

According to Victor Marshall (1980), the social character of death remained relatively constant until about 100 years ago. It is in the past century that dying has become more privatized and bureaucratic. The attending on death has moved from the family and community to the control of experts and institutions (Blauner, 1966; Shorter, 1977). Today, for everyone—including the old—death is characterized by a fear of the unknown. For the old, it usually occurs in unfamiliar institutionalized surroundings, such as hospitals or nursing homes. Before the twentieth century few older people died in hospitals, and most died without medical attention (Haber, 1983; Leming & Dickinson, 1985). Institutional settings can be strange and uncomfortable places to die, as documented in many recent works on death (Aries, 1974b; Blauner, 1966; Marshall, 1980).

As life expectancy at birth is extended still further in the future, it is likely that older people will be increasingly associated with death and dying. Unless we become more open to the topic and the presence of death and dying, however, older people will continue to experience death with great uncertainty—even more uncertainty, in fact, than in the past. It is possible that movements such as hospice will alleviate this trend and have a positive influence on how we die. But only time will tell if hospice and other alternative, less institutional ways of caring for the dying will have a lasting and major impact.

SUMMATION

In closing, we must ask what we have learned from artists about older people in the past. A few ideas seem to characterize all the reviewed images at a high level of abstraction. First, there is the persistent sense of duality. Older people have almost always been viewed in both positive and negative terms at the same time. They can be admired for their wisdom, yet ridiculed for their foolishness.

Second, societies have been fairly restrictive in what they define as appropriate behavior for older people. Besides all the generally applicable prescriptions of society, older people have had to deal with additional expectations not applied to younger people. This is particularly true for older women.

Third, as just intimated, there are clear differences between the sexes. Historically, older men have had a different social image from older women. Older men were characterized (dualistically) by artists as fools, religious leaders, wise, feeble, venerable, esteemed, contemplating, lustful, and honored. Older women—whose images are less common in Western art—were shown as helpers, feeble, evil, pious, and grandmotherly. The connotations and uses of these sex-specific images differed on many dimensions.

Fourth, regardless of epoch, old age has never been the desired state of being. Most images convey a bias toward more youthful states. People have desired to remain young or middle-aged and to postpone old age. They have, however, wanted to live as long as possible—perhaps to the point, anyway, at which infirmity would make death welcome.

Finally, one is struck by the great variety that exists among images of older people. The vast, colorful array of Western art—once its value to scholarship is fully recognized—should remain a rich source of information about older people in prior times. In all this variety, however, clear contradictions can be found, making any sorts of conclusions tenuous. As the research work in this area develops, undoubtedly some of the themes proposed here will find continued support while others will need correction. It is hoped that the approach in itself will be inspirational and that scholars will continue to explore and study the use of art as a means of understanding older people in the past and present.

REFERENCES

Achenbaum, W. A. (1978). *Old age in the new land: The American experience since 1790*. Baltimore: Johns Hopkins University Press.

Achenbaum, W. A., & Kusnerz, P. A. (1978). *Images of old age in America*. Ann Arbor: University of Michigan and Wayne State University.

Altherr, T. (Ed.). (1983). *Procreation or pleasure: Sexual attitudes in American history*. Malabar, FL: Robert E. Krieger.

Anderson, M. (1971). *Family structure in nineteenth century Lancashire*. Cambridge, England: Cambridge University Press.

Aries, P. (1962). *Centuries of childhood: A social history of family life*. New York: Vintage Books.

———. (1974a). *Western attitudes toward death: From the Middle Ages to the present*. Baltimore: Johns Hopkins University Press.

———. (1974b). The reversal of death: Changes in attitudes toward death in Western societies. *American Quarterly, 26*, 536–560.

———. (1985). *Images of man and death*. Cambridge, MA: Harvard University Press.

Aries, P., & Bejin, A. (1985). *Western sexuality: Practice and prescription in past and present times*. Oxford, England: Oxford University Press.

Arluke, A., Levin, J., & Suchwalko, J. (1984). Sexuality and romance in advice books for the elderly. *Gerontologist, 24*, 415–419.

Back, K. W. (1977). The ambiguity of retirement. In E. Busse & E. Pfeiffer (Eds.), *Behavior and adaptation in late life*. Boston: Little, Brown.

Banzinger, G. (1979). Intergenerational communication in prominent Western drama. *Gerontologist, 20*, 69–73.

Barash, D. P. (1983). *Aging: An exploration*. Seattle: University of Washington Press.

Barker-Benfield, G. J. (1983). The spermatic economy: A nineteenth century view of sexuality. In T. L. Altherr (Ed.), *Procreation or pleasure: Sexual attitudes in American history*. Malabar, FL: Robert E. Kreiger.

Bell, I. P. (1980). Thd double standard. In B. Hess (Ed.), *Growing old in America*. New Brunswick, NJ: Transaction Books.

Benedek, T. G. (1978). Beliefs about human sexual function in the Middle Ages and Renaissance. In D. Radcliff-Umstead (Ed.), *Human sexuality in the Middle Ages and Renaissance*. Pittsburgh: University of Pittsburgh Press.

Beresford, J. C., & Rivlin, A. (1969). The multigenerational family. In *Occasional papers in gerontology*. Ann Arbor: University of Michigan and Wayne State University, Institute of Gerontology.

Berg, G., and Gadow, S. (1978). Toward more human meanings of aging: Ideals and images from philosophy and art. In S. F. Spicker, K. M. Woodward, & D. D. Van Tassel (Eds.), *Aging and the elderly: Humanistic perspectives in gerontology*. Atlantic Highlands, NJ: Humanities Press.

Berger, S. E. (1982). Sex in the literature of the Middle Ages: The fabliaux. In V. Bullough & J. Brundage (Eds.), *Sexual practices and the medieval church*. Buffalo, NY: Prometheus Books.

Berkner, L. (1972). The stem family and the development cycle of the peasant household: An eighteenth century Austrian example. *American Historical Review, 77*, 398–418.

Berman, L., & Nelson, J. (1987). Voltaire's portrayal of old age. *International Journal of Aging and Human Development, 24*, 161–169.

Bever, E. (1982). Old age and witchcraft in early modern Europe. In P. N. Stearns (Ed.), *Old age in preindustrial society*. New York: Holmes & Meier.

Bishop, J. M., & Krause, D. R. (1984). Depictions of aging and old age on Saturday morning television. *Gerontologist, 24*, 91–94.

Blauner, R. (1966). Death and social structure. *Psychiatry, 29*, 378–394.

Boswell, J. (1980). *Christianity, social tolerance, and homosexuality*. Chicago: University of Chicago Press.

Brandon, S. G. F. (1975). *Man and God in art and ritual*. New York: Charles Scribner's Sons.

Braunstein, P. (1988). Toward intimacy: The fourteenth and fifteenth centuries. In G. Duby (Ed.), *A history of private life: Revelations of the medieval world*. Cambridge, MA: Belknap Press.

Bullough, V. L. (1973). An early American sex manual, or, Aristotle who? *Early American Literature, 7*, 236–247.

———. (1976a). *Sex, society, and history*. New York: Science History Publications.

———. (1976b). *Sexual variance in society and history*. New York: John Wiley & Sons.

———. (1979). *Homosexuality: A history*. New York: Meridian Books.

———. (1982). Postscript: Heresy, witchcraft, and sexuality. In V. L. Bullough & J. Brundage (Eds.), *Sexual practices and the medieval church*. Buffalo, NY: Prometheus Books.

Bullough, V. L., & Brundage, J. (Eds.). (1982). *Sexual practices and the medieval church*. Buffalo, NY: Prometheus Books.

Bullough, V. L., & Bullough, B. (1977). *Sin, sickness, and society: A history of sexual attitudes*. New York: Garland Publishing.

Burgess, E. W. (Ed.). (1960). *Aging in Western societies*. Chicago: University of Chicago Press.

Burnside, I. M. (Ed.). (1975). *Sexuality and aging*. Los Angeles: University of Southern California Press.

Burrow, J. A. (1984). *Essays on medieval literature*. Oxford, England: Clarendon Press.

———. (1986). *The ages of man: A study in medieval writing and thought*. Oxford, England: Clarendon Press.

Butler, R. (1975). *Why survive? Being old in America*. New York: Harper & Row.

Cannadine, D. (1981). War and death, grief and mourning in modern Britain. In J. Whaley (Ed.), *Mirrors of mortality: Studies in the social history of death*. New York: St. Martin's Press.

Carlton, C. (1978). The widow's tale: Male myths and female reality in 16th and 17th century England. *Albion, 10*, 118–129.

Chandler, A. R. (1948). Aristotle on mental aging. *Journal of Gerontology, 3*, 220–224.

Charles, D. C. (1977). Literary old age: A browse through history. *Educational Gerontology, 2*, 237–253.

Charles, D. C., & Charles, L. H. (1979–1980). Charles Dickens's old people. *International Journal of Aging and Human Development, 10*, 231–237.

Chartier, R. (1989). The practical impact of writing. In R. Chartier (Ed.), *The history of private life: Passions of the Renaissance*, Volume 3. Cambridge, MA: Belknap Press.

Chew, S. C. (1962). *The pilgrimage of life*. New Haven, CT: Yale University Press.

Choron, J. (1963). *Death and Western thought*. New York: Collier Books.

———. (1964). *Death and modern man*. New York: Collier Books.

Christensen, C. V., & Gagnon, J. H. (1965). Sexual behavior in a group of older women. *Journal of Gerontology, 20*, 351–356.

Chudacoff, H. P., & Hareven, T. K. (1978). Family transitions into old age. In T. K. Hareven (Ed.), *Transitions: The family and the life course in historical perspective*. New York: Academic Press.

Clark, J. M. (1950). *The dance of death in the Middle Ages and the Renaissance*. Glasglow: Jackson, Son.

Coffman, G. R. (1934). *Old age from Horace to Chaucer: Some literary affinities and adventures of an idea*. *Speculum, 9*, 249–277.

———. (1937). Old age in Chaucer's day. *Modern Language Notes, 52*, 25–26.

Cole, T. R. (1984). Aging, meaning, and well-being: Musings of a cultural historian. *International Journal of Aging and Human Development, 19*, 329–336.

Cole, T. R., & Gadow, S. (Eds.). (1986). *What does it mean to grow old?* Durham, N.C.: Duke University Press.

Collomp, A. (1989). Families: Habitations and cohabitations. In R. Chartier (Ed.), *The history of private life: Passions of the Renaissance*, Volume 3. Cambridge, MA: Belknap Press.

Comfort, A. (1965). *The process of aging*. London: Weidenfeld and Nicolson.

———. (1976). *A good age*. New York: Crown Publishers.

Copplestone, T. (1983). *Art in society*. Englewood, NJ: Prentice-Hall.

Corby, N., & Zarit, J. M. (1983). Old and alone: The unmarried in later life. In R. B. Weg (Ed.), *Sexuality in the later years: Roles and behavior*. New York: Academic Press.

Cott, N. F. (1983). Passionlessness: An interpretation of Victorian sexual ideology, 1790–

1850. In T. Altherr (Ed.), *Procreation or pleasure: Sexual attitudes in American history*. Malabar, FL: Robert E. Krieger.

Coupe, W. A. (1967). Ungleiche liebe—a sixteenth-century topos. *Modern Language Review, 62*, 661–671.

Covey, H. C. (1988). Historical terminology used to represent older people. *Gerontologist, 28*, 291–297.

———. (1989a). Perceptions and attitudes toward sexuality of the elderly during the Middle Ages. *Gerontologist, 29*, 93–100.

———. (1989b). Old age portrayed by the ages-of-life models from the Middle Ages to the 16th century. *Gerontologist, 29*, 692–698.

Cuffe, H. (1607). *The differences of the ages of man's life; together with the original causes, progress, and end thereof*. London: Hatfield.

Dahlin, M. (1980). Perspectives on the family life of the elderly in 1900. *Gerontologist, 20*, 99–107.

Dannenfeldt, K. H. (1987). Andre Du Laurens (1558–1609): An early French writer on the aged. *Gerontologist, 27*, 240–243.

Davidson, G. (1971). Histories and rituals of destiny: Implications for thanatology. *Soundings, 54*, 415–434.

de Beauvoir, S. (1972). *The coming of age*. New York: G. P. Putnam's Sons.

Degler, C. N. (1974). What ought to be and what was: Women's sexuality in the nineteenth century. *American Historical Review, 79*, 1467–1490.

———. (1980). *At odds*. New York: Oxford University Press.

Demos, J. (1970). *A little commonwealth: Family life in Plymouth Colony*. London: Oxford University.

———. (1978). Old age in early New England. *American Journal of Sociology, 84*, 248–287.

———. (1986). *Past, present, and personal*. New York: Oxford University Press.

de Rougemont, D. (1974). *Love in the Western world*. New York: Harper & Row.

Dieck, M. (1980). Residential and community provisions for the frail elderly in Germany: Current issues and their history. *Gerontologist, 20*, 260–272.

Douglas, A. (1974). Heaven our home: Consolation literature in the northern United States, 1830–1880. *American Quarterly, 26*, 496–515.

Dove, M. (1986). *The perfect age of man's life*. London: Cambridge University Press.

Dublin, L. E. (1965). *Factbook on man*. New York: Macmillan.

Duby, G. (1978). Medieval marriage: Two models from twelfth-century France. Baltimore: Johns Hopkins University Press.

Duby, G., Barthelemy, D., & de La Ronciere, C. (1988). The aristocratic households of feudal France. In G. Duby (Ed.), *A history of private life: Revelations of the medieval world*. Cambridge, MA: Belknap Press.

Edel, L. (1977–1978, Winter). Portrait of the artist as an old man. *American Scholar*, pp. 52–68.

Erikson, E. (1963). *Childhood and society*. New York: Norton.

Evans, G. (Ed.). (1974). *The Riverside Sheakespeare*. Boston: Houghton Mifflin.

Fabre, D. (1989). Families: Privacy versus custom. In R. Chartier (Ed.), *The history of private life: Passions of the Renaissance*, Volume 3. Cambridge, MA: Belknap Press.

Faragher, J. (1976). Old women and old men in seventeenth-century Wethersfield, Connecticut. *Women's Studies, 4*, 11–31.

Farge, A. (1989). The honor and secrecy of families. In R. Chartier (Ed.), *The history of private life: Passions of the Renaissance*, Volume 3. Cambridge, MA: Belknap Press.

Field, P. J. (1970). Chaucer's merchant and the sin against nature. *Notes and queries, 215*, 84–86.

Finucane, R. C. (1981). Sacred corpse, profane carrion: Social ideals and death rituals in the later Middle Ages. In J. Whaley (Ed.), *Mirrors of mortality: Studies in the social history of death*. New York: St. Martin's Press.

Fischer, D. H. (1977). Growing old: An exchange. *New York Review of Books, 124*, 47–48.

———. (1978). *Growing old in America*. Oxford, England: Oxford University Press.

Flandrin, J. L. (1975). Contraception, marriage, and sexual relations in the Christian West. In R. Forster & O. Ranum (Eds.), *Biology of man in history*. Baltimore: Johns Hopkins University Press.

———. (1976). *Families in former times*. Cambridge, England: Cambridge University Press.

———. (1979). *Families in former times: Kinship, household, and sexuality*. Cambridge, England: Cambridge University Press.

Folts, J. D. (1980). Senescence and renascence: Petrarch's thoughts on growing old. *Journal of Medieval and Renaissance Studies, 10*, 207–237.

Foote, T. (1968). *The world of Bruegel*. New York: Time-Life Books.

Foucault, M. (1978). *The history of sexuality*. New York: Pantheon Books.

Fowler, D. H., Fowler, L. J., & Lamdin, L. (1982). Themes of old age in preindustrial Western literature. In P. N. Stearns (Ed.), *Old age in preindustrial society*. New York: Holmes & Meier.

Freedman, E. B. (1982). Sexuality in nineteenth-century America: Behavior, ideology, and politics. *Reviews in American History, 10*, 196–215.

Freedman, R. (1978). Sufficiently decayed: Gerontophobia in English literature. In S. F. Spicker, K. M. Woodward, & D. D. Van Tassel (Eds.), *Aging and the elderly: Humanistic perspectives in gerontology*. Atlantic Highlands, NJ: Humanities Press.

Freeman, J. T. (1965). Medical perspectives in aging (12th–19th century). *Gerontologist, 5*, 1–24.

Friedmann, E. (1960). The impact of aging on the social structure. In C. Tibbitts (Ed.), *The handbook of social gerontology*. Chicago: University of Chicago Press.

Fritz, P. S. (1981). From public to private, the royal funerals in England, 1500–1830. In J. Whaley (Ed.), *Mirrors of mortality: Studies in the social history of death*. New York: St. Martin's Press.

Gauthier, M. (1964). *The Louvre: Paintings*. New York: Meredith Press.

Gay, P. (1986). *The tender passion*. New York: Oxford University Press.

Gies, F., & Gies, J. (1978). *Women in the Middle Ages*. New York: Thomas Y. Crowell.

Gilbert, C. (1967). When did a man in the Renaissance grow old? *Studies in the Renaissance, 14*, 7–32.

Goldscheider, C. (1971). *Population, modernization, and social structure*. Boston: Little, Brown.

Goldthorpe, J. E. (1987). *Family life in Western societies*. Cambridge, England: Cambridge University Press.

Goody, J. (1969). *Comparative studies in kinship*. Stanford, CA: Stanford University Press.

———. (1974). Death and the interpretation of culture: A bibliographic overview. *American Quarterly, 26*, 448–455.

———. (1976). Aging in nonindustrial societies. In R. Binstock & E. Shanas (Eds.), *Handbook of aging and the social sciences*. New York: Van Nostrand Reinhold.

———. (1983). *The development of the family and marriage in Europe*. Cambridge, England: Cambridge University Press.

Gordon, M. S. (1960). Aging and income security. In C. Tibbitts (Ed.), *The handbook of social gerontology*. Chicago: University of Chicago Press.

Gorer, G. (1965). *Death, grieving, and mourning*. Garden City, NY: Doubleday.

Greven, P. J. (1970). *Four generations: Population, land, and family in colonial Andover, Massachusetts*. Ithaca, NY: Cornell University Press.

Griffin, J. J. (1946).The Bible and old age. *Journal of Gerontology, 1*, 464–471.

Haber, C. (1983). *Beyond sixty-five: The dilemma of old age in America's past*. Cambridge, England: Cambridge University Press.

Hanawalt, B. (1986). *The ties that bound*. New York: Oxford University Press.

Hareven, T. K. (1979). The last stage: Historical adulthood and old age. In D. Van Tassel (Ed.), *Aging, death, and the completion of being*. Philadelphia: University of Pennsylvania Press.

Harthan, J. (1977). *The book of hours*. New York: Thomas Y. Crowell.

Hendricks, J., & Hendricks, C. D. (1977). *Aging in mass society: Myth and realities*. Cambridge, MA: Winthrop.

———. (1977–1978). The age old question of old age: Was it really so much better back when? *Journal of Aging and Human Development, 8*, 139–154.

Herlihy, D. (1967). *Medieval and renaissance Pistoria*. New Haven, CT: Yale University Press.

———. (1982). Growing old in the quattrocento. In P. N. Stearns (Ed.), *Old age in preindustrial society*. New York: Holmes & Meier.

———. (1985). *Medieval households*. Cambridge, MA: Harvard University Press.

Hinton, J. M. (1967). *Dying*. Baltimore: Penguin Books.

Hofstatter, H. H. (1968). *Art of the late Middle Ages*. New York: Harry N. Abrams.

Holmes, R. (1974). *Witchcraft in British history*. London: Frederick Muller.

Hotvedt, M. (1983). The cross-cultural and historical context. In R. B. Weg (Ed.), *Sexuality in the later years: Roles and behavior*. New York: Academic Press.

Hughes, P. (1965). *Witchcraft*. Baltimore: Penguin Books.

Huizinga, J. (1952). *The waning of the Middle Ages*. London: Edward Arnold.

Jacobowitz, E. S., & Stepanek, S. L. (1983). *The prints of Lucas Van Leyden and his contemporaries*. Princeton, NJ: Princeton University Press.

Johns, C. (1982). *Sex or symbol: Erotic images of Greece and Rome*. Austin: University of Texas Press.

Kalish, R. (1985). Death and dying in a social context. In R. Binstock & E. Shanas (Eds.), *Handbook of aging and the social sciences*. New York: Van Nostrand-Reinhold.

Kamen, H. (1976). *The iron century: Social change in Europe, 1550–1660*. London: Sphere Books.

Kammen, M. (1980). Changing perceptions of the life cycle in American thought and culture. *Proceedings of the Massachusetts Historical Society, 91*, 35–66.

Kastenbaum, R. (1969a). The foreshortened life perspective. *Geriatrics, 24*, 126–133.
———. (1969b). Death and bereavement in later life. In A. H. Kutscher (Ed.), *Death and bereavement*. Springfield, IL: Charles C. Thomas.
———. (1979). Exit and existence: Society's unwritten script for old age and death. In D. Van Tassel (Ed.), *Aging, death, and the completion of being*. Philadelphia: University of Pennsylvania Press.
Kastenbaum, R., & Ross, B. (1975). Historical perspectives on care. In J. G. Howells (Ed.), *Modern perspectives in the psychiatry of old age*. New York: Brunner-Mazel.
Kaufmann, C. M. (1975). *Romanesque manuscripts: 1066–1190*. London: Harvey Miller.
Kebric, R. (1983). Aging in Pliny's letters: A view from the second century A.D.. *Gerontologist, 23*, 538–545.
Kellogg, J. H. (1881). *Plain facts for old and young*. Burlington, IA: Segner & Condit.
Kett, J. (1971). *Rites of passage: Adolescence in America, 1790 to present*. New York: Basic Books.
Kingsley, C. (1880). *The water babies*. New York: Macmillan.
Kinsey, A. C., Pomeroy, W. B., & Martin, C. E. (1948). *Sexual behavior in the human male*. Philadelphia: Saunders.
Kubler-Ross, E. (1969). *On death and dying*. New York: Macmillan.
Larner, C. (1984). *Witchcraft and religion: The politics of popular belief*. Oxford, England: Basil Blackwell.
La Ronciere, C. (1988). Tuscan notables on the eve of the Renaissance. In G. Duby (Ed.), *A history of private life: Revelations of the medieval world*. Cambridge, MA: Belknap Press.
Laslett, P. (1965). *The world we have lost*. London: Methuen.
———. (1976). Societal development and aging. In R. Binstock & E. Shanas (Eds.), *Handbook of aging and the social sciences*. New York: Van Nostrand Reinhold.
———. (1977). *Family life and illicit love in earlier generations*. Cambridge, England: Cambridge University Press.
———. (1984). *The world we have lost further explored*. New York: Charles Scribner's Sons.
Laslett, P., & Wall, R. (Eds.). (1972). *Household and family in past time*. New York: Cambridge University Press.
Lawton, A. (1965). The historical developments in the biological aspects of aging and the aged. *Gerontologist, 5*, 25–32.
Lebrun, F. (1989). The two reformations: Communal devotion and personal piety. In R. Chartier (Ed.), *A history of private life: Passions of the Renaissance*, Volume 3. Cambridge, MA: Belknap Press.
Leming, M. R., & Dickinson, G. E. (1985). *Understanding dying, death, and bereavement*. New York: Holt, Rinehart, & Winston.
Lewinsohn, R. (1956). *A history of sexual customs*. New York: Bell.
Leyser, K. J. (1979). *Rule and conflict in early medieval society*. London: Ottonion Saxony.
Litchfield, R. B. (1978). The family and the mill: Cotton mill work, family work patterns, and fertility in mid-Victorian Stockport. In A. S. Wohl (Ed.), *The Victorian family*. London: Croon Helm.
Loughman, C. (1980). Eros and older people: A literary view. *Gerontologist, 20*, 182–187.

McKee, P. L., & Kauppinen, H. (1987). *A celebration of old age in Western art*. New York: Human Sciences Press.

McManners, J. (1981). *Death and the enlightenment: Changing attitudes to death among Christians and believers in eighteenth century France*. New York: Oxford University Press.

Maier, R. A. (1984). *Human sexuality in perspective*. Chicago: Nelson Hall.

Maoz, B., & Landau, E. (1983). Womanhood in the climacterium and old age. In R. B. Weg (Ed.), *Sexuality in the later years: Roles and behavior*. New York: Academic Press.

Markson, E. (1980). A hiding place to die. In B. Hess (Ed.), *Growing old in America*. New Brunswick, NJ: Transaction Books.

Marshall, V. (1980). *Last chapters: A sociology of aging and dying*. Monterey, CA: Brooks-Cole.

Martindale, A. (1979). *Gothic art*. London: Thames & Hudson.

Masters, W. H., & Johnson, V. E. (1966). *Human sexual response*. Boston: Little, Brown.

Mather, C. (1950). *On witchcraft, being the wonders of the invisible world*. Mount Vernon, NY: Peter Pauper Press. (Originally published in Boston in 1692.)

Maxon, J. (1970). *The Art Institute of Chicago*. London: Thames & Hudson.

May, W. F. (1986). The virtues and vices of the elderly. In T. R. Cole & S. Gadow (Eds.), *What does it mean to grow old?* Durham, NC: Duke University Press.

Mayhew, H. (1950). *Mayhew's characters*. London: Spring Books. (Original work in 1851.)

Metress, S. P. (1985). The history of Irish-American care of the aged. *Social Service Review, 59*, 18–31.

Mignon, E. (1947). *Crabbed age and youth: The old men and women in Restoration comedy of manners*. Durham, NC: Duke University Press.

Miles, W. R. (1965). Human personality in perpetuity. *Gerontologist, 5*, 33–39.

Mitterauer, M., & Sieder, R. (1982). *The European family*. Chicago: University of Chicago Press.

Moody, H. R. (1986). The meaning of life and the meaning of old age. In T. R. Cole & S. Gadow (Eds.), *What does it mean to grow old?* Durham, NC: Duke University Press.

Morgan, E. (1983). The Puritans and sex. In T. L. Altherr (Ed.), *Procreation or pleasure: Sexual attitudes in American history*. Malabar, FL: Robert E. Krieger.

Mullins, E. (1985). *The painted witch: How Western artists have viewed the sexuality of women*. New York: Carroll & Graf.

Murray, L. (1967). *The late Renaissance and mannerism*. New York: Frederick A. Praeger.

Nissenbaum, S. (1980). *Sex, diet, and debility in Jacksonian America*. Westport, CT: Greenwood Press.

Noonan, J. T. (1986). *Contraception: A history of its treatment by the Catholic theologians and canonists*. Cambridge, MA: Harvard University Press.

Oaks, B. F. (1978). "Things fearful to name": Sodomy and buggery in seventeenth century New England. *Journal of Social History, 12*, 268–278.

O'Conner, B. L. (1979). Albert Berne and the completion of being: Images of vitality and extinction in the late paintings of a ninety-six-year-old man. In D. D. Van

Tassel (Ed.), *Aging, death, and the completion of being.* Philadelphia: University of Pennsylvania Press.

Ozment, S. (1983). *When father ruled.* Cambridge, MA: Harvard University Press.

Palmer, B. (1978). To speke of wo that is marriage: The marital arts in medieval literature. In D. Radcliff-Umstead (Ed.), *Human sexuality in the Middle Ages and Renaissance.* Pittsburgh: University of Pittsburgh Press.

Panofsky, E. (1939). *Studies in iconology: Humanistic themes in the art of the Renaissance.* Oxford, England: Oxford University Press.

Parsons, T. (1942). Age and sex in the social structure of the United States. *American Sociological Review, 7,* 604–616.

Pearsall, R. (1976). *Public purity, private shame.* London: Weidenfeld & Nicolson.

Pfeiffer, E. (1977). Sexual behavior in old age. In E. W. Busse & E. Pfeiffer (Eds.), *Behavior and adaptation in later life.* Boston: Little, Brown.

Pfeiffer, E., Verwoerdt, A., & Wang, H. S. (1969). The natural history of sexual behavior in a biologically advanced group of aged individuals. *Journal of Gerontology, 24,* 193–198.

Philibert, M. (1974). The phenomenological approach to images of aging. *Soundings, 57,* 33–49.

Praz, M. (1971). *Conversation pieces: A survey of an informal group portrait in Europe and America.* University Park: Pennsylvania State University Press.

Premo, T. (1984). A blessing to our declining years: Feminine response to filial duty in the new republic. *International Journal of Aging and Human Development, 20:* 69–73.

Preston, S. H. (1977). Mortality trends. *Annual Review of Sociology, 3,* 163–178.

Quadagno, J. (1982). *Aging in early industrial society: Work, family, and social policy in nineteenth century England.* New York: Academic Press.

Quinones, R. J. (1972). *The Renaissance discovery of time.* Cambridge, MA: Harvard University Press.

Randall, O. A. (1965). Some historical developments of social welfare aspects of aging. *Gerontologist, 5,* 40–49.

Ranum, O. (1989). The refuges of intimacy. In R. Chartier (Ed.), *The history of private life: Passions of the Renaissance*, Volume 3. Cambridge, MA: Belknap Press.

Ravensdale, T., & Morgan, J. (1974). *The psychology of witchcraft: An account of witchcraft, black magic, and the occult.* New York: Arco.

Regnier-Bohler, D. (1988). Exploring literature. In G. Duby (Ed.), *A history of private life: Revelations of the medieval world.* Cambridge, MA: Belknap Press.

Richardson, G. (1979). *Iconology*, Volumes 1 & 2. New York: Garland. (Originally published in London in 1779.)

Riley, J. W., Jr. (1970). What people think about death. In O. G. Brim, Jr., H. E. Freeman, S. Levine, & A. Scotch (Eds.), *The dying patient.* New York: Russell Sage Foundation.

Riley, M. W., & Foner, A. (1968). *Aging and society*, Volume 2. New York: Russell Sage Foundation.

Robin, J. (1984). Family care of the elderly in a nineteenth century Devonshire parish. *Ageing and Society, 4,* 505–516.

Robinson, P. K. (1983). The sociological perspective. In R. B. Weg (Ed.), *Sexuality in the later years: Roles and behavior.* New York: Academic Press.

Roebuck, J., & Slaughter, J. (1979). Ladies and pensioners: Stereotypes and public policy affecting old women in England, 1880–1940. *Journal of Social History, 13*, 105–114.

Rosand, D. (1978). *Titian*. New York: Harry N. Abrams.

Rosenmayr, L. (1971). Family relations of the elderly. In F. G. Scott & R. M. Brewer (Eds.), *Perspectives in aging*. Corvallis: Oregon State University.

Rosenthal, J. T. (1973). Medieval longevity and the secular peerage, 1350–1500. *Population Studies, 27*, 287–293.

Rossiaud, J. (1985). Prostitution, sex, and society in French towns in the fifteenth century. In P. Aries & A. Bejin (Eds.), *Western sexuality: Practice and prescription in past and present times*. Oxford, England: Oxford University Press.

Sandler, L. F. (1983). *The psalter of Robert de Lisle*. London: Harvey Miller.

Scarre, G. (1987). *Witchcraft and magic in sixteenth and seventeenth century Europe*. Atlantic Highlands, NJ: Humanities Press International.

Schiller, G. (1971). *Iconography of Christian art*. Greenwich, CT: New York Graphic Society.

Scot, R. (1973). *Discoveries of witchcraft*. Yorkshire, England: Rowmand & Littlefeld. (Original work in 1584.)

Shanas, E. (1977). Living arrangements and housing of old people. In E. Busse & E. Pfeiffer (Eds.), *Behavior and adaptation in late life*. Boston: Little, Brown.

Shanas, E., Townsend, P., Wedderburn, D. Friis, H., Milhoj, P., & Stehouwer, J. (1968). *Old people in three industrial societies*. New York: Atherton Press.

Shorter, E. (1977). *The making of the modern family*. New York: Basic Books.

Sill, G. G. (1975). *A handbook of symbols in Christian art*. New York: Macmillan.

Simmons, L. W. (1945). *The role of the aged in primitive society*. New Haven, CT: Yale University Press.

Skultans, V. (1970). The symbolic significance of menstruation and the menopause. *Man, 5*, 639–651.

Smith, D. S. (1973). Parental power and marriage partners: An analysis of historical trends in Hingham, Massachusetts. *Journal of Marriage and the Family, 35*, 419–429.

———. (1978). Old age and the great transformation: A New England case study. In S. F. Spicker, K. M. Woodward, & D. D. Van Tassel (Eds.), *Aging and the elderly: Humanistic perspectives in gerontology*. Atlantic Highlands, NJ: Humanities Press.

Smith, S. R. (1976). Growing old in early Stuart England. *Albion, 8*, 125–141.

———. (1978a). Death, dying, and the elderly in seventeenth-century England. In D. Van Tassel, S. Spicker, & K. Woodward (Eds.), *Aging and the elderly: Humanistic perspectives in gerontology*. Atlantic Highlands, NJ: Humanities Press.

———. (1979). Age in Old England. *History Today, 24*, 172–178.

———. (1982). Growing old in an age of transition. In P. Stearns (Ed.), *Old age in preindustrial society*. New York: Holmes & Meier.

Smith-Rosenberg, C. (1983). Davey Crockett as trickster: Pornography, liminality and symbolic inversion in Victorian America. In T. L. Altherr (Ed.), *Procreation or pleasure?: Sexual attitudes in American history*. Malabar, FL: Robert E. Krieger.

Sokoloff, J. M. (1986). Character and aging in *Moll Flanders*. *Gerontologist, 26*, 681–685.

Sommers, T. (1978). The compounding impact of age on sex. In R. Gross, B. Gross, & S. Seidman (Eds.), *The new old*. Garden City, NY: Anchor Books.

Spisak, J. W. (1978). Medieval marriage concepts and Chaucer's good lovers. In D. Radcliff-Umstead (Ed.), *Human sexuality in the Middle Ages and Renaissance*. Pittsburgh: University of Pittsburgh, Center for Medieval and Renaissance Studies.

Stannard, D. (1977). *The puritan way of death*. New York: Oxford University Press.

Starr, B. D. (1985). Sexuality and aging. *Annual Review of Gerontology and Geriatrics, 5*, 97–126.

Stearns, P. (Ed.). (1976). *Old age in European society: The case of France*. New York: Holmes & Meier.

————. (1980). Old women: Some historical observations. *Journal of Family History, 5*, 44–57.

————. (1981). The modernization of old age in France: Approaches through history. *International Journal of Aging and Human Development, 13*, 297–315.

————. (Ed.). (1982). *Old age in preindustrial society*. New York: Holmes & Meier.

Stern, K., & Cassirer, T. (1946). A gerontological treatise of the Renaissance. *American Journal of Psychiatry, 102*, 770–773.

Stewart, A. G. (1979). *Unequal lovers*. New York: Abaris Books.

Stone, L. (1975). The rise of the nuclear family in early modern England: The patriarchal stage. In C. E. Rosenberg (Ed.), *The family in history*. Philadelphia: University of Pennsylvania Press.

————. (1977). Walking over grandma. *New York Review of Books, 24*, 10–16.

————. (1979). *The family, sex, and marriage in England, 1500–1800*. New York: Harper & Row.

Streib, G. F. (1976). Social stratification and aging. In R. Binstock & E. Shanas (Eds.), *Handbook of aging and the social sciences*. New York: D. Van Nostrand-Reinhold.

Tannahill, R. (1980). *Sex in history*. New York: Stein & Day.

Tashjian, D., & Tashjian, A. (1974). *Memorials for children of change: The art of early New England stonecarving*. Middletown, CT: Wesleyan University Press.

Taylor, G. R. (1970)., *Sex in history*. New York: Harper & Row.

Thomas, K. (1971). *Religion and the decline of magic*. New York: Scribner.

————. (1976). Age and authority in early modern England. *Proceedings of the British Academy, 62*, 205–248.

————. (1978). *Religion and the decline of magic*. London: Peregrine.

Thomlinson, R. (1976). *Population dynamics: Causes and consequences of world demographic change*. New York: Random House.

Thompson, R. (1986). *Sex in Middlesex: Popular mores in a Massachusetts county, 1649–1699*. Amherst: University of Massachusetts Press.

Tristram, P. (1976). *Figures of life and death in medieval English literature*. New York: New York University Press.

Troyansky, D. (1982). Old age in the rural family of enlightened provence. In P. Stearns (Ed.), *Old age in preindustrial society*. New York: Holmes & Meier.

Van Tassel, D. D. (Ed.). (1979). *Aging, death, and the completion of being*. Philadelphia: University of Pennsylvania Press.

Vinovskis, M. A. (1971). The 1789 life table of Edward Wigglesworth. *Journal of Economic History, 31*, 570–590.

Waldemar, C. (1960). *The mystery of sex*. New York: Lyle Stuart.

Walker, A. (1987). The poor relation: Poverty and old woman. In C. Glendinning & S. Millar (Eds.), *Women and poverty in Britain*. Brighton, England: Wheatsheaf.

Walker, B. (1985). *The crone: Woman of age, wisdom, and power*. San Francisco: Harper & Row.

Wall, R. (1984). Residential isolation of the elderly: A comparison over time. *Ageing and Society, 4*, 403–503.

Wall, R., Robin, J., & Laslett, P. (1983). *Family forms in historic Europe*. Cambridge, England: Cambridge University Press.

Warthin, A. S. (1931). *The physician of the dance of death*. New York: Paul B. Hoeber.

Weg, R. B. (1975). Physiology and sexuality in aging. In I. M. Burnside (Ed.), *Sexuality and aging*. Los Angeles: University of Southern California Press.

————. (Ed.). (1983). *Sexuality in the later years: Roles and behavior*. New York: Academic Press.

Weinstein, D., & Bell, R. M. (1982). *Saints and society: The two worlds of Western Christendom, 1000–1700*. Chicago: University of Chicago Press.

White, L. (1962). *Medieval technology and social change*. London: Oxford University Press.

Whittick, A. (1972). *Symbols for designers*. London: Crosby Lockwood & Son. (Original work in 1935.)

Woodward, K. (1978). Master songs of meditation: The late poems of Eliot, Pound, Stevens, and Williams. In S. F. Spicker, K. Woodward, & D. D. Van Tassel (Eds.), *Aging and the elderly*. Atlantic Highlands, NJ: Humanities Press.

Zimmerman, M. (1980). Old age poverty in preindustrial New York City. In B. Hess (Ed.), *Growing old in America*. New Brunswick, NJ: Transaction Books.

Zucker, P. (1963). *Styles in painting: A comparative study*. New York: Dover.

INDEX

ABOUT THE AUTHOR

HERBERT C. COVEY is a postdoctoral fellow in the Bureau of Sociological Research at the University of Colorado at Boulder. He received his Ph.D. from the University of Colorado at Boulder in 1979 and has taught at the University of Nebraska at Omaha and the University of Colorado.

Dr. Covey coauthored a book on theories of the sociology of education and has written more than 30 refereed journal articles on gerontology as well as criminology. His work has appeared in the *Gerontologist, Research on Aging, Educational Gerontology,* the *Journal of Research in Crime and Delinquency,* the *Social Science Journal,* the *Journal of Crime and Justice, Justice Quarterly,* and *Social Service Review.* He is currently writing a book on youth gangs.

Dr. Covey's research interests include the social history of aging, crimes committed by older people, criminal victimization of older people, and youth gangs.